Memoir
with
Grykes and Turloughs

Patricia Burke Brogan

WORDSONTHESTREET

First published in 2014 by
Wordsonthestreet
Six San Antonio Park,
Salthill,
Galway, Ireland.
web: www.wordsonthestreet.com
email: publisher@wordsonthestreet.com

© Copyright Patricia Burke Brogan

The moral right of the author has been asserted.
A catalogue record for this book is available from the British Library.

ISBN   978-1-907017-29-2

Cover design, layout and typesetting: Wordsonthestreet
Cover photo: Joe Shaughnessy
Printed and bound in the UK

Memoir
with
Grykes and Turloughs

Dedication

To my sisters Claire, Teresa and Philomena, and to the memory of my brother Fr Brendan and my parents Mary (née O'Beirne) and Joseph Phelim Burke.

Acknowledgements

Mike Diskin, Thomas Kilroy, John McGahern, Michael Harding, John O'Donoghue, Gerald Dawe, Tom Kenny, James Harrold, Ann and Gabe Walshe, Charlotte Headrick, Eileen Kearney, Patricia Kennedy, Mika Funahashi, Margaret Faherty, Carla de Petris, Member of Galway Writers' Workshop, Bernard Kirk with committee members of Galway Education Centre, Fintan O'Toole, Rebecca Bartlett, Eugene McCabe, Bernard Farrell, Tyrone Guthrie Centre, Dermot Duncan, the editors at Wordsonthestreet Gerardine Burke and Tony O'Dwyer, my nephew Padraig, my husband Edward and members of my family: Fr Brendan, Claire, Teresa and Philomena.

Reviews of *Eclipsed* by Mephisto Theatre Company 2013

It is an absorbing experience, more humane than browbeating, yet it is chilling that Burke Brogan's play met the world four years before the last laundry closed.... The decades of slow exposure since haven't diminished this play's impact or its clear-sighted political indignation. If anything, in a year of government reports and apologies, it seems more urgent.
Peter Crawley. The Irish Times

Mephisto Theatre Company's production of Eclipsed, directed by Niall Cleary, is a beautifully paced and poignant event that tells of the histories and experiences of women (unmarried mothers, orphans, those 'mentally unfit', but 'fit for work') in Ireland's Magdalen laundries... It leads the audience from recognition of an institution, to in-jokes about a culture, and, finally, ..., to tears about a tragic history that is still not fully unearthed. This play does not end on stage, but follows an audience out the door, prompting them to further action.
Miriam Haughton. Irish Theatre Magazine

The play is extraordinary brave for its time ... Watching the play now, I was immediately struck by how relevant it remains... the production suggests that this country's underlying power structures – involving gender and social class in particular – may not be all that different from what they were twenty years ago.
Prof. Patrick Lonergan's blog, From Magdalene to Slane

Extraordinary Eclipsed gets new staging ... This is a moving, thought-provoking play and Mephisto's production should be seen.
Judy Murphy. Irish Independent

The power of humour and imagination to bring light into the most inhuman situation is demonstrated in Mephisto Theatre Company's new production of Patricia Burke Brogan's powerful play, Eclipsed.
Judy Murphy. The Connacht Tribune

A punchy, provocative production that finds a high emotional tenor and makes for first- class theatre.
Pádraic Killeen. Irish Examiner

Reviews of earlier productions of *Eclipsed*

On rare occasions theatre goes beyond its walls and rises to the level of myth. Patricia Burke Brogan's original and powerful play Eclipsed ... touches the black of the human soul.
Worcester Magazine Mass USA 1994

... the play's real themes are about change, courage, hard times, grace and listening to the still small voice that tells us what we should do when things fall apart and the old signposts disappear... Eclipsed is a play with many levels: spiritual, feminist, even Irish too; about dreams gone sour for the unwanted and outcasts ... not unlike those who gave Christ such a bad name as He consorted with tax collectors, outsiders, losers and adulterous women.
Middlesex News Mass. USA 1994

Audiences walk away from Eclipsed with a communal knot in their stomachs – a sour feeling from having seen a piece of Irish history that people rarely talk about and a slice of Irish culture many would rather not remember ... This is a story about judgement and it is a story about Ireland. But it is for anyone with compassion in their hearts and the conditions of women in their minds.
Southbridge News Mass USA 1994

Her stage play, Eclipsed, changed everything. A play that was as faithful to the lives of the characters represented as it was to the hidden stories could almost not have had another author.
Michael D. Higgins T.D. Minister for Arts, Culture and the Gaeltacht.

This subversive and devastating play, Eclipsed, won her international recognition as a writer of courage and finely tempered imagination.
John O'Donohue author of Anam Cara.

Mothers for a moment, then cloistered forever. A charming play, powerful and thought-provoking.
The New York Times 1999

Patricia Burke Brogan's historically compelling and vividly staged new Irish drama unearths little known story ... A sterling ensemble achievement, alternately scalding and magical in its theatricality.
Los Angeles Times

Total Eclipse of the Heart – a tremendous play – many people are just overwhelmed by its power.
Colin Lacey, Arts Section, Irish Voice NY 1995

Ms. Brogan paints a canvas filled with vivid portraits that reveal the full tragedy not only of the penitents but of the emotional price paid by their carers and keepers.
Elyse Sommer, Curtain Up

Eclipsed contains a great dramatic force, a cry of horror for a life that slips away without a chance of being lived.
Mauro Martinelli of Sipario, Firenze (Translation) 1995

Eclipsed is a celebration of Life, of Freedom, an exaltation of survival at any cost. It is a story of women united, joined by the same pain and sad destiny, women who were strengthened by their tragic experiences. I was struck by its chorality, by the idea of a group which is always on stage – every character is finely drawn and all roles are really beautiful – by the fact that it is a play for eight women, very unusual in theatre.
Massimo Stinco, Dottore in Discipline delle Arti, della Musica, dello Spettacolo, Associazione Teatro Firenze

To deal with such a difficult subject requires both the skill and sensitivity of the artist ... Perhaps it is the kind of subject only the artist is really capable of exploring. By dealing with those dark corners of our collective social and historical experience, the dramatist has the chance to bring light, compassion and understanding in a way no one else can quite achieve.
Jeff O'Connell, The Galway Advertiser, February 1992

This is powerful and moving theatre, all the more powerful because it is understated.
Evening News, Edinburgh Theatre Festival 1992

A compelling Irish play called Eclipsed brims over with darkness and light, rising from Ireland's boggy soil like a wailing banshee ...
Ray Loynd, Los Angeles Times, 21 April 1995
A sterling ensemble achievement, alternately scalding and magical in its

theatricality.
Los Angeles Times April 23 1995

Well written, witty and poignant, Eclipsed unfolds like a young rose, each petal revealing the sad, sad stories of these forgotten women.
The Nine Mass USA 1994

Despite a seemingly bleak and dark subject matter, the play is filled with humour and celebration ... and the script is well-crafted and subtly poetic. This is a fine piece of work and deserves a large audience.
Seattle Fringe Review Rag 1995

A small masterpiece.
Sr. Ailbhe in The Galway Advertiser.

If you do nothing else with your life, Patricia, you did that. Michael D. Higgins, then Minister for Arts, Culture and the Gaeltacht, (After the first night of Eclipsed in Punchbag Theatre.)

A fair treatment of an unfair time.
Ciara Dwyer Irish Independent.

Eclipsed is a play which demands to be seen, not just from the Irish perspective, but as a universal exploration of suffering and insidious cruelty within society.
Adrian Byrne, The Irish Arts Review July 1998.

Patricia Burke Brogan's plays have always seemed a little ahead of their time.
Prof. Patrick Lonergan, Irish Times.

Notes from the catalogue of *Pilgrimage*, a retrospective exhibition of my art work.

_____

Patricia Burke Brogan - Artist

I first met Patricia Burke in the 1960's, not long after I came to Galway. A meeting had been organised by Dr. John Heskin of College Road which had the intention of forming a branch of Tuairim. That organisation was facilitating discussion and publishing pamphlets on the numerous sacred cows which had survived into the Ireland of the First Programme for Economic Expansion. Among the aims of the half dozen or so who came was the advancement of music and art in the city. As to the cows – some wanted them to continue in sacred sleep.

It was long before Galway acquired its present reputation for innovation in the arts but I am clear about the quiet presence that was there at this meeting, and others like it, before the beginning of the contemporary surge in the arts in Galway. That presence was Patricia Burke-Brogan. I recall her making the case for creativity and the arts in education. If the history of Galway in the modern period is written it will include the patrons who stood at the long Burmese teak counter of the Tavern. The Lenihan family establishment was the location for one of Patricia's first exhibitions and had the advantage that we could discuss the pictures and the event with Pat and Eddie, in what had become a familiar space.

Even now I recall being struck by the perfection she sought. This showed particularly in her approach to what was for her a new medium – graphics. Laura Vecchi's large printing press was an emblem of the times – a piece of art equipment in search of a home – like everything else artistic in the City at the time. There were of course the exceptional voluntary efforts including the Galway Art Club that brought such work as that of Hubert Broderick in watercolour and gouache to the fore. Exhibitions were rare however and Brian Bourke's first Galway Exhibition in the Kenny Gallery had yet to take place.

At the same time as there were stirrings in the visual arts, literary festivals were being established, the leading one of which was Listowel Writers Week.

Among the first to participate was Patricia. Poetry followed short stories and meanwhile the painting was changing in terms of theme, composition and method. It was reflecting the regular visits made to Italy and Spain. The abstract work now emerging had for me the darkness of the costumes of a Lorca play, the colours of dried blood and the obsessive turns of memory – evidenced in the tones and textures of the work.

Her first stage play "Eclipsed" changed everything. A play that was as faithful to the lives its characters represented as it was to the hidden stories could almost not have had another author.

In that play the risks were taken, of writing out of one's own life experience because, in touching other's lives, one had encountered a hidden story of grief and enforced silence. It represented a drawing back of the veil in many senses. It is appropriate that "Eclipsed" and the later work have received recognition abroad, particularly in the U.S. where they are regular choices for University and Studio performance.

The Award of an Arts Council Creative Writing Bursary, and an Award from the European Script Writers Fund were recognition of a talent that was original and important.

Such awards are only some of the recognition given to the work of Patricia Burke-Brogan. They are all well merited and it is hard to think of anybody who has moved through all the different art forms with such insight and artistic success.

But behind all the artistic achievement, as I have said, was the painting. To me it is a backdrop to all of the work. It itself, like the artist, has moved through several phases. Each phase, however, gives a sense of a departure with such a sense of attention to detail and perfection as will make a return possible. The painting has also changed, in intent. From visual impact it has moved through emotional tides that have included the emerging liberation of the female in Ireland that has respected memory and the resonance of place.

An exhibition of Patricia Burke-Brogan's work will always be rich in the sources to which it may return but it will also hold the prospect of a new departure. She is truly at the centre of innovation and experiment in the artistic life of Galway.

For her presence so long before Galway's contemporary artistic reputation was established, her work right through it in such an integrative way, with the visual, the aural, lyrical and the dramatic, for her seeking excellence and sharing it, as artist, teacher and sensitive human being, it is appropriate that we pay tribute to Patricia Burke-Brogan – and I with many are grateful to her and may the onward march of her curiosity and achievement in the arts continue into the new century.

Michael D. Higgins.

Looking Back - Looking Forward

Time is on loan, month by month, day by day it emerges and vanishes. The artist is alert to the urgency of time. She endeavours to hold moments of experience or vision in an artistic form which transience cannot reach. The artist imagines sifts of time to discover its concealed eternity. Every real artist is haunted by that rupture between time and eternity, known and unknown, seen and unseen. It is on this tense and second threshold that the intuitions, whispers and glimpses are gathered which foster creation. Patricia Burke is a true artist. In terms of personality, she is quiet and unostentatious. In terms of the art imagination, she is wild, endowed with a raging, experienced art intellect. A retrospective exhibition is always special. It affords both the artist and public the opportunity to "look back" over a whole chronology of art exploration and growth. A retrospective assembles in sequence all the different phases of the artwork. By any standard, this retrospective concerns the prodigious creativity of Patricia Burke. It also illustrates the great inner division of her work. The exhibition includes paintings and etchings of Old Galway, City Pilgrimages, the Normans, Music, the Ocean, An tOilean, An Doras and Landscape and its various presences. This retrospective spans 40 years of artwork. Galway is now a flourishing and encouraging art centre. It was not always thus. In earlier decades there was no encouragement and often little welcome for the fruits of the imagination. It is a testimony to the integrity of Patricia Burke that she continues her quiet meticulous art and craft regardless of the times.

In recent years, she has published a fine collection of poetry "Above the Waves, Calligraphy" and the subversive and devastating play "Eclipsed" which won her international recognition as a writer of courage and finely tempered imagination. The focus on her as a writer almost made us forget what a wonderful painter she is. This retrospective exhibition affords Galway an opportunity to recognise and acknowledge her. A characteristic of this retrospective is Patricia Burke's continual request for new and challenging forms of expression. It shows a great trust in the unknown and a fierce unwillingness to settle for what is complacent or successful. She submits the depths of her individuality to the full rigours of art exploration. This is the secret to the luminosity, originality and subtle darkness of this wonderful exhibition of exhibition. Often a retrospective denotes the closure of a career; however, these paintings witness to a restless and resourceful visual imagination, which has closed nothing. In actual fact, the logic of this retrospective could be the launch of a new imaginative pilgrimage for Patricia Burke. A Pilgrimage in which truth and individuality would be key qualities. As the poet Wallace Stevens said: "Anyone with a passion for truth will of necessity be original".

John O'Donohue

List of Early Exhibitions

Solo Exhibition Stone Art Gallery, Spiddal 1984.
Solo Exhibitions United Arts club, Dublin 1985, 1989.
Women in Action Group Exhibition, Nuns Island Arts Centre, Galway 1984, 1985.
Invited to Fredrikstad print Biennalo, Norway 1982.
Listowel Third International Biennale 1982, Honourable Mention.
Solo Exhibition, Stone Art Gallery, Galway 1982.
Two-person Exhibition, Ostan Carraroe1982.
Group Exhibitions Stone Art Gallery, Spiddal, 1982, 1983, 1984.
Galway Arts Centre (with Grafica 11 Ireland) 1982.
Arts Council Travelling Exhibition, Co. Mayo and Dublin Airport 1983.
Listowel National Graphic Exhibitions 1982, 1983, 1984.
Galway based Artists, Stone Art Gallery, Galway 1981, 1982.
Listowel Second International Biennale, 1980.
Alliance Francaise de Dublin (with Grafica 11 Ireland) 1980.
Tuam Theatre Arts Centre (with Grafica 11 Ireland) 1980.
University College Galway (with Grafica 11 Ireland) 1980.
Third National Fine Arts Exhibition, Claremorris 1980.
Group Exhibition, Project Gallery, Dublin 1980, 1984.
Bank of Ireland, Baggot St. Dublin Exhibition (with Grafica 11 Ireland) 1979.
Galway Arts Festival Exhibition 1978.
Exhibition of Visual Arts, Limerick EVA, 1978.
Listowel International Biennale in Listowel and Belfast 1978.
Douglas Hyde Gallery, Dublin (with Grafica 11 Ireland) 1978.
Arts Society Lavitts Quay, Cork (with Grafica 11 Ireland) 1978.
Oireachtas Exhibition, Municipal Gallery Dublin and Arts Council Belfast 1977.
National Exhibition Women's Art, Kenny Gallery, Salthill 1975.

CONTENTS

Thorntree

The wind from the Burren is against me as I take my bicycle from under the thorntree at Kilcolgan crossroads. Head down, I push and push on creaking pedals towards the cut-stone school framed by a cut-stone wall in Ballinderreen. The air is needle-sharp with sleet on my face and limbs.

'Just because I'm leaving the Novitiate shouldn't mean that I'll lose my position in the convent school, Mother Superior!' I had protested.

'Once you leave, we'll have nothing more to do with you, Sister. You'll never get a teaching job in this diocese.'

Waxed floorboards, incense, starched veils, custody of the eyes are in a world of the past.

Without the protection now of coif and veil, I pull my woollen scarf down over my ears and starting-to-grow auburn hair.

Ballinderreen is on the edge of the diocese of Galway and Kilmacduagh. Ballinderreen is on the edge of the Burren.

'You say you wish to leave our Novitiate! You've no vocation, Sister! No vocation!' Mother Superior's six-foot frame had overshadowed my kneeling figure.

'There are different kinds of vocation, Mother Superior.' I stood up.

'On your knees, Sister! You must wait for permission from Rome. You mustn't tell anyone of your intention. I put you under obedience! A mortal sin if you tell.'

Truth disappeared like water from turloughs in Burren limestone.

The walls of the schoolroom are a sludge-colour, the floorboards do not fit together; soot falls from the chimney with a thump.

The children are bright and happy. They bring gifts, bags of turf, pieces of driftwood and oysters from the sea.

I light a fire.

I encourage them to paint their stories on old newspapers with their fingers, sticks and feathers using ashes and soot bound with paste.

When boxes of powder-paints I had ordered from Dublin arrive, we cover the classroom walls with their story-paintings. Ultramarines, chrome yellows, alizarin crimsons resonate and blaze in fractured sunlight.

I post their paintings to a Children's Art Competition in Dublin. They win first, second and many other prizes. When this is announced in the *Connacht Tribune*, a member of the local branch of the teachers' union objects to the fact that the success of another member is publicised. Though this causes me pain, I continue with my own teaching methods and the children win prizes annually at local and national levels.

We sing Plain Chant and Irish ballads.

One stormy morning the *Cigire* sits in his grey Volkswagen outside the school gate.

From Kilcolgan, I push and push creaking pedals against the southwest gale, but I'm still two minutes late.

'Are those your own paintings, *a mhúinteoir?*' the *Cigire* stares at the classroom walls. The children raise their hands and point: 'Mine, that's mine, that's mine, *a dhuine uasail.*'

'That's King Guaire and his soldiers eating a big feast in his castle beyond in Kinvara!' Seósamh comes forward.

'That's King Guaire's brother, St. Colman, and his holy monks in Kilmacduagh. His holy monks are starving with the hunger,' Carmel points with both hands. 'St. Colman is down on his knees praying to God to send food for his holy monks. All of a sudden, every one of King Guaire's dinner plates, packed full of sausages and Christmas pudding and ice-cream and jelly, rise up and fly away to St. Colman in Kilmacduagh,' she continues.

'But King Guaire's soldiers jump on their horses and race and race and race after the plates,' Pádraig says as he pretends he's riding a horse. 'When they come to *Bóthar na Mias*, the horses' hooves get stuck to the rocks just outside St. Colman's monastery. They can't move an inch, no matter how the soldiers shout and roar at them.'

'St. Colman and his holy monks have a huge big party and they don't forget to say thank you to God for the sausages and Christmas pudding and ice-cream,' Caitlín insists.

'And jelly!' shouts Pádraigín.

'You can still see the tracks of the horses' hooves in the rocks, if you go over to *Bóthar na Mias!*' the children point towards Bell Harbour.

Seán is wide-eyed with wonder as he says, 'That's what *múinteór* told us.'

On the next stormy morning, the *Cigire's* grey Volkswagen splashes past me as I pedal against another southwesterly. When I reach Ballinderreen, the *Cigire*, spectacles down over his sharp nose, stands at the school gate. He writes in his diary and says, 'Three minutes late, *a mhúinteóir!*'

Suddenly his hat flies off towards Kinvara.

I pray to St. Colman of Kilmacduagh to send a tornado.

We sing our new song, *Va Pensiero*. The *Cigire* doesn't understand Italian and cannot sing.

'It's the *Slaves' Chorus* and Verdi made it up and wrote it all down beyond in Italy!' Tomás tells the *Cigire* as Pearl points to Italy on the globe beside the fireplace.

He writes in his diary and drives away in his grey Volkswagen.

The children paint pictures of the *Cigire's* hat lost among the grykes and turloughs of the Burren.

'That ice-cap must be very huge, *a mhúinteóir*, to make such great big scratchy grykes in the Burren as it squashed away into the sea. Was it huger than our church across the road?' asks Seán as he pushes more ultramarine mixed with burnt umber around his grykes painting.

'It could've been ten times, maybe a thousand times, bigger than our church, a Sheáin,' I answer.

'It must have reached away up, up, up to the sky, *a mhúinteóir!*' Caitlín says, raising her arms.

'A monster of an icy-cap, so it was,' shouts Tomás.

I cycle to Kilcolgan and park my bicycle once again under my thorntree. I give it a goodbye pat. It's the bicycle my parents bought me for my tenth birthday.

A lay teacher, cousin of the Superior, sits at my desk in the convent school.

Her Ford Zephyr is parked at the school gate.

In Galway City my mother is battling with cancer.

Ten years later, the *Árd Cigire* himself will introduce me to the 'three-minutes-late' *Cigire* at the Department of Education in Dublin. I want to smile, but instead I look him in the eyes and say, 'How do you do?' before I turn to the *Árd Cigire* to be congratulated on my commitment to the Arts in Education.

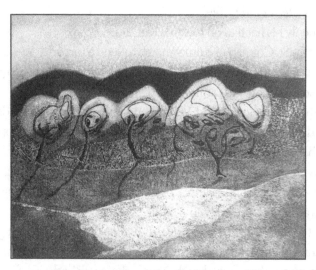

Thorntrees 1980
Soft ground relief colour etching

Crossroads

On a snowy afternoon in February our *Sagart Paróiste*, a saintly clergyman, knocks at our classroom window. I promise to bring him the usual supply of white clerical collars and a box of black shoe polish from the *siopa mór* in Galway City.

Should I also suggest that he order a new pair of shoes? The *Sagart Paróiste* doesn't know that when he leaves his shoes outside his bedroom door, his housekeeper loans them to her boyfriend for their ballroom-dancing sessions in Gort.

'What size shoe do you take, *a athair*?' I ask.

'Size seven, wide, black and laced, but this pair will do me for the rest of my days.'

He blesses me and blesses my journeys to and from the city.

That evening as I approach Kilcolgan crossroads, I see the bus flash past.

It's too far to cycle the fifteen miles home. I leave my bicycle under my thorntree, stand by the roadside and pray to St. Jude, patron of hopeless cases.

The *Gárda Siochána*, who lives nearby, notices my predicament. He holds up a safe-looking car and asks the driver to give me a seat to Galway City. The driver is dressed in a dark suit, gaudy shirt and tie. He wears horn-rimmed spectacles and smells of stale cigarette smoke. There are cardboard boxes with red lettering on the back seat. Embarrassed by taking a seat from a stranger, I revert to custody of the eyes as practised in the Novitiate, and I try to take up as little room as possible in the passenger seat.

'So you missed the Galway bus, young lady!'

'Yes, by a few minutes. Thank you for giving me a seat.'

'Are you interested in fashion?' he looks sideways at my home-made cycling outfit.

'Yes. I'm very interested in fashion.'

'Good! I can see that you're a smart young lady. Do you make your own clothes?'

'Yes, I like to sew dresses, but jackets and coats are difficult.'

'Then you must buy one of my Conqueror sewing machines! You'd have no difficulty with jackets, even heavy coats. I'm Agent for Conqueror in the West of Ireland.'

'But we've a good sewing machine at home, my mother's Singer.'

'A Singer machine! Singers are finished, are archaic! With my Conqueror you can embroider with satin-stitch, chain-stitch, lazy-daisy, blanket-stitch and all in colour!'

'But I prefer to embroider by hand.'

'By hand! Why should you waste your time, when you could be walking the Prom and admiring the fellas swimming and diving in Salthill!'

He takes his left hand from the steering wheel and stretches it towards me. I scrunch myself away from him against the passenger door.

'Here, look at these beautiful samples.' He twists towards a box as we turn a corner.

'Watch out!' I scream. He swerves, narrowly avoiding a petrol lorry.

'You can show me those samples when we get to Galway City. This road surface is dangerous!' I protest.

'I've never had an accident. Never! Stop worrying!'

'But, you almost –'

'My sewing machines work even when you're not watching them. Just set up your colours, press a button and they're off. It's magic!'

In the Novitiate, some of our recreation sessions were spent embroidering badges and holy pictures.

'I'm not really interested in embroidery,' I say.

'What pretty young woman isn't interested in embroidery? It's the latest fashion in Paris, New York and Washington. Jackie Kennedy embroiders every day of her life. She uses one of our Conquerors.'

'Who's Jackie Kennedy?' I ask.

'Jackie Kennedy! Do you not read newspapers? Her husband, John

F. Kennedy, is the President of our nearest neighbour across Galway Bay. Jackie and John F. will visit Ireland this summer. I've been asked to set up one of our sewing machines in Dublin, so that she can keep up her embroidery when John F. is busy. She's the best-dressed woman in the world!'

We slither into Clarinbridge. Suddenly he puts on the brakes and nearly collides with a lamppost.

'Great big fat oysters in Paddy Burke's with homemade brown bread and a pint of Guinness will warm the cockles of your heart.' He salivates. 'Would you like a few oysters, my young lady? To put some flesh on your bones!'

'No, no, thank you very much.'

'That's a pity. Are you sure?'

'Yes, thank you. I am sure.' I pray to his guardian angel.

He drives on faster and begins to hum tunelessly. I pray to my own guardian angel.

Relieved that we've got through Oranmore safely, I plan an escape. Should I say I live near Merlin Park? Then I could walk home the rest of the way. No. That'd be a lie. I pray again to St. Jude.

As we pass the triangular field in Roscam, where the last duel in Ireland was fought, I remember that love story, but dare not distract him. He might swerve again and hit the Red Railway Bridge.

'Are you related to that *Gárda* in Kilcolgan, my young lady?'

'No, but whenever I miss the bus, he flags down a car for me.'

'Nice man.'

'He's very kind. A real Christian. I've promised him a copy of *The Thomas Davis Lectures*, as a thank-you token.'

'A real Christian, you say! Not many of those around. Are there?' He looks sideways at me again. I decide not to answer him and I keep my eyes on the icy road. It's not the time for staring at tree-shapes at Merlin Park or at cloud formations above Ballyloughane. If only that bus had been a few minutes late!

'If you like, I'll give you a good cut on a span new Conqueror and I'll take away that useless old Singer of yours. What do you say?'

'It's my mother's sewing machine! I'm busy making dresses for my sisters and myself.'

In my mind's eye, I see myself, a six-year old seamstress, making dresses for my dolls. I cut and rip silk frills from my mother's shell-pink ball gown and tack them into skirt-shapes. Mother doesn't scold me, but folds her best gown of salmon-pink crepe-de-Chine in lavender tissue paper and places it in a large cardboard box.

'In case our little dress designer cuts this up for her dolls!' she says to Dad. 'Please keep it in your office.'

Mother's porcelain skin, which suited those delicate pinks, is now yellowed with cancer. I must get home to her immediately.

'Stop here at Calvary Hospital. Just here, please. Our house is quite near.' I put my hand on the handle of the door. 'Thank you very much for the offer of a Conqueror sewing machine and thank you for the seat.'

The car skids to a halt as he pulls in at Duggan's shop-on-the-corner. I get out quickly. He grins and winks through his horn-rimmed spectacles.

'Young lady, you'll have changed your mind when we meet again at that crossroads!' he insists.

Delighted to be free from his sales talk, I promise myself that from now on, hail, rain or snow, I'll be in time for that bus at Kilcolgan. Tomorrow I'll ask our *Sagart Paróiste* for another blessing.

Lady Ampthill

It's Catechism Time and we're preparing for the annual Plain Chant Festival in Gort.

We make and decorate a banner with our school's name, *Scoil Náisiúnta le Naomh Sourney.*

We chant the Gregorian *Missa de Angelis, Kyrie eleison, Kyrie eleison, Christe eleison, Christe eleison.*

'They're funny words, *a mhúinteóir.*'

'They're Greek words from a far-away land.'

'Mhúinteóir, a mhúinteóir, is that the Holy Land where Jesus was born?'

'No, it's not the Holy Land. It's a place where, long, long ago, people made beautiful statues -- sculptures they're called. They built great buildings with marble columns and wrote wonderful story-plays. They were able to run faster and jump higher than anyone else in the world. Who wants to visit Greece when they've grown up?'

'Me, me, me, *a mhúinteóir!'* they shout in chorus.

We find Greece on the globe and then point out the Holy Land.

'Can we pretend we're in Greece now and dress up, a *mhúinteóir.'*

With scarves draped around our shoulders we chant, *Kyrie eleison, Christe eleison.*

'Now, children, we're going on a visit to the Holy Land. It's Palm Sunday. Jesus rides through Jerusalem on a donkey. That's why every donkey has a big mark like a cross on its back. We'll stand on each side of the classroom and, with the people of Jerusalem, wave our copybooks like palm trees. Now we'll chant the Latin words.'

'Latin words? What's Latin words, *a mhúinteóir?'*

'Pope Gregory used Latin words every day. He lived in Rome and his choir sang in Latin. Our *Sagart Paróiste* uses Latin words during Mass.'

'Gloria in excelsis Deo. Et in terra pax hominibus –

Sanctus, Sanctus, Sanctus,' we continue.

'Can we pretend we're in Rome now, *a mhúinteoir?*'

'Tomorrow we'll talk about Pope Gregory and Rome. Are we ready to sing *Benedictus qui venit in nomine Domini?*'

A sharp knock on the front window distracts us.

Lady Ampthill, her blonde hair straying from under a crimson scarf, her sparkling eyes outlined with lime green eye-shadow, beckons. I open the window. Her red sports car, with horse box attached, is parked at the school gate.

'Tell the little creatures that I'll give them a party at my castle in Kinvara! Next Saturday at twelve noon my coach will pick them up here.'

Leaving a whiff of lavender and cigarette smoke in the air, she bounces out the gate and into her car.

'A party with Lady Ampthill next Saturday if you're here at noon,' I announce.

'Lady Ampthill, Lady Ampthill, lives in a castle.

She gives us lollipops and banana sandwiches,' the children chant.

'She's a very kind lady and she takes great care of her castle, *Dún Guaire.*

We must practise the *Credo.* The Plain Chant Festival takes place in three weeks,' I insist. With the help of the tuning fork, I find the right note and we chant.

Credo in unum Deum, Patrem omnipotentem, factorem caeli et terrae,

visibilium omnium et invisibilium. Et in unum Dominum –

'My Daddy says that Lady Ampthill is a desperate bad driver, a *mhúinteóir!*

She's afraid to pass out anyone cycling on the road.'

The children wear their Sunday clothes for the Plain Chant Festival in Gort. Knitted berets, patent buckled shoes and navy anoraks on the girls, boys in navy Confirmation suits with green rosettes. Holding our banner high, we march through streets decorated with flags and bunting. Towns-people wave as we turn towards the church hall.

The ghosts of King Guaire and his horsemen ride beside us.

Lady Gregory, Yeats, Synge and a host of famous writers, holding quills and ink-spattered notebooks, glow amongst the shadows.

Lady Ampthill's sports car is parked near the church. One of the Gort boyos leaps into the driver's seat and tries to start the engine. Lady Ampthill, scarf flying, jumps into the passenger seat and asks him his name. In her notebook, she writes his answer, *Colman Ó Guaire.*

'I'll report you to the police, young ruffian!' She pushes him out, slides into the driver's seat and, engine roaring, races towards the *Gárda* Barracks.

(The young ruffian is the son of a local *Gárda.*) As she approaches the Barracks, she sees our *Sagart Paróiste* and brakes abruptly. Our *Sagart Paróiste* listens to her complaint and gives her his blessing.

For three minutes Lady Ampthill, scarlet gloves on steering wheel, sits statue-like in her sports car.

Does she see the spirits of King Guaire and St. Colman as they ride past?

Suddenly, she puts on even more crimson lipstick, turns her car and slowly drives towards the church.

While the first choir chants the *Credo,* I hear, '*Mhúinteóir, mhúinteóir!* That choir made a mistake! They sang, *visibilum omnium instead of visibilium omnium, a mhúinteóir!*'

When our choir chants the *Credo,* I spot Lady Ampthill at the door of the church hall.

The adjudicator praises us and says that our voices are sweeter than those of the Galway choirs. Lady Ampthill applauds and announces, 'Another party for the little creatures!'

'Lollipops, lollipops,' whisper our little angels.

'Say, 'Thank you, Lady Ampthill', I insist.

'Thank you, Lady Ampthill', they say with a smile.

I remind the children that another Lady called Lady Gregory had lived nearby.

'Did that Lady live in a castle too, *a mhúinteóir?*'

'Lady Gregory didn't live in a castle. But in her big house at Coole Park, she gave parties for famous visitors, people who wrote poems and story-plays. W. B. Yeats, Sean O'Casey, Douglas Hyde and John Millington Synge. Lady Gregory wrote story-plays too. Lady Gregory will be remembered forever.'

'Will Lady Ampthill be remembered forever, *a mhúinteoir?* Does she write story-plays?'

'No, she doesn't write story-plays, but she takes great care of *Dún Guaire*.'

The *Príomh Oide* treats us to lunch of chicken, chips and dessert in Glynns' Hotel beside the convent's cloistered walls. We eat, not in novitiate-like silence, but with peals of excited laughter. The ice-creamed faces of the children are reflected in the wall-mirrors.

On the road home, we pass Coole Park and wave to the spirits of Lady Gregory and her famous visitors.

'Lady Gregory with her special friends founded the Abbey Theatre in Dublin. On our next outing to Dublin we'll visit the Abbey Theatre,' I promise.

'But a *mhúinteóir*, why can't we go to the Zoo? I want to see the huge big elephants, the stripey tigers and the monkeys with funny faces. Please, *a mhúinteóir*.'

'Of course we'll visit the Zoo. But we'll also pass by the Abbey Theatre and wave our hands in memory of those great writers.'

'But *a mhúinteóir, a mhúinteóir*, Lady Ampthill is driving after our bus!'

'She will not pass!' says the *Príomh Oide*. 'She was furious, when two of our boys cycled slowly, one on either side of the road, all the way from Kilcolgan to Ballinderreen. She couldn't or wouldn't overtake. When our two boys reached the crossroads in the village, one swerved off on the road to the left and the other took the road to the right. I had to allow her check an identity parade in my *seomra ranga*, while her green eye-shadow melted with emotion. Later, I found the two boys hiding under coats in the girls' cloakroom! Of course, I didn't report them to her Ladyship.'

'*Mhúinteóir, a mhuinteóir*, Lady Ampthill's gone off down that side-road to Kinvara!'

As the sun sets in Galway Bay, the sleeping-elephant forms of the Burren are melting into crimson cloud-shapes. From the honeycombed limestone grykes, a tide of gentian, bloody cranesbill and bee-orchid spills towards our school walls.

To the south flows the River Shannon on its way to meet the sea.

The Crimson Parlour

The Superiors travel to Dublin to buy an outfit for my return to secular life.

In Clerys of O'Connell Street they choose a coffin-brown coat and a scarf of red gauze. They know nothing about fashion, having been enclosed in black and white armour for most of their lives. Afterwards they enjoy a substantial lunch in the Gresham Hotel and return in triumph bearing the scarf and shroud-like garment.

The following evening, I'm called to the Crimson Parlour to meet His Lordship, the Bishop. He sits at the rosewood table surrounded by three Superiors. The human-hearted Mother of Novices is not present. Reluctantly I obey the signal to kneel.

'God bless you, my child.' His Lordship extends his ruby ring to be kissed.

Mother Superior pushes a document towards me.

'Now sign here.' His Lordship offers me his golden fountain pen. Thinking that this is my freedom letter from Rome, I'm shocked to read that I'm asked to sign away all rights to payment for my work as a teacher in the convent schools.

Six months earlier I had told the Mother Superior that I wished to leave the community immediately. Her words echo in my mind. 'No vocation? So you've no vocation, Sister! I put you under Obedience, a mortal sin if you tell anyone of your decision. You must wait for permission from Rome.'

I believed that I had to wait for some faceless official in some musty office in the Vatican to sign a slip of paper. In fact I could have walked out the hall door at any time.

Truth disappeared like water from turloughs in Burren limestone.

I read in this document that a fee of fifty pounds will be paid to His

Lordship for his presence. Taking up the bishop's pen, I sign the document. I'd sign anything to get out.

'Come with me,' the Superior's dark voice orders as, smiling sweetly, she returns the pen to His Lordship. We walk across the incense-drenched corridor to the Blue Parlour.

'Your lay clothing is there on that armchair. Leave your habit, coif and veil with your ring, rosary beads and belt in this sideboard. Do not attempt to return to the cloister or speak to any of the sisters. A taxi waits at the hall door. Goodbye.'

'Goodbye, Mother Superior.'

For the last time I remove that starched half-circle from my heart. I fold my black habit and slip the silver ring engraved with Christ Crucified from my finger. Untying the tapes of my coif, I pull a length of thread from my veil and roll it into my handkerchief.

I place veil, habit, coif, guimpe, rosary beads, leather belt and ring in the already opened walnut sideboard. A gauze scarf? This scarf will not conceal my ragged scalp.

I put on the ugly coat and secure my rolled-up handkerchief in one of its empty pockets.

Retreating glaciers at the end of the Ice Age had cut grykes into Burren limestone and left treasures in their depths.

Outside the hall door my father gives me a big hug and opens the taxi door for me.

'I'll be back in a few minutes, love,' he says and rings the convent doorbell.

My father doesn't tell me what he said to the Superiors on that December evening.

He is a hero of the War of Independence and a courageous Christian.

The Angelus bell rings as the taxi brings me back to my family and to the world outside. Next day my mother takes me to a shop in Eglinton Street. There she buys me a smart cream wool coat and a beret to match. We go to the GBC for coffee and cakes.

People recognise me on the street. There are nudges and whispers as I pass.

At Moon's Corner a schoolchild says, 'Mammy! Look, Mammy! Has my *múinteór* turned into a woman?'

Later a friend advises me, 'Walk up and down Shop Street every day for a week and after that nobody will stare at you.'

Bad diet in the Novitiate and lack of fresh air on my scalp slows down the re-growth of my hair. I visit a hairdresser called Beverley.

'What style would you like?' She stands, scissors ready.

'Just a trim to give it shape,' I reply.

I hear again the strange words of that stony-faced Superior – 'This gives me the greatest pleasure' – as, scissors steel-sharp against my skull, she shears away my long auburn hair. I can still feel those starched coif-tapes tighten on my skull. I raise my hands to loosen them.

'Sorry, Beverley.' I jump up, pull off the robe, grab my shopping bag and rush out of the salon.

Cancer

My mother visits a consultant in the Crescent. The following week, she has a surgery procedure in Calvary Hospital. This surgery weakens her further. My only brother, a Roman Catholic priest in Surrey, returns home for a visit. We realise that mother is gravely ill. A cloak of sadness envelops our family. Aunt Clara comes from her convent of St. Louis in Monaghan and prays with us. Uncles and aunts from Dublin, Cork and Longford arrive. Mother's cousin, Ciarán Bairéad, folklorist, brings healing water from a Holy Well.

Weeks go by as we take care of mother. The Blue Nuns from Calvary Hospital visit her once a day. I cook her favourite meal – duckling, garden peas and baked potato. Propped by pillows, she sits up and tries to eat.

During those last weeks of her life I travel to teach in Ballinderreen. I rest for a few hours on my return home and sit beside her during the night.

When the Reverend Diocesan Inspector pays his annual visit to Ballinderreen, he praises the children's religious artwork and their singing of Plain Chant.

'I'll be going back to Galway at three o'clock and I can give you a seat home, if you wish, *a mhúinteóir*,' he tells me before he writes a report in his diary.

'Thank you very much, *a athair*.'

As we drive past Kilcolgan, he says, 'If you see an important-looking black car coming towards us, please crouch down out of view, in case His Lordship is taking a cruise around his diocese!'

'Yes. I'll become an invisible woman, *a athair*! But shouldn't you be wearing your black hat too?' He reaches for his hat of velour and puts it on at an angle.

'You're right. His Lordship chastised an archbishop from the USA last week for walking the Prom without a hat. But that archbishop was well able to squash him with a belt of his American crozier, when he displayed his newly-acquired Cardinal's colours!'

As we reach Renmore Road, I look anxiously at the windows of my home and am relieved to see that the drapes are not closed.

'Thank you very much, *a athair*. This gives me extra time with mother.'

'I'll say Mass for her tomorrow morning. *Slán agus beannacht*.'

I take my portfolio, get out of the car and he drives away.

Mother drifts in and out of coma. Her heart continues to beat strongly, though I can lift her with one arm. Singing her favourite hymn, *Salve Regina*, I sponge and apply lotions and oils to her emaciated body.

When her condition worsens I telephone my brother's presbytery to say that it's time to come. His Parish Priest responds with, 'How am I going to manage the Easter Ceremonies without my curate?'

My father, sisters, brother and I keep watch as mother passes away on that Monday evening before Easter Sunday. Because it's Holy Week, a Requiem Mass is not allowed.

'This can't be true,' I whisper, as shivering in a bitter March wind, we follow mother's body to The New Cemetery above *Loch an tSáile*.

Years earlier, I had sat beside my pregnant mother in a car parked outside the gate of Cloonmorris graveyard. Inside beneath the white marble family monument, Granny O'Beirne's coffin was being lowered into the earth. That sound of clay on board, punctuated by mother's sobs, still echoes in my mind.

Here again there's that thud of clay on coffin, that drone of rosary-prayer.

No! That's not my mother down there in that coffin. No. No!

I look up.

A jet weaves a cloud-prayer above Burren limestone.

Outside

In spite of my work in painting and music, the 'in the nuns' stigma attaches itself to me like a barnacle. After a period of mourning for my mother, I venture to dances in Seapoint Ballroom with my student sister. One gossiping holy-water-hen remarks, 'With you leaving the convent, it's no wonder your mother got cancer and died!'

Before I entered the Novitiate, there were many admirers wanting to 'do a line' with me. Some now give me a 'duty dance' and move on quickly. My most attractive feature, my Titian hair, hasn't grown back yet. I'm the same person, but with that bruised stigma.

I spend a lot of time on the balcony, as I pull my hair to make it grow faster. A farmer from east Galway asks me to dance. As we quickstep under a revolving sphere, he sings the hymn, *Tantum ergo Sacramentum, Veneremur cernui* ... I'm too polite to walk away.

One night I decide to go home early. As I go down the balcony steps to get my coat from the Ladies' Cloakroom, a handsome farmer asks me for a dance. I had often danced with him before I entered the Novitiate. After the usual two dances and a lemonade, he takes me home and offers to meet me in Seapoint the following Sunday night. We meet on the balcony as arranged and dance to the rhythms of Dickie Rock and his band. I then decide to accept his offer of a seat home. When we arrive at my garden gate, he turns to me and says, 'You're a nice girl, Patricia, but, you see, my two brothers are priests. I'm sure you'll meet someone else.'

'My only brother is also a priest and my cousin is a cardinal. I hope you'll meet another nice girl. Goodbye,' I say as I hurry out of his mud-splattered Volkswagen.

After a few weeks, I return to the balcony in Seapoint. The stench of unwashed bodies mixed with cigarette smoke and cheap perfume rises on quick-step-waltzing air. In the Ladies' Cloakroom, girls drink from small bottles of whiskey or vodka before going downstairs to wait at floor-edges for dance partners. Aching bachelors arrive from nearby public houses. Full of alcoholic courage, they grab the nearest girls and dance cheek-to-cheek. Brendan Bowyer's body rocks to his song, *You put your right foot in and your right foot out. You do the Hoky Poky and you turn around. That's what it's all about.*

Starry-eyed couples leave the ballroom early. The blaring music softens. The last dance is announced to the crooning of *Love thee dearest, love thee …*

In Seapoint a few years later, a tall man comes up the balcony stairs, takes my hand and leads me into the Dance of Life.

On holidays

Choirs

I'm organist in the Abbey Church and I also play the harmonium for our parish choir. At weekends I'm therefore obliged to rush from a ceremony in the Abbey to another ceremony in the church on Renmore Road.

A vacancy arises for an assistant teacher in one of our parish schools.

I send my CV and references to our *Sagart Paróiste*, the Reverend Manager. During the interview he treats me to tea and biscuits in his presbytery. He compliments me on my work with the choirs and talks about my other accomplishments. The fact that I had left the Novitiate and no longer teach in the convent schools is not mentioned. As I leave, he smiles as he says, 'I hope you'll get that teaching job.'

Truth disappears like water from turloughs in Burren limestone.

He fails to tell me that the vacancy has already been filled by a friend of his family. When I hear of this appointment a few days afterwards, I become even more disillusioned. I resign from the parish choir.

I make a resolution that from now on attendance at Mass will be my only form of worship. The first Mass was celebrated by Jesus, the son of God, on that first Holy Thursday before the Imperial Institution of the Church added its own rules.

Oratorio

I'm a member of the Franciscan Choral Society. We rehearse Handel's *Messiah* in an ouside-the-cloister room of the Abbey. We give recitals to music lovers in the Dominican Hall, Taylor's Hill. Sopranos and contraltos wear long black dresses softened by white shawls. Tenors and base-baritones wear black dress-suits.

Together we sing, 'Despised and rejected, a man of sorrows and acquainted with grief.'

Brian Boydell conducts us in Haydn's *Creation*, 'Let there be light – and there was light!'

Orchestras and conductors arrive from Dublin, Bristol and London. Strings, brass and percussion instruments encircle our Choral Society with harmony.

The famous European conductor Tibor Paul races his red Jaguar over from Dublin to conduct the Irish Symphony Orchestra and our Choral Society in *Mozart's Requiem in D Minor*. Bernadette Greevy and Eithne Troy sing soprano and contralto arias.

I'm comforted by the *Benedictus*.

Benedictus qui venit in nomine Domini –

We get an enthusiastic review in *The Irish Times*.

Burren grykes are being filled with treasures left by melting ice.

We rehearse Elgar's *Dream of Gerontius*. Our Franciscan choirmaster is moved to Cork. There are no further recitals.

With my sister Philomena I join a non-political group called *Tuairim*. Members include Dr. John Heskin, and a young Michael D. Higgins. We discuss current affairs.

We organise lectures by prominent Irish business men. One male speaker questions the morality of the earnings of young

Irish women who have emigrated to England. Philomena objects strongly to his remarks. A heated discussion follows.

A few weeks afterwards we organise a conference at which Garret FitzGerald and Tony O'Reilly are the main speakers. Finance assistance runs low. Some members of *Tuairim* move away, meetings become irregular and eventually cease.

Images

With canvases, sable brushes and oil paints, I continue to make visual images. In the Art Club's premises above the River Corrib, members meet weekly to draw or paint from a live model. Gradually I build up a body of work and put on a solo exhibition in the Corrib Hotel, Oughterard. It's a sell-out. From another exhibition in the Ryan Hotel, canvases move to homes in Dublin, Los Angeles, France, Germany and New Zealand.

The editor of the *Sunday Independent* buys one of my paintings and publishes my photograph together with words of praise.

'This is a change from your last experience with a daily newspaper,' Dad says.

'You mean that neighbour of ours who used my pen and ink illustration for her articles in the *Irish Press*, but excluded my name, Dad. This makes up for that bad experience.

One morning the hotel manager telephones to say that one of my oils, *Girl Thinking*, has been ripped with a sharp knife. Though I'm shocked by this vandalism, I'm glad that it's not a live girl's body.

The hotel manager telephones again. 'Your large painting, *Irish Musicians in Concert*, has disappeared overnight, Patricia.'

'Stolen! At least it wasn't vandalised,' I reply.

Old Galway scenes are much loved by Galwegians who live abroad. *The Long Walk, Buttermilk Lane, Galway Market, The Spanish Arch* are in constant demand. Aware that I could fall into a repetitive money trap and in spite of many requests for more, I develop new shapes, new images. And all the time I'm writing stories and hiding them away in drawers and on bookshelves.

At boarding school, I had written story-essays. My teachers had often encouraged me to read out my work to the different *ranganna*.

Full of confidence, I submitted my first essay to the Professor of English in Teacher Training College. He dismissed it with a curt, 'Not an essay'. From then on I conform and submit humdrum work. If only he had added, 'This is a story.'

My real stories remain hidden until I enrol for an Extra Mural Course in Creative Writing at University College Galway. Having had many different life experiences, my stories change, but still contain vibrant images. The tutors, Thomas Kilroy and Gerald Dawe, encourage me.

My short stories *Over the Bridge* and *Collage* are published in *Writing in the West,* the Arts Page of the *Connacht Tribune.*

I learn to type.

Sunflowers, my short story set in a Magdalen Laundry, wins First Prize in the *Writing in the West* competition, 27th June 1980. At a literary ceremony, the chief executive of the paper presents me with a cheque for fifty pounds. When he comments, 'Of course this type of thing happened a long, long time ago,' I want to shout, 'Our Galway Magdalen women are still washing our dirty linen.'

The following week a Sister from the local convent laundry, smiling sweetly under the shadow of her black veil, tells me, 'The nuns have complained to the editor and management of the *Connacht Tribune!*'

'Why?' I ask.

'That story of yours should never have been published, nor should you have won a prize,' she spits through her smile.

'Have you read my story?' I ask.

Rosary beads rattling, she flips her leather belt and scurries back to her laundry.

Truth disappears like water from turloughs in Burren limestone.

Regatta

Our *Loch an tSáile* Association plans a regatta. The programme is discussed at committee meetings held in the Grammar School. One new member, his leather portfolio stuffed with paper, announces in a loud voice, 'My friends will arrange for a flotilla of Tall Ships to sail from Plymouth into Galway Bay and arrive in *Loch an tSáile* for our regatta!'

Truth disappears like water from turloughs in Burren limestone.

Eyebrows are arched, one committee member looks up to heaven, while another covers his face with his fingers.

'Sure that'd cost thousands! Our budget is limited,' Tom, the chairman, objects. 'We'll have a show of hands. How many for Tall Ships?' He counts. 'One – For Currach Racing another show of hands.' He counts again. 'Seven. Yes! That's the choice of our members. We'll also have a funfair and amusements near *Móinín na gCiseach.*'

Pointing his finger towards me, he says, 'You'll take charge of the Arts Programme, Patricia!'

A stripey marquee is erected on the lakeshore and I oversee art workshops for junior and senior schoolchildren.

'No colouring books, please! We have plenty of paper and paints and imagination!' I announce to the parents. There are looks of disbelief.

'Please do not try to help these young artists. Let them show us their own vision of the world.' I continue. 'Pablo Picasso himself said he wished he could paint like a five-year-old child!'

Brushes and fingers are soon busy.

'Look at my big bad toothache!' Mairéad shouts. 'That's my tears too,' as she blobs purple paint on her yellow image.

'And here's my Daddy with the monster fish he caught beyond in *Inis Oirr.*' Dónal's paper is vibrant with viridian, magenta and crimson fish-blood.

'These paintings would win prizes in Dublin!' one parent says.

'That's not really a good idea,' I answer.

'If each child is expressing herself or himself, how can we say that this painting is better than that one? Competition always means winners and losers!'

'But you used to send the Ballinderreen children's art to competitions!'

'Yes, that's true. I'm much wiser now. If you wish to send off your child's painting, feel free to do so.'

'Aren't they all just wonderful, wonderful!' I say as I look around at paintings ablaze with colour.

My mind goes back to a few years earlier when two of my pupils, Tomás and Séamus, won prizes in a National Child Art Competition. The prize-winners, their mothers, Mary and Nuala, and myself travelled to Dublin by train.

'I've never been to Dublin,' Mary admitted.

'I've been many times and to New York too.' Nuala swung her designer handbag to and fro.

'You can make a wish, Mary,' I said. Mary smiled and closed her eyes for a moment.

After the prize-giving ceremony for Tomás aand Séamus and a light lunch, we went to the National Gallery. There I introduced them to Rembrandt's *Flight into Egypt.* We gazed and gazed in silence at the magical chiaroscuro. Suddenly, Mary put out her hand and touched the painting, saying, 'Blessed Mary, the poor girl and baby Jesus must have …

A steward jumped forward from what seemed like nowhere, grabbed her arm and shouted, 'That painting is worth more than a million pounds, woman! Nobody is allowed to touch these precious works!'

We moved away quickly, followed by suspicious stares from the other stewards. In the foyer Mary turned to me and said quietly, 'Sure that's the only chance I'll ever get to touch a million pounds!'

'Rembrandt, who painted that canvas, died penniless and was buried in a pauper's grave, Mary,' I told her. She looked at me and said, 'He must have been very hungry. He must have been like Mary and Joseph with baby Jesus running away from Herod on dark rocky boreens with only a donkey to carry them.'

Standing now in that stripey regatta marquee surrounded by children's crimsons ultramarines and chrome yellows, I ask myself what would Rembrandt himself have said to that Galway woman.

Writers

I invite writers who meet in University College Galway to read from their work during the Regatta. Eva Bourke and her husband Eoin accept my invitation. An American writer, Jessie Lendennie, fails to respond, even though she rents an apartment nearby in College Road. The Regatta is a success and there are plans for an annual *Loch an tSáile* Festival.

New members join the UCG group of writers.

'Women only!' one feminist poet proclaims, but the others don't agree.

Later, Jessie Lendennie and her partner, Mike Allen, join the group. She had worked as assistant in the Poetry Library in London. They soon realise that there are only a few outlets for publishing women's poetry in the West of Ireland. Jessie plans to set up a publishing business. She starts by printing a broadsheet, which evolves into *Salmon Poetry Magazine*. I'm delighted when she chooses *Claddagh*, one of my black and white etchings, for a cover design. She also publishes *Stop*, my anti-racism poem.

The writers' group moves its meeting place to a room above a public house in Dominick Street. There I meet Anne Kennedy, a writer and photographer from Los Angeles. Joan McBreen, a poet from Tuam, brings along her own work. Eventually the group takes the title of *Galway Writers' Workshop*. The poems of a new writer, Rita Ann Higgins, are first published in the broadsheet and in *Salmon Poetry Magazine*.

Salmon Poetry Magazine evolves into *Salmon Poetry Ltd*.

Now and again, I meet Anne Kennedy and, over coffee in the Great Southern Hotel, we discuss my own collection of poems.

'A few months ago *Galway Writers' Workshop* moved to a room on the first floor of the Bridge Mills,' Ann tells me at one of our meetings.

'Is it to that cut-stone building on the River Corrib, Anne?'

'Yes. *Salmon Poetry* was renting a room on the top storey of the same building, but has now moved again to a house in Upper Fairhill, the Claddagh. It seems that Jessie is settling in to life in Galway.'

I decide to absent myself from the poetry meetings. Instead I develop my work-in-progress stage play, *Eclipsed.*

'PETching/Aquatint: Claddagh I' Patricia Burke 1980

Cell

Veils of black rain wrap Galway City on this October afternoon, the feast of St. Teresa of Avila. I say goodbye to my tearful family and walk from the Blue Parlour through that ancient door into silent, stone-cold cloisters.

Climbing a wooden stairs, I read messages painted in black on white-washed walls: *Blessed are the poor in spirit for theirs is the kingdom of heaven.*

In my narrow cell a creaky bed is covered with a blue and white counterpane. A lone candlestick sits on a wooden bureau. On the wall hangs a black crucifix. Near the small window a washstand holds an enamel jug and basin.

Stripped of worldly colours, I put on postulant's long black dress, thick black stockings and shoes black-laced and flat. Without the help of a mirror, I fix a white-banded black net veil over my long hair. I add a white collar and cuffs and waist-length black cape.

Blessed are they that mourn for they shall be comforted.

Beneath my cell window, the voice of the River Corrib rejoices as it rushes to meet the Atlantic. Across Galway Bay, the Burren raises its textured limbs towards Black Head.

Three months ago, alone on top of Diamond Mountain in Conamara, I had pledged my life to working with Christ for the poor.

In the refectory, rows of black-veiled nuns, eyes lowered, eat at tables set along white walls. There is the clink of thick white mugs, glass butter-dishes and coarse cutlery. At the top table in this stony room, four Superiors sit and watch. White-veiled novices serve dinner on plates under steel covers with black-painted numbers. My number, 27, once belonged to a nun who is now dead. A white-veiled novice stands at the lectern and reads, *Blessed are they that hunger and thirst after justice for they shall have their fill.*

Will I ever paint again? I stare at masticating black-white shapes.

The Novitiate is that part of the convent which is set aside for postulants and novices. From its special workroom, a tall window looks out on a garden recreation-space.

Centre floor is a long table with sewing boxes. An upright piano stands near bookshelves stuffed with spiritual books. I decide to play a Schubert *Impromptu* on black and white keys.

Sister Charles, one of the white-veiled novices, shows her displeasure by rattling her large rosary beads and shishing with down-turned mouth.

A spiritual friend had told me that entering a Novitiate is like jumping from a cliff into the sea. To me it seems more like taking off in a spaceship.

The first months are of exultation. I write my motto, *God is Love*, on parchment.

It's my turn to give morning call to the community. At five-thirty the shriek of the alarm clock pierces the dark. I roll out of bed, kneel on waxed floorboards and try to pray. My skin squirms as I splash cold water over my body and pull on the coarseness of my black serge garments.

Holding bell and lighted candle, I walk along shadowed corridors. *'Benedicamus Domino!'* I knock at each cell door, ring the bell and wait for the answer, *'Deo Gratias.'* My words echo and re-echo through ancient cloisters. Am I calling back spirits of long-dead nuns?

Descending the spiral staircase to unfold wooden shutters, I let in the morning.

In the chapel the sanctuary lamp glows against white marble. For five minutes I lie prostrate before the tabernacle, then move to my *prie-dieux* near the altar. I hear the percussive jangle of rosary beads, swish of habits and suppressed sighs as, one by one, nuns shuffle in to genuflect and kneel at their *prie-dieu*. From ornate stalls inside the chapel door, the Mothers Superior watch for latecomers.

Meditation before Mass means distractions, distractions.

I fall asleep and dream of home. Startled by the nuns' chant: *Magnificat anima mea Dominum. Et exultavit Spiritus meus, In Deo salutari meo. Quia respexit humilitatem ancillae sua: ecce enim ex hoc beatam me dicent omnes generationes. Quia fecit mihi magna qui potens est et sanctum nomen ejus.* My soul doth magnify the Lord. And my spirit hath rejoiced with God my Saviour. Because He hath regarded the humility of His handmaid. I smile at *Dispersit superbos mente cordis suae. Deposuit potentes de sede: et exaltavit humiles.* He hath scattered the proud in the conceit of their heart. He hath put down the mighty from their seat and hath exalted the humble.

I smile again, distracted by what I had heard about Mary's two-thousand-year-old hymn of praise. 'The Congress of Vienna, the Hapsburg Ruler of Austria and the King of England wrote to the Pope in 1816 requesting him to delete the Magnificat from all possible usage, because 'it spoke the language of the French Revolution.'

Sunrise through the stained glass windows offsets crimsons, ultramarines, saffrons on this black and white interior. The bell tolls as the priest in vestments of magenta enters from the sacristy and begins to celebrate Mass. Pangs of hunger make me dizzy. I breathe deeply and pray for strength.

'Credo in unum Deum, Patrem omnipotentem, factorem caeli et terrae, visibilium omnium, et invisibilium,' I whisper with the celebrant. After Mass we kneel in meditation for what seems like two hours. In the refectory we eat breakfast in silence before beginning our daily work of teaching or of cleaning the cloisters.

During recreation, a walk in the garden, Sister Justin, one of the white-veiled novices, tells of a Mother Superior in a nearby convent who lines up her novices every evening. Holding a tall jug full of brewing senna-pods, she orders each novice to drink a cupful of the liquid as she insists, 'Obedience, obedience! You're preparing to take vows, Sisters! Poverty, chastity and obedience. Obedience! That's the difficult one. It encompasses all three.'

Sister Barnabas, our tallest novice, returns from Mother Superior's office. In tears, she whispers, 'The result of my tests has come from the hospital. Mother Superior told me the consultant's letter says that my womb has not developed, that I'm lucky I'm not married, because I can never bear children. She then gave me one of her icy smiles.'

Truth disappears like water from turloughs in Burren limestone.

'Are you sure? Ask for a second opinion, Sister Barnabas,' I say in shock.

'Ask Mother Superior herself to spend more money on a novice! It's her way of keeping you here for the rest of your life!' Sister Ambrose whispers.

'I couldn't face herself again.' Sister Barnabas pulls out a handkerchief.

How could this woman, this Mother Superior, be so cruel to one of her novices?

'But you must have been regular when you entered, otherwise you wouldn't have been accepted in the Novitiate,' Sister Ambrose argues.

''Yes, I was regular as a clock,' Sister Barnabas dabs away her tears.

'Just as entrants to seminaries must be full sexual males,' Sister Ambrose adds.

Another novice, Sister Gregory, digresses and speaks of her brother, who is curate to a Reverend Canon in an English diocese.

'Before Sunday Mass offerings are counted, the Reverend Canon pockets the biggest notes, leaving a small amount to be divided between himself and his curate!'

'Such worldly talk! Shhh!' a professed Sister admonishes.

We stop and breathe in the perfume of lily-of-the-valley, which is clustered around the carved Norman doorway. The doorway has now half-sunk into umber earth.

I think of my father's garden in full bloom. Elegant lupins and delphiniums nudge sunflowers. Fragrant sweetpea and albertine roses wrap the trellis near hives of honey-bees. I, too, dab tears from my eyes.

At supper time we stand in silence, our faces turned in towards the refectory walls, as we drink tea from thick mugs and chew stale bread.

'Our seven o'clock cocktail party! Don't overdo the G and T,' I whisper.

Our giggles are cut short by the tolling of a prayer bell.

One evening I notice that Evelyn, one of the postulants, is not at recreation.

'Evelyn has gone home. Mother of Novices told me,' Sister Gregory announces.

'Sent home,' Sister Ambrose whispers.

'Why?' I ask.

'We're forbidden to talk about, or ask questions about, anyone who leaves our congregation,' Sister Barnabas interjects.

'She must be terribly upset, sent back into the world again!' I say.

'We'll pray for her,' Sister Barnabas murmurs as we continue to embroider altar-cloths.

Mea culpa. I must try to accept these rules without questioning.

Christmas Trees

On Christmas Eve I'm polishing the long corridor when the Mother of Novices' bell summons me to the Noviceship. I put aside my polishing block, take off my blue check apron, hurry along the tunnel-like corridor, knock and wait for the call to enter.

'*Benedicite!*'

I open the door. Mother of Novices, her black veil pinned back, is mending an old habit at her desk near the bookshelves. I kneel. If a Superior is sitting, any Sister who approaches her must kneel so that their head is lower than that of the Superior. She turns towards me and says, 'Mother Superior has told me that a gentleman, a Mr. Mikey Walshe, from your home town arrived at lunchtime with a large Christmas tree for you, Sister Patricia. She has given orders to have it put outside in the garden.'

'Outside in the garden! But Mother of Novices, poor Mikey must have come more than twenty-five miles on the bus to give me my annual Christmas tree! Then Mikey had to walk all the way from the bus station and he's overweight!'

'Mother Superior says that your tree would certainly shed needles in the Noviceship and all over the cloisters, Sister! What would His Lordship say if some of those needles drifted into his Crimson Parlour, into his buckled shoes?'

'But I promise to sweep up every needle from that tree. I'm sure Mikey expected at least a cup of tea from our community. My mother always gave him tea in a china cup and fruitcake on a china plate when he called, especially at Christmas time. He likes four spoons of sugar in each cup.'

'We don't entertain strange men in our convent, Sister.' Mother of Novices' hazel eyes are smiling as she continues, 'If you go over to that window, you can see your tree propped against the garden wall.' She points to the Noviceship window.

'Thank you, Mother of Novices.' I rise from my knees and hurry to the window.

Through tears, I see that the rejected Christmas tree has slipped from the support of the wall beside the Norman doorway and now lies on wet clay.

'You may return to work on the long corridor now, Sister,' Mother of Novices remarks as she checks her fob watch. She then bends over her sewing.

'Thank you, Mother of Novices,' I give one last glance at my fallen Christmas tree.

Head down, eyes tear-swollen, I walk back slowly through the Noviceship doorway to that tunnel-like corridor, to my polishing block and blue check apron.

'Maybe my tree will take root in the garden in spite of being thrown away,' I whisper.

Debite nobis debita nostra, sicut et nos dimitimus debitoribus nostri.

Forgive us our trespasses as we forgive them who trespass against us.'

Hope rises like water into dried-up turloughs in Burren limestone.

The following Saturday Mother of Novices smiles, but makes no comment when she hands me my father's opened letter. Incoming and outgoing Novices' letters are censored.

My father writes of Mikey Walshe's visit to the convent.

'According to Mikey, Tomás O'Brien brought him and your Christmas tree in his hackney as far as the nearest Longford-Galway bus stop. That's just where your much-loved Esker Riada meets the main road at Horse Leap. Jimmy, the bus conductor, allowed him to put it at the end of the bus. Mikey carried your Christmas tree on his back all the way from the bus station in Galway City around by Eyre Square, over by Moons' Corner, down Eglinton Street and Francis Street to the Salmon Weir Bridge and the main door of the convent. He says he rang that doorbell at least ten times before a nun in crooked shoes opened the barred door.

Mikey proclaimed expectantly, 'I want to see Sister Patricia, because I've brought her annual Christmas tree all the way from Cooloo!'

Staring at him from under her black veil, the nun twisted her mouth, sniffed loudly, then grabbed the tree and banged the door in his face.

'Not even a thank you from crooked shoes!' said Mikey as he sat in our kitchen beside the range with his special doubly-sweetened tea and an enormous amount of homemade mince pies.'

My father adds in a P. S.

'You'll be pleased to hear that Mikey has now developed an interest in collecting antique china.'

Mikey's tree does not take root in that convent garden. I do not take root in that cloister. My Christmases are now spent outside in the world again.

In May 2004 my friend, Fr. John, who had visited my mother during her illness, calls to say he's being sent to do research in Rome. He'll have an office in the Papal Palace.

In December 2005 Fr. John emails me.

'Dear Patricia, A Christmas tree from Tubingen together with German sausages and boxes of selected foodstuffs has arrived in the Vatican.'

'Dear John, Congratulations on your appointment! Is it a real Christmas tree for Pope Benedict the Sixteenth?' I email back.

'Dear Patricia, I'll tell you what His Holiness does. He now leaves his *Appartamento Pontifico*, walks past lines of Swiss Guards down towards the domestic area and receives the gifts with open-armed blessings.'

I hit reply. 'Will The Roman Curia allow His Holiness bring his Christmas tree into his Apostolic Palace? Remember those convent rules I told you about?'

He answers, 'Some pine needles fall from the tree. His Holiness picks them up, inhales their greenness, kisses them and stuffs them into the inner pocket of his white soutane.'

Will those Benedictine nuns in the Apostolic Palace object? I ask myself.

Another email arrives from Rome.

'His Holiness takes a tin of German cat food from a delivery box and hurries to feed Mozart, his cat. Mozart is not allowed into his *Appartamento Pontifico*, but remains in the apartment across St. Peter's Square, where His Holiness lived before he was elected Pope.

There His Holiness puts some of the green needles into a silver vase, opens the tin of cat food, and empties it into a dish of Dresden china. He then sits at his grand piano and plays *Stille Nacht*, while Mozart purrs between rhythmic mouthfuls. That's all for now, Patricia.'

'*Nollaig Shona* to you, John, to the spirits of Peter and Paul, of Bernini, Raphael and Michelangelo, to Pope Benedict and his cat, Mozart,' I reply.

Spiritual Year

After six months as a postulant, Reception Day has come. In the small parlour near the sacristy I put on my white dress and veil.

'You will now be a bride of Christ,' Sister Ambrose says and hands me a bouquet of lilies. The last time I dressed in white for a religious ceremony was for my Confirmation in the Cathedral of *Tuaim Dhá Ghuallainn*.

Dramatic in crimson robes, the mitred Archbishop
anoints row after row of young foreheads.
Round scent of oil on skin.
Our shining whiteness in stony distances.
Veils flutter over satin dresses, while the choir chants,
Veni, Creator Spiritus.

But my love of swimming drew me to the river for my daily dip.

Shedding veil and dress in the afternoon,
from the river bank I dive into watery greenness.
I swim without fear through an emerald tunnel.
With pilgrim heron and kingfisher, with pike and salmon,
I carve watery images.
Miracles of water anoint my body.
A strong and perfect Christian, my fingers break through watercress.
Chant of the river throbs in my ears.
Taste of viridian, incense of meadowsweet stretching my senses,
I glory in my limbs.
Joy undiminished, my body is no prison
to contain my spirit.
I swim and swim with dearógs and minnows,
with brown trout and otters through cloisters of malachite.
Candelabra of wild iris light the banks.

Water-lilies float with me as I salute the clouds.
I write my name in water.

'His Lordship has arrived for your reception ceremony! Stop dreaming, Sister! You're miles away!' Sister Jarlath nudges me.

'Your parents and sisters are in the side-chapel,' she adds and rushes off to ring the Mass bell.

Bride of Christ! I'm on that mountain-top in Conamara again where I dedicated my life to work with Christ for the poor.

His Lordship, the Bishop, in crimson robes and decorated mitre, holds his crozier aloft as he presides at Mass. Fragrance of incense and candle-wax with reek of unwashed habits floats through the chapel.

During the Offertory one of the altar boys falls in a faint. His Lordship, pointing towards the collapsed body, stares at one of the priests. The priest lifts the still body, carries it like a piece of luggage to the sacristy and rushes back for *Sursum Corda, Sanctus* and *Benedictus qui venit in nomine Domini.* Blessed is He who comes in the name of the Lord.

A novice rings the consecration bell before the celebrant repeats Christ's two-thousand-year-old words. I am overjoyed yet again to take part in this sublime sacrifice, which reaches upwards through space and outwards to all of creation. The celebrant raises the consecrated Host in memory of Him. We kneel in adoration. He consecrates the chalice of wine and raises it.

'Bride of Christ,' I whisper.

When Mass is over, head bowed, I move from the back of the chapel to the altar steps and lie prostrate.

'What do you seek, my daughter,' His Lordship asks.

I rise, then kneel and answer, 'The grace of God and the habit of holy religion.'

'And do you intend to persevere faithfully in all the rules and constitutions of this Order?'

'With the help of Divine grace I do intend to and thus hope to persevere.'

His Lordship's voice is stern as he asks, 'And do you truly desire to enter the state of holy religion?'

'I desire it with all my heart,' I reply.

He makes the sign of the Cross over me as he says, 'What God has begun in you, may He Himself make perfect.'

His Lordship blesses my habit, veil, coif, guimpe, large black rosary beads and belt.

The choir chants,

Te Deum laudamus: te Dominum confitemur.

Te aeternum Patrem, omnis terrra veneratur.

Tibi omnes angeli, tibi caeli, et universae potentates:

I kneel and kiss His Lordship's ring, which glows ruby in fractured sunlight.

Sanctus, Sanctus, Sanctus Dominus Deus Sabaoth.

Pleni sunt caeli et terra majestatis gloriae tuae.

I kiss the newly blessed items of clothing and holding them on outstretched arms, I return to the back of the chapel. I kneel again as Mother Superior, with scissors steel-sharp on my scalp, roughly shears off my long hair. She whispers, 'This gives me the greatest pleasure.'

Why does she take pleasure in cutting off my hair I wonder, as clumps of my auburn tresses drop into an enamel basin.

'Forgive us our trespasses as we forgive those who trespass against us,' I say to myself. She places the coif on my skull and tightens the starched tapes, then fastens the white veil and domino to the coif with special pins. I take the guimpe and tie its tapes under my veil at the back of my neck.

In the small parlour, my heartbroken parents and sisters sit down to tea and slices of iced reception cake. I'm not allowed to eat with them. His Lordship enjoys lunch in the Crimson Parlour.

My head is now truly enclosed in starched linens. The discomfort of my coif makes me long for bedtime and the loosening of the starched coif-tapes from my shaven scalp.

I try to focus on the fact that Christ wore a crown of thorns as he stumbled under that cross on His way to Calvary.

Spiritual Year means that I'm not allowed to go out to teach in any of the convent schools and not allowed visits from members of my family. Enclosed, enclosed for twelve months in starched linens. Enclosed in the Novitiate.

Unknown to me, His Holiness, Pope John the twenty-third, has called bishops and cardinals to Rome for Vatican Two. During a number of their Council meetings, they discuss life in monasteries and convents. They suggest that the clothing of Sisters, who go out to teach or nurse, should be modernised, brought into the twentieth century. The starched coif and veil should be replaced by a simple veil of shoulder length. Hair should not be shorn and may be partly visible under the veil. A dark dress and jacket or suit should take the place of the unwieldy habit.

In my cell at bedtime, I untie my pinned-together veil-coif-domino in one piece and place it on the bureau. It sits there, a faceless headdress on a wooden stand.

Should my face fill that empty space? I struggle with this thought. After breakfast next morning I put on my blue apron and prepare for kitchen work.

'Mother Superior has opened this letter,' Mother of Novices says as she hands me an envelope.

'Thank you, Mother,' I bow my head and recognise the handwriting.

'It's a love letter from one of your boyfriends, Sr Patricia. His father has died and he's upset. You may take time off for meditation.'

I hurry to the chapel and read my letter. After the hour bell rings, I place the tear-stained letter in my missal, genuflect and return to the kitchen,

Keeping custody of the eyes, I clean and polish corridors, wash and chop vegetables in the kitchen, carve meat for the following day. While re-heating dinners for the refectory, I decide to put the best slices of meat under the novices' plate-covers.

'The Superiors at the top tables have vows of poverty, so they should practise poverty. Novices are the future members of this congregation and need extra nourishment,' I remark to another novice.

Next morning I'm ordered to leave the kitchen and take up duties in the sacristy.

There I polish brasses, scrape away candle-wax, push used altar-cloths, corporals, purificators and communion-cloths into blue laundry bags. I set out vestments for morning Mass and arrange the ribbons in the Missal.

As I carry the laundry bags into the sacristy, my stiffly starched coif-tapes dig deeper into my skull and neck. I loosen the tape-knots and lift off the whole pinned-together headdress. Turning to the mirror above the sacristy basin, I see my lacerated neck and scalp.

Bruised blood comes away on my fingers. I run cold water over a corporal. As I ease it to my abrasions, a sudden rattle of keys and rosary beads alerts me and I pull on my headdress quickly and rinse the corporal.

'We are forbidden to admire ourselves in mirrors, Sister!' Mother Superior glares at my image in the mirror.

'But, Mother Superior, I –'

'His Lordship will be here for Mother Bursar's Feast Day next week! Check his Carrickmacross lace surplice. Make sure there's sufficient incense for Benediction and polish that thurible again, Sister!'

'Yes, Mother Superior', I push the bloodied corporal into my apron pocket and lift the thurible from its stand.

'Mend that cigarette scorch on Fr. John's chasuble during recreation this evening. Straighten your coif and veil – without the help of his Lordship's mirror, Sister! I'll be back!'

'Yes, Mother Superior.' I polish the thurible again and tie my coif-tapes loosely, before filling the incense-holder.

I take extra care with the sacred vessels, chalices, ciboria, patens and monstrance.

Privileged to hold them, it's worth the loneliness, the suffering. I'm alone with God.

I try to keep distractions away by polishing, mending, sewing, re-polishing.

Incense, candle-wax and brasso smells mix with stale cigarette smoke from the vestments.

I believe. Help my unbelief.

If I truly believe that the Real Presence is in the tabernacle, nothing should annoy or distract me.

My confessor advises, 'A vocation to the religious life is not about feelings, Sister. Put your trust in God. He'll look after you.'

'But God has got mixed up with rules and regulations, Father.'

'For your penance say the *Credo*, Sister. *Visibilium omnium et invisibilium.*'

'*Invisibilium*,' I say to myself.

'You must clean between those door crevices again, Sister!'

'Polish the sanctuary lamp and refill with oil, Sister.'

As I banish these echoes, I'm reminded of a university graduate from my home town, who chose to work as a chimney-sweep.

'When I'm cleaning chimneys,' he'd told me, 'my mind is free, so I can think of King Louis the Fourteenth of France admiring a newly purchased tapestry for his throne-room in Versailles. Or I can imagine him in his dressing-room as he chooses lace ruffles to wear for lunching with his Queen. While I select my brushes for special chimneys, I see him selecting wines for dinner.'

When I scrub, sweep and polish in the sacristy, my own mind should be free to concentrate on becoming closer to God.

'Check the Carrickmacross lace on His Lordship's surplice again, Sister! And check his special Benediction cope!' These orders echo in the cloisters.

I ask myself if His Lordship has replaced God in this place.

Schools

Spiritual Year passes and I return to teach at Secondary and Primary levels.

'See that these girls are awarded honours in Leaving Cert Art, Sister. They must get into University.'

I want to reply that Art is too important to be used in that way.

After lunch in the refectory I look at my history students and wonder if any of them will, in the future, continue to ask questions and challenge social injustices or will regurgitated off-by-heart lists stifle them for life.

I'm delighted when one of the students in my geography class asks, 'Why do nuns wear those old black habits and strange covers on their heads, Sister? They look like Muslim women from the east.'

'How do you know you should be in this convent, Sister?' another asks.

'Vocation? How can you be certain? Why don't the Poor Clares go out to teach?'

When the Leaving Cert results are announced, I'm pleased to hear that my Art students are awarded honours. However, they all go on to study medicine and science in University College, Galway.

In order to go across to the primary schools, I use the tunnel, which runs from the convent grounds under Francis Street.

A stench of dried urine hits my nose as I walk into classrooms full of junior and senior infants. These are the most important years of their lives, I remind myself, as I struggle with being an actor, a singer, a nurse, a psychologist, a clown. Sticky fingers pull my veil, but luckily the Rule orders us to wear black veils instead of white in the classrooms.

During Catechism time we compose plays from stories in scripture.

'Our story-play today is about Adam and Eve in the Garden of Paradise!' I begin.

Tusa Samantha, you'll be Eve, so stand near that table with the big green plant. Damian, you'll be Adam. Stand in the sunshine near that big window.'

'Today you can be God and here's your special apple tree,' I tell little Trevor, as I give him a picture of a tree laden down with apples.

'Yes, I'm God Himself!' Trevor raises his arms and stands tall.

'You are the angels around God in Heaven.' I hold out both arms towards the other children. Adam and Eve, you are both very happy in this beautiful garden!'

From the prop box I take out a patched tablecloth, which acts as a stage-curtain.

Tusa, a Rosanna, take this end of our stage-curtain. And you, Cyril, hold the other end. Wait until I give you the signal to fold the stage-curtain away and then our story-play begins.'

'Yes, Sisther-*Mhúinteóir*,' they smile.

'Ready! Rosanna and Cyril, *a haon, a dó, a trí*, please fold down the stage-curtain. Fold. Now listen to what God has to say to you!' I announce.

'You can eat apples from every tree in my beautiful garden,' Trevor points his right hand towards Adam and Eve. 'But you mustn't, mustn't ever, ever take and eat any apple from my special tree with my gorgeous apples.'

Adam runs up to Trevor and pretends to grab and eat one of God's apples.

Grace interrupts and, rushing forward, she stands beside Adam.

'But, but, Sisther-*Mhúinteoir*, my Daddy says that it was Eve that gave Adam a big juicy apple and then Adam took a big greedy bite out of it. And Eve said, 'Good man, Adam! You're a great fella!' Then Adam did his best to swallow it, but it stuck in his neck. That's why all the men in the whole world have a big lump in the front of their necks. That's what my Daddy says!'

'*Go raibh maith agat*, Grace! Remember that's a story, a story from long, long ago.'

'A story, Sisther-*Mhúinteoir?* My Daddy says it's only a made-up story!' Grace says.

'Tomorrow we'll make a halo for God from silver paper. I'll bring apples from the convent and we'll sing *The Bells of the Angelus,*' I promise with a smile.

'But why can't we sing *Báidín Fheidhlimidh,* Sisther-*Mhúinteóir?*' asks Nicola.

Trevor contradicts, 'No! No! That's for Noah in his big boat full up of huge elephants and stripey tigers and gr-gr-growly lions and giraffes with mile-long necks!'

'A Mammy elephant and a Daddy elephant. A Mammy tiger and a Daddy tiger. A Mammy lion and a Daddy lion,' Grace adds.

'You must have Mammies and Daddies! That's what my Daddy says,' Ciarán explains.

'Tomorrow we'll sing both. *The Bells of the Angelus* and *Báidín Fheidhlimidh. Am lóin anois, a pháistí.* We'll march like angels without pushing one another.' I move towards the playground door followed by a line of children, their arms moving like wings.

'Can I be God again tomorrow, Sisther-*Mhúinteóir?*' Trevor pleads.

'Next week, we'll wait until next week,' I reply.

As I walk back to the Noviceship through the under-the-road tunnel, I meet two black-veiled Sisters. They keep custody of the eyes and walk close to the tunnel wall.

Novices are not allowed to speak to professed Sisters. I think of our home-place where everyone speaks to one another when they meet on the street or road.

In our village traffic passed to and from Tuam and Galway City and some even to and from Dublin. One busy afternoon my sister Philomena decided that half of the main road through the village belonged to herself and her school pal, Kitty Colleran. They took possession of one half of the road and refused to give way to oncoming traffic. A lorry-driver pulled in.

'Get out of my way, you lttle ruffians,' he shouted.

'This is our half of the road! We've every right to it!' they shouted back.

When he asked them their names, my sister proclaimed, 'Philomena Josephine Agnes Burke and we own this half!'

Kitty changed her surname to Corcoran.

'I'm reporting you both to the Guards. You'll be thrown into jail!' the lorry-driver roared. When he went into the Gárda Barracks, he met my father, who was about to go out to post dispatches to the Depot.

'I'll deal with this,' my father said as he turned to the Barracks Orderly.

He then listened to the lorry-driver's complaint, took notes and said, 'I'll warn those two youngsters. Thank you for this information and don't worry, it won't happen again.'

'We've a young rebel on our hands,' he told my mother later that evening.

Keys

During school holidays, Mother Superior calls me to her office. I knock and wait for her response. She sits on a throne like chair. On her desk an ornate silver frame holds a photograph of His Lordship, the bishop. His ruby-ringed hand emerging from crimson robes, edged with delicate lace, is raised in blessing. I kneel with head bowed.

'Tomorrow morning I'm sending you to our branch-house on the other side of the city. Mother Romanus will inform you of your duties there, Sister.'

'Yes, Mother Superior.' I stand and turn to leave. I get a whiff of *Eau de Parfum* as she points her hand towards me.

'On your knees, Sister!'

I kneel.

'You'll be accompanied to your new place of work by Sister Mary Gregory. And remember to keep eyes downcast, custody of the eyes at all times, Sister!'

The phone rings. Mother Superior lifts the receiver. Her stylish shoes shift under the rosewood desk.

'Yes. – Yes, Father. I'll hold on! – Oh, good morning, my Lord!' She softens her voice. 'Yes, my Lord. I'm working on the ledgers now. – I should have them finished tomorrow, my Lord. – Yes. I'll send the cheque too. – Thank you, my Lord.'

I'm amazed by her change of attitude.

She puts down the receiver with care and turns towards me. Her smile disappears. 'Custody of the eyes, Sister! You may leave now!'

'Thank you, Mother Superior.'

I close the door on that exotic fragrance and return to my life of worn-out shoes and waxed-floor smells.

Next morning, Sister Mary Gregory and I walk from the side door of the convent novitiate along Francis Street to Eglinton Street, around Eyre Square to Forster Street and through the fortified gates of the branch house called the Magdalen Convent.

On the western side of the convent building, a tall chimney belches clouds of dark smoke.

'This is the richest branch-house of our Order,' Sister Mary Gregory says as she rings the brass doorbell. I turn to the right and stare at the circular stained glass window high on a cutstone wall.

'That's Mary Magdalen by Evie Hone,' Sister Mary Gregory informs me and rings that doorbell again.

With a rattle of keys, the Sister Portress bows to Sister Mary Gregory and leads me to Mother Romanus's office. The walls of this office are lined with shelves holding stacks of ledgers. Again a photograph of His Lordship, the bishop, is positioned beside the telephone on the mahogany desk. Again his ruby-ringed hand edged with delicate lace is raised in blessing.

'Follow me, Sister!'

Mother Romanus takes a bundle of large keys from a drawer in her desk. We walk to the end of the waxed hallway. Using those large keys, she opens a heavy door. We enter. She double-locks and bolts the door after us. We walk down a long dark-umber corridor.

She opens another heavy double-locked door. A deafening noise hits us. We're in a room with huge machines from which steam hisses. Prison bars pattern the roof-windows. The grey walls are sweating. There's a stench of soiled clothing. Bleach fumes sting my throat. I gasp for air.

Gradually I see that the room is full of women. Elderly women, middle-aged women, and young girls all seem to merge with the grey of womb-like washing machines.

'Your duty is to supervise their work, Sister.' She takes a blue-white check apron from a shelf and holds it towards me.

Along the walls rows of women bend over porcelain sinks. Some wear small white caps and mumble prayers as they scrub mounds of dirty clothes.

'Pin back your veil now. Hook up your outer habit. On no account are you to speak to these women, except to give orders, Sister.'

'But Mother Romanus, why are the women in here?'

'These women are penitents, Sister.'

'Penitents?'

'They're weak. They've no control, Sister. They've broken the sixth and ninth commandments!'

'But, how – who put them–?'

'No one wants these women. We protect them from their passions. We give them food, shelter and clothing. We look after their spiritual needs.' She hands me the bundle of large keys.

'These keys must remain attached to your girdle at all times, Sister! Keep your eyes wide open. Be careful! The consecrated penitents, those wearing white caps, shouldn't cause any trouble, but watch out for the others!'

'Why are they called consecrated penitents, Mother Romanus?'

'They've accepted their lives of penance and they've made a solemn promise not to try to escape, Sister!'

With a rattle of rosary beads and heavy keys, she opens and then double-locks the door behind her. She returns, I presume, to sit beside the bishop's photograph in her ledger-stacked office.

Have I slipped down into Dante's Purgatorio?

Many pairs of eyes are watching me, their white-veiled jailer. Eyes. Eyes. Everywhere sad, sad eyes are watching, staring, glaring. I want to turn and run. Obedience, obedience, obedience! Isn't God a loving Father, a forgiving Father? The bundle of keys is on my girdle. Should I open that door now and lead these women out?

I take up and clasp the crucifix attached to my large rosary beads.

Despised and rejected, a Man of Sorrows and acquainted with grief.

My spiritual life has changed forever.

Under double lock, within this pious cage these women live a penitential life.

I walk over to an arthritic woman, who is bowed over a sink. I take her scrubbing brush and board and I begin to scrub a dirty shirt collar.

'But, Sister, no, no! This is my work.'

'I must do this!' Christ would have taken pity on this woman, would have helped her.

Scrub. Scrub! Smell of soiled shirts and woolly socks. My fingers grow raw against the rough board. Scrub. Scrub.

I hear the clang of door-bolts and the rattle of keys as Mother Romanus returns.

'Stop! Stop immediately, Sister!' she shouts from the door. 'Back to work now, Katie! I'm surprised at you, a consecrated penitent. Not your first time in trouble, is it? You'll do without your blessed cap for the next two weeks! And you, Sister, come with me!' Watched by eyes, eyes, eyes, I follow her through that double-lock door.

'I told you to supervise the penitents, not to do their work, Sister!'

'But they are our Sisters in Christ, Mother Romanus!'

'Our sisters!'

'Yes, Mother Romanus! Part of His Mystical Body.'

She hands me another work-ledger and pencil.

'You are preparing to take vows, Sister! A Vow of Obedience. Keep aloof from those fallen women! When I was a novice I wanted to free the penitents – some of them were mothers of women in the laundry now. You see, this weakness for sins of the flesh stays in the blood for seven generations. From now on you'll just check their work, Sister!'

'But how can I check work that I'm not allowed to do myself, Mother Romanus?'

'Obedience, Blind Obedience, Sister! Go now to the sorting area. The Athlone baskets have arrived. If any incoming article hasn't got its owner's name, order the women to initial it with red thread.'

'They are bond-women. They are slaves, Mother Romanus!'

'To the sorting area now, Sister!' She points towards a doorway.

Baskets full of laundry bags. Bags full of soiled garments. Baskets full of bags full of smells. My stomach heaves. I turn aside and throw up.

'Here y'are, Sister.' A white-haired woman offers me a clean towel.

With work-roughened hands, she then makes a fan from a piece of cardboard.

'It's fresh air you need, Sister! I'll wash your apron now and iron it dry, you poor cratiur. You'll get used to the smells if you stay long enough in this scummy hell.'

'No, No! Thank you very much, but I'll wash this towel and my apron myself. You shouldn't have to clean up after me.'

But she grabs the soiled items and limps away into steam-filled twilight.

Next morning in the main laundry, two young women stop work and approach me.

'We're all going on strike, Sister! No more of this filthy, dirty work. You can run over now and tell that to big-toothy dragon, Romanus!'

A strike in this place of horrors! No! No! I say to myself.

At a signal from the two ring-leaders, all of the women, except for the white-capped consecrated penitents, sit down on the flagstone floor. Some hold baby clothes in their arms and rock their bodies as they sing lullabies.

Seoithín Seo hó, mo stoirín, mo leanbh. Mo sheód gan cealg, mo chuid den tsaol mór.

Suddenly, three consecrated penitents join the mothers on the floor. To and fro, to and fro. Mothers grieve for their babies.

Why shouldn't they protest? No, I won't report them to Mother Romanus.

I walk slowly towards the centre of the work area.

I sit down on the floor beside the women.

Again clasping my crucifix in both hands, I pray silently.

Blessed art thou amongst women and blessed is the fruit of thy womb. Pray for us sinners now and at the hour of our death.

Surprised eyes of the women focus on me.

Slowly, slowly, one after the other, the women stand up and return to work.

The Magdalen Laundry over the years,
as a novice, and outside the walls.

Gifts

I'm ordered to take up a teaching position in a new school on the outskirts of Galway City Accompanied by the School Principal, Sister Martin, I go there by bus.

Children who live in caravans nearby arrive in my classroom. I ask Mother of Novices for permission to sew items of clothing for the girls, Maureen and Nora. I also ask Mother Superior to write to the City Manager requesting him and the Corporation to provide proper housing for the caravan families.

'Because of your request, Mother Superior will write a formal letter to the City Manager, Sister,' Mother of Novices says with a smile.

After about a week, the children, Maureen, Nora and their brother, Jamsie, arrive at school every morning carrying gifts. One morning it's a bundle of old postcards, another morning it's a yellowed and tattered paperback, another morning it's a broken vase full of paper flowers. Collections of coloured cards and old photographs, shiny ribbons, framed pictures are presented to me with excited smiles.

'*Go raibh míle maith agaibh,*' I thank the children and put the gifts away in one of the empty classrooms.

Every evening I kneel before Mother of Novices and, keeping to the Rule, say, 'May I keep and dispose of presents given to me by my caravan children?'

'Yes, Sister, you may dispose of them.' After a few weeks she adds, her hazel eyes sparkling, 'That extra classroom must be full by now.'

One morning I see Jamsie, Maureen and Nora struggle under the weight of a huge volume as they come through the school gate and along the pathway.

'Here y'are, Sisther!' they gasp for breath as they hand me a bible.

'Thank you very much. But this is much too heavy for you little ones.' I notice that the usual fusty smell is much stronger from this gift.

Back in the Novitiate during recreation a novice whispers, 'Those children live in caravans beside the city dump and every evening after school they search in the dump for treasure-presents for you, Sister.'

On my Feast Day, when I sit down to dinner in the refectory, I find, to my delight, that my side plate is adorned with paper flowers like those made by traveller women.

When I look along the refectory table, each novice has her head bowed and her eyes cast downwards, pretending not to notice my surprise.

I say, 'Deo Gratias'.

Grykes in Burren limestone grow deeper and richer.

Angels (Circa 1980)

Come, Holy Spirit. Creator blest and in our hearts take up Thy rest. We begin morning prayers in our primary school. Ameena, my new pupil, throws herself down on the classroom floor and shouts, 'I'm a Muslim, *mhúinteóir!* I'm not allowed!'

Natasha rushes from her desk, plaits flying. With hands on hips, she stands in front of Ameena and yells, 'Join yer hands and say yer prayers, ya sooty-faced pagan!'

Ameena jumps up, dashes to the classroom door and out into the corridor. I rush after her and persuade her to return. She does so reluctantly.

Once she's inside the classroom door, Ameena glares at Natasha, then sits at her desk, eyes closed, fingers wedged into her ears. Are we about to have an Islamic-Christian war?

Later that day during Art Class, I announce, '*Anois a pháistí,* we're going to make angel faces from these sheets of white paper!' With much swishing and rustling, we tear out oval-shaped faces.

'We'll now paint the faces in different colours. Here are your paints and brushes!'

On their desks I place pots of earth-coloured paints in pale to dark tones of raw umber, yellow-ochre, sienna, alizarin and burnt umber mixed with ultramarine.

Excitement grows as they paint some faces burnt sienna, others raw umber, others ochre with slanted eyes, others pink-crimson, others pale olive. While they work, I make paper wings and flowing paper skirts. I then attach wings and skirts to each face and mount them high on the main wall facing the big window.

'Show me your angel, Ameena,' I say.

She stands under the pale brown angel and points. 'That's my own Muslim angel, a *mhúinteóir.*'

'*Go raibh maith agat,* Ameena. Isn't she beautiful? She has a lovely smile. And that's a Chinese angel from Peking in China,' I point to a yellow ochre-faced angel.

'Has anyone been to the Chinese restaurant in the city?'

Cleo and Karen hold up their hands. Karen smacks her lips and says, 'My Daddy brings home Sweet 'n' Sour Chinese every Friday night.'

'Noodles and stir-fry!' Cleo exclaims.

'Go raibh maith agaibh, Cleo agus Karen.'

I point to a red-skinned face. 'Here's a Red Indian angel from America. We'll make a feathered headdress tomorrow!'

I point to a jet-black face with white teeth. 'That's an African angel from Nigeria.'

'Just like the black babies in Granny's prayer-book,' Rosanna says and smiles at the black-faced angel.

'What about the tigín children? Have they angels, a mhúinteóir?' Natasha asks.

'Of course, they do, Natasha. Now, we'll make more faces!'

There's another excited rustle of paper as more face-shapes are torn. I put pots of cadmium yellow paint on the desks, as I say, 'The children in the tigíns have golden hair and golden earrings.'

'They've freckles all over their faces too, a mhúinteóir.' Cleo paints umber spots on her angel's face.

'But some of them have black hair and black eyes,' Zoe protests and splashes black paint on her angel's eyes and hair.

I arrange a number of golden-haired angels with hooped paper-earrings and black-haired cherubs beside the others on the main wall.

'Look, a pháistí, all of our angels are praying. Ameena's Muslim angel is praying to Allah. The Chinese angel is praying to Buddha. The Japanese angel from Hiroshima is praying to Buddha too. Our pale-faced angels are praying to our own God. They have great fun together.'

'A mhúinteóir! Can we sing our Christmas song, mhúinteóir, please?' Cleo pleads.

'You'll take each other's hands and our angels will sing with us.' I sit at the piano. My fingers move on ivory and ebony keys, as I accompany the voices of the children.

Angels we have heard on high,
sweetly singing o'er the plain
and the mountains in reply
echo back their joyous strain.
Glo – ooria Gloo – oria in excelsis Deo.'

'Aa – Aa – Aaallah', sings Ameena as she bends to the floor.

I finish with a number of harmonious chords.

In Burren limestone grykes a variety of new plants deepen their roots.

Amsterdam

As our plane descends towards Schiphol Airport, the landscape resembles a Wagemaker painting, shapes of bronze-umber in bas-relief now softened by rain.

This is my first time in Continental Europe. As we pass through customs, I'm amazed to see armed airport police watch from a balcony.

Two women from The Long Walk in Galway City greet us as we gather our luggage and move towards the taxi rank.

'We're on our way to Switzerland!' they tell us.

'Have a wonderful trip. We'll see you at the Galway Races!' I reply.

Ten days earlier, our travel agents had contacted us to say that our chosen Museum Hotel was not available, but that they had booked another, which was very central. Rather than cancel our trip, we accepted.

Next morning, carrying easel, canvases and paint box, we walk from our hotel, which is close to Dam Square. We turn left and move through a narrow cobbled side-street towards the canals.

'Here? -- Oh, no!'

'Here? – No! No!'

I stop suddenly.

'It's quiet here, Eamon. Look at those colours, those shapes, tones!'

'Are you sure? But why are those shop-fronts closed?'

'It's just right!' I make visual notes with my hands.

Eamon sets up easel and canvas, unfolds my small painting stool.

I open my paint box with acrylic paints for quick drying.

'All set now? *Slán.* Back in an hour, love.'

'*Go raibh míle maith agat.* See you for lunch, love.'

We like to speak Gaelic when we are abroad.

On the water below, barges full of tourists pass under curved bridges overshadowed by tightly-packed-together tall narrow houses.

Clatter of trams, distant hum of city life is punctuated by shrillness of bicycle bells.

I choose earth colours for my palette. Even the shadows are warm, reflections in the canal waters are warm too, except for small areas of sky-water.

I half-close my eyes. With knife and brush I mix yellow ochres, burnt siennas, raw umbers with a little alizarin, curve of bridges, texture of buildings, mirror-images, a concerto of colours.

I work quickly. Brushes, knife, paints, fingers, looking out intensely, looking back at canvas, set up compositions, more gamboge, less crimson, scrape off paint here. Dab on, scratch with fingernail. Smooth. I use details on one area, letting the eye imagine the rest.

Eamon brings coffee and cheese. Still immersed in and excited by the cityscape, we lunch silently.

'The organ-grinder should be playing in the Kalverstraat this afternoon. I might take some pictures. Back before six, love.'

Cameras across his shoulder, cigarette in hand, he moves away towards Dam Square.

Shadows under the bridges deepen and I push more ultramarine on to my palette.

More burnt umber, more sienna, indigo, a touch of viridian. To focus on a bell tower I change my position and try to catch the glow of fading light. Shadows lengthen and I work faster.

Suddenly, hands on my shoulders make me jump. A man speaks in a language I do not understand. The peculiar expression in his eyes and his sleazy gestures makes the hair stand up on the back of my neck. I snap shut my paint box, grab hold of my canvases and easel and, dropping my brushes on cobbles, run to our hotel.

Grykes in Burren limestone grow sharper and darker.

'I shouldn't have left you alone, my love. There, there, you're safe now. To-morrow we'll visit the house of Rembrandt,' Eamon comforts me.

Later that evening we join a sightseeing group.

We listen to the guide as she relates the history of the Royal Palace in Dam Square and then we move to the Diamond Centre.

It's getting dark as we walk down a side street towards the canals.

'This street! Is it? Doesn't it look familiar, Eamon?' I take his hand in mine and move closer.

'Yes, it's the same street, love, but now the shop fronts are open.'

'This is our famous Red Light District,' our guide announces.

In each neon-lit window a woman poses. Some sit or stand doll-like, others move slowly to loud music. We stop and stare as cruising men ask questions or bargain with the window-women, then a few walk through the chosen doorway. Others move on.

'It's the oldest profession. A variety of women to suit all tastes,' says our guide.

An argument erupts between a young window-woman and a sailor.

'Get lost! I don't do S. and M.,' she shouts as he slinks away towards another window and goes through the doorway. The curtain closes.

'That's an Irish accent,' Eamon remarks.

'Her pimp will beat that woman up. That's why some women have bruised faces,' our guide explains.

'But why do they stay on here?' another Irish voice echoes along the street.

'Money for drugs. Most of the women are now addicted to drugs.'

The colours in my mindscape have now changed to purples, magentas, aubergines.

Grykes in Burren limestone grow deeper and darker.

Cyclists push pedals over cobbled streets as we make our way to Rembrandthuis, which is now a museum.

In Rembrandt's darkened studio, we see his etching press and special copper plates.

I stand at the window, where he worked with etching needles.

'Look, Eamon, this is Rembrandt's burin and this is his burnisher!

He held these tools in his hands. His spirit is here, is still here. He may have sat on this chair as he worked on that silverpoint of his beloved Saskia.'

'Or his Prodigal Son, his Christ Preaching which he reworked so many times,' the caretaker adds.

Shelves hold supplies of his resin, waxes, inks and his acid-baths.

'Master of chiaroscuro,' I say.

'He wanted to be the best and he was the best,' a Dutch voice adds.

'His special method of gradually treating and finishing his etched plates will never be known.'

'The invention was buried with him. Buried in an unmarked pauper's grave, but now the grave of Rembrandt, one of the greatest artists of all time, has been rediscovered in Westerkirk,' the caretaker announces.

'We'll take a tram to Westerkirk tomorrow,' Eamon takes my hand.

'Shouldn't we see his great paintings first and then visit his grave?'

In the Rijksmuseum I sit, shoeless, on the floor for hours and hours.

I'm entranced by the major works of Rembrandt, by his Self Portraits which show him as libertine, as suffering man and as ageing master. Magnificent!

'We must come back to the Vermeers after we visit Westerkirk.' My voice is choking with emotion as we drink white wine in the outside café.

Another day at special exhibitions in the Stedelijk Museum, I again sit, shoeless, on the floor all day and absorb the Abstract Expressionists' world of colour, vitality.

De Kooning, Kokoschka, Jasper Johns, Rothko.

I fall in love with 'Portrait of a Pierrot' by Rouault.

In the bar of the Krasnapolski Hotel in Dam Square, we chat about Dutch art with Tom, our tall, sad-eyed barman.

'Our usual Amstel beers, Tom, please,' Eamon orders.

'We're going to try Indonesian to-night,' I add.

As Tom serves us, a silver-haired, fine-boned man in a well-cut grey suit sits beside us at the bar. He presents Tom with a ribbon-wrapped parcel.

'From Leningrad for you and Miriam.' They speak in Dutch for a few moments.

We sip our cool drinks and examine street-maps.

Our Irish accents attract the stranger and he joins in conversation about the Troubles in our country. He mentions Bernadette Devlin and Dr. Ian Paisley and we realise that he has an extensive knowledge about breaches of human rights in Northern Ireland.

In a calm voice, he says, 'I'm against discrimination of every kind.'

Insisting on buying us a drink, 'Because I am old, I drink Young Genever. You are young, so I buy you Old Genever.'

Later, he says goodnight with, 'I fly to Basle very early tomorrow morning.'

'Slán leat agus go néirigh an bóthar leat.'

We shake hands and he leaves to go to his bedroom.

'Do you know who that is?' Tom is full of emotion.

With our eyes, we ask him.

'That is the father of Anne Frank.' Tom's voice is hushed.

Behind a revolving bookcase were those hidden stairs to that secret annexe in Prinsengracht, the wall-map on which he charted the advance of the Allies from Normandy.

Betrayal, Betrayal, Betrayal.

Spat on, kicked down that narrow stairs by jack-booted Gestapo.

The twisted cross of iron on hell-like trains to Auschwitz.

Separation from his wife, Edith, and from his daughters.

Anne and Margot to Bergen-Belsen.

Typhus. Gas-chambers. Death. Death. Death.

In silence, we turn and watch Otto Frank walk up the wide stairs of Hotel Krasnapolski.

Otto Frank, only survivor from that family, died in Basle in 1980.

At Rembrandthuis, Amsterdam.

Piano Music

'We're going to Ennis to buy goodies for your birthday, love.'

'Jelly and ice-cream and crunchy biscuits? Mmmm. Can I come too?'

'We'll be back very soon. Nell will take care of you.'

Both Mammy and Daddy give me a big hug and leave. They take my brother, Brendan, with them. I'm sad.

Nell Hurley brings me into her cat-smelly parlour.

Her curly hair bounces, as she sits on her special twisty stool and plays the piano.

'Listen to my beautiful music, little one!'

Her fingers run up and down the black and white keys. Her foot presses a big shiny button on the flowery carpet.

I take out my blue pencil and make up and down music on the walls. Up, down, around and around, I push my pencil, keeping time, dancing with the music. My pencil skips and twists in circles, Mammy's face, Daddy's face, Mammy's big blue eyes, Daddy's smile, angels with shiny haloes dance into Heaven.

'Stop! Stop that scribbling. Stop now, you bold, bold child! You've destroyed my beautiful wallpaper! Wait until I tell your Mammy and Daddy about you.'

She grabs my blue pencil, breaks it into pieces and smacks my fingers with her bony hands.

I scream and scream. 'I'll tell my Mammy and Daddy about you!'

Then I sob and sob. I'm almost three years old. Nobody has ever slapped me before.

We're in a small squeaky boat on the River Shannon. I pretend that I'm rowing the boat with my Daddy.

Row, row, backwards and forwards, row, row, row.

'Daddy, Daddy, look at the huge big fishes!'

'Dolphins. They're called dolphins, a *stór*. They've come in from the big sea away out there. Look, they're dancing special birthday wishes for you.'

'Can I sing my new song for the dolphins, Daddy?'

'Yes, *a stór*. We'll sing together.'

'Hello big shiny fishes. Hello, Hello, Helloo-ooo big shiny fishes. Hello-oo-ooo.' I wave my hands in delight.

'Daddy! Look, Daddy! The River Shannon is coming into our boat.'

Daddy scoops up water with a tin and empties it with a splash.

'Splash! Splash! Splash, shiny fishes. Splash, splash!' I shout.

'Time to go home to Mammy. Say goodbye to the dolphins.'

'Can I bring them to my birthday party, please, Daddy?'

'Dolphins don't eat jelly or cake. They love to stay outside and swim where the River Shannon meets the sea.'

'Bye, big wavy fishes. Bye. Bye. Bye.'

Daddy is writing on big books in his office. I sit under the table with my dolls.

'Please, Daddy, bring me and Bren out in the squeaky boat to see the wavy fishes.'

'Daddy is very busy. No time to go on the River Shannon, love.'

He gives me blue crayons and a copybook. I write letters to the wavy fishes.

When Daddy goes to collect post from the letterbox, I climb on his chair and write on his big books.

'Why are you putting all my dolls into those big boxes, Mammy?'

'We're going to another house next week, love.'

'But why are we going to another house, Mammy? I like this house.'

'Daddy has to go to another house and we'll all go with him.'

'But why has Daddy to go to another house?'

'Because the Big Boss says so, love.'

'I don't like that Big Boss, Mammy.'

'Mammy, Mammy, I want to go home now.'

'But you are at home, my love.'

'No, Mammy, no huge big wavy fishes, no squeaky boats, no squishy sand, no big splashy waves of the River Shannon.'

'You're here with us, with Daddy and Mammy.'

She lifts me up and hugs me.

'Could we walk back, Mammy?'

'It's too far, love. But we might go on a visit soon.'

'But when is soon, when will we go on a visit? Show me where it is and I'll walk.'

Mammy points to distant mountains.

'It's away, away over those mountains. Close your eyes and we'll fly together, love.'

Mammy holds me in her arms and we fly, fly, fly over the mountains and down to the big splashy waves and the big wavy fishes.

In my mother's arms

Knocknarea

Christy, our favourite driver, pulls up at our front door.

'We're off on our holidays to Strandhill,' says Mammy.

Daddy checks the door locks, then sits in beside Christy. Mammy sits with Brendan and me in the back. We clap hands and chant, 'Holidays. Holidays. We're going on our holidays!'

'Suitcases and lunch basket are packed into the boot,' Daddy assures Mammy.

We swing out through the gates and drive away on roads edged with speckled stone walls.

'Strandhill. Isn't that where the Calm Sea is?' says Christy. 'It's safer than Bundoran for children.'

'Will we see the hobby horses?' I ask.

'We'll see Queen Maedbh's mountain, Knocknarea,' Daddy answers.

'Who's Queen Maedbh, Daddy? Has she hobby horses?'

'She was a famous Queen of Connaught,' Christy says and lifts his cap.

'She lived long, long ago. We'll be passing by her castle, Rath Cruachán. She owned a huge farm with lots and lots of cattle and horses. But she wasn't happy because she wanted to be richer than her husband, Ailill,' Daddy adds.

'Was Ailill richer than Uncle James?' Brendan asks.

'Yes, love. He was much, much richer. He wore gold collars and gold brooches.'

'But Uncle James has a gold chain,' I contradict.

'And a gold watch and he lives in a castle,' Brendan says.

'Uncle James works at his desk in Dublin Castle, but he goes home to Aunt Kathleen in the evenings, love,' Mammy says.

'Ailill had a precious white bull,' Daddy continues.

'With curly horns,' Christy says and twists his cap.

"Curly horns, curly horns," we chant.

'We've left stone-wall country. Now we've hedges with thorntrees,' Mammy observes.

'We're halfway to Sligo now.' Christy begins to whistle tunelessly.

'Look! That's Rath Cruachán over there.' Mammy points to the right. 'And that's Oweynagcat where hundreds of cats live in a fairy cave.'

'Hundreds of cats, Mammy! Is our cat in that cave?'

'Our Beauty is asleep under the rosebush in our garden, love.'

'But she's asleep for ages and ages, Mammy!'

'Our Beauty doesn't want to wake up,' Brendan announces.

'Rath Cruachán is older and bigger than Tara! Imagine that!' Daddy turns to Christy.

'Are there hobby horses in Tara, Daddy?' I interrupt.

'We'll take you and Brendan to Tara on our way to visit Uncle James,' Mammy promises.

'Queen Maedbh was a mighty woman! A warrior. She gathered her army and invaded Ulster. Didn't she come back with the Brown Bull of Cuailgne! A warrior was that woman!' Christy says and lifts his cap again.

'A warrior indeed! The Táin Bó Cuailgne, Christy!' Daddy says as he turns around and gives us Crunchie bars. 'I must climb Knocknarea during the week. There's a cairn on top. Everyone who climbs adds an extra stone to that cairn.'

'Can we climb with you, Daddy, please?' I ask.

'I'll bring up a stone for each of us. One for Mammy, one for you, one for Brendan and one for myself.'

'And one for Beauty,' I insist.

'She was a mighty woman. She was!' Christy announces.

'Buried on top of Knocknarea,' says Daddy.

We eat the Crunchie bars and fall asleep. I dream of Queen Maedbh with her gold brooches and rings and hobby horses with curly horns.

When I wake up, Daddy and Christy are standing outside the car.

'Strandhill at last,' Mammy says as she helps us out.

'Look! Knocknarea! There it is.' Daddy points upwards, while Christy opens the boot and lifts out our luggage.

'It's very big and dark,' I say as I rub sleep from my eyes.

'A warrior of a woman! She's buried up there under that cairn with all her gold collars and brooches,' says Christy.

'Up there beside the stars, Daddy?'

'Yes, love. Up there on top of Knocknarea near the moon and the stars!'

The Last Post

We gather for Christmas dinner with my father as he lies in a hospital bed.

Tinsel and holly pierce my brain
Not a star
but a twist
of black pain
is pinned
above each shining crib.

The earth is frozen as we follow father's body on its way to rest beside mother.

We stand to attention while The Last Post echoes over Galway Bay, along by Black Head, through the Burren and southwards to Killadysert.

In my mind, I announce the following:

Company Officer, Third Battalion, North Roscommon Brigade. Old IRA, survivor of the last hunger strike under British Rule in the twenty-six counties.

Released from Death Wing, Mountjoy Jail after the Treaty was signed in December 1921.

The national flag is folded, green on top, and handed to us.

We gather spent bullet cases.

Falling snowflakes, frozen tears, wrap his grave in tricolour light.

Sinn Féin, the Old IRA

At home later, I reread the following notes taken before Dad died in January 1981.

My father sits in his favourite armchair. I'm ready with my pen and notebook.

'Most of what I want to tell you is in those ledgers on my desk, but now my writing is no longer clear, love,' he says, as turning to pat his dog, Tuflis, he hides his sadness.

My father's brothers who left for the USA in 1915
Back L-R William Burke, Thomas Burke
Front L-R Peter Burke, John Burke

'But your writing was copperplate, Dad, and you were such a great reader!'

'Sit down here, love. You are now my eyes!'

'Of course, Dad. You want to talk about that time when you were a member of Sinn Féin, the Old IRA.' I turn away to hide my own tears.

'Yes, I was Company Officer, Third Battalion, North Roscommon Brigade, Old IRA,' He emphasises each word as I write.

'North Roscommon, Old IRA,' I add.

'North Roscommon Brigade, Old IRA,' he corrects me.

'Yes, Dad, I'm writing Brigade here now. Brigade.'

'I've told you that four of your uncles, William, Thomas, Peter and John Burke, had emigrated to the USA. They wrote regularly to our mother and father. Their letters, which expressed their great love for our parents and family, are still in the old farmhouse. Your two uncles, James and Pakie Burke, and myself, the youngest, went on the run after taking part in the ambush at Scramogue near Strokestown.'

'Scramogue. Yes, Scramogue.' I spell out each letter.

'Captain Peeke was shot dead in that ambush. Other Auxiliaries too,' Dad says.

'Afterwards we hid in dugouts in the hills above Kilglass Lake, but sometimes we were able to wash, eat and sleep in what we called safe houses.'

'Dugouts, Dad? Down into the earth?' I shiver. 'Like an animal's burrow.'

'Yes, love. Small and very cold. We had to keep on the move all of the time. Friends of the Cause left food and warm clothing under Mass rocks on the hill of Mullagh. Guerilla warfare. We, the Old IRA, brought about the first fracture in the British Empire.'

'That's amazing! Guerilla warfare toppled an Empire, Dad!'

'Yes, daughter. One evening we got another urgent message. This time it was from what we thought a trusted medical source, saying that our mother, Brigit Burke, was very ill and was asking for us. We rushed home.'

'Of course you did,' I say as I write.

'But when we ran into our farmhouse it was full of Black and Tans. Twenty or thirty of them! Tans everywhere, so we had no chance, even though we were fully armed.

I was carrying a revolver that belonged to an officer shot dead in the Scramogue ambush. They arrested us, tied us up, kicked and spat on the three of us and threw us into their lorries. Their lorries had been well hidden down a boreen.'

'Oh, Dad! That's horrible!' I look at my ailing father. Until recently he had kept silent about his early life.

'The Tans beat up your grandfather, William Burke, so badly that he never recovered. They smashed his ribs, his collarbones and injured his spine. The Tans told your grandmother that we, her three sons, would be shot dead before they got us as far as Longford. They then shot all the cows in the byres and took away all of the turkeys and geese that my mother, your grandmother, was rearing for Christmas.'

'Such inhuman behaviour!' I gasp. 'Take a rest, Dad!' I say as I hold his hand.

'My mother,' he continued, 'told me that when the Black and Tans' lorries, holding us, had gone, she cleaned the blood and spittle from my father's face. She then went out to the Penal Cross near the house. She knelt there for hours and prayed and prayed.

Your Uncle James and Uncle Pakie and myself were brought first to Rooskey RIC Barracks, then on to Athlone. James and Pakie were chained and sent up to Ballykinlar Camp in Co. Donegal. I was sent under heavy guard to Mountjoy Jail, where I was brought before a military court and sentenced to death. I was kept in D. Wing, Mountjoy, the condemned wing, for twelve months – until the Treaty. I could have been executed at any time.'

'For twelve months not knowing when that call would come!'

'Yes, love,' he says as he wipes sweat from his forehead.

'On the morning of an execution, the prisoner whose turn had come was given a glass of whiskey. Another prisoner called Kenny always drank any whiskey left in the dead man's cell.'

'He went around and drank the leftover whiskey, while the prisoners were being executed, Dad!'

'Yes, love. Kenny always drank all of those very last drops. It's strange, but prisons are strange places. Have you got that down?'

'Nearly all of it – yes – I have it now. But Dad, how did you survive?'

'I was very young. I was full of ideals and full of love for my country.'

'Tell me about your attempt to escape from D. Wing, Mountjoy.'

'Three of us, Simon Moynihan, Con Coughlan and myself, managed to get a hacksaw into our cell. During a concert in Mountjoy, Coughlan cut through an iron upright. This left enough space to enable a few of us to get out into the compound.

We then got into the basement, but the hacksaw broke just as Coughlan tried to cut another iron bar. We couldn't go any further without a hacksaw, so we had to return to the cells.'

'Yes. Hacksaw. I've all of that.'

'After our escape attempt, an Auxiliary, using a car starting handle, regularly checked the bars on the high window of our cell.'

'A car starting handle, Dad?'

'In those days, cars and lorries were started by twisting an iron bar into the front of the engine. But now I must tell you that the British had spies among the prisoners. We couldn't trust certain men in D. Wing.'

'Spies pretending to be prisoners. Double agents? Did any of the prisoners escape?'

'A prisoner with the alias Gerald Dixon, a medical student, managed to get an Auxiliary's coat and beret with pom-pom, two ribbons and an RIC badge. He walked out of the jail unchallenged.'

'Good for him.'

'With me in Mountjoy at that time were Sean Mac Eoin, Arthur Griffith, Eoin Mac Neill, Sean Kavanagh and Eamon Duggan. There was great excitement when Emmet Dalton and his pals tried to rescue Sean Mac Eoin.

Ernie O'Malley was with us too. He had been a student in Trinity College in 1916. His father was a Clerk of the Crown. When captured, he said his name was Bernard Stuart. His captors brought him to Dublin Castle and gave him a glass of whiskey. As he walked about they shouted "Bernard". He was caught on the hop and didn't respond. Now I must tell you that Ernie's uncle was a landlord's man. He used to call to Irish farmhouses saying, "Be at such a place at such a time and pay me such an amount of rent for your landlord."

'So Ernie was a new-style republican?'

'Ernie himself was a member of our North Roscommon Brigade Old IRA and he organised the whole countryside for the IRA.'

'You were Company Officer North Roscommon Brigade Old IRA. I have it right this time, Dad!'

'Yes, love,' he says as I continue to write.

'Ernie was sent over to Kilmainham Jail. After a while he escaped from Kilmainham. Corporal Roper got ten years for allowing Ernie to escape. Patrick Moran from Roscommon didn't go to Kilmainham with Ernie. Although Patrick Moran claimed he was an innocent man, he was hanged afterwards in Mountjoy.'

'May he rest in peace.'

'Did I tell you that anyone, a woman or even a child, caught with the booklet *An tÓghlach* got six months in jail? Write that down, love.'

An tÓglach – six months in jail.'

'I painted a portrait of Robert Emmet while I was in Mountjoy. That helped to keep my spirits up. A number of us decided to go on hunger strike. We refused solid food, but took a little water. After ten days on hunger strike, we succeeded in getting permission for prisoners to attend Mass without the presence of prison guards. That gave us a chance to plan an escape. This was the last hunger strike under British Rule here in the South, in what we now call the Twenty-Six Counties. Make sure you write that down!'

'Yes, Dad. That's very important,' I write and underline.

'I didn't escape in spite of so many attempts. The Anglo-Irish Treaty was signed at 2.20 a.m. in 10 Downing Street on December 6, 1921. Having spent twelve months in Mountjoy, I was released on 12th December 1921. Mrs. Sheehy Skeffington met us as we were released. Our clothes were worn out, so she gave us money to buy new suits.

On my first night of freedom in Dublin, a cousin of ours from Kilglass asked me what I'd like to do. "The Abbey Theatre! Take me there", I replied.'

'Such a contrast! The stage, the set-design – was it good?'

'The stage was much, much bigger than ours in Killglass. The set was very interesting. Yes, the acting was very good too.'

'Did you take your Robert Emmet portrait out with you, Dad?'

'Yes, love. It's hanging in the parlour of our old home. I'll show it to you next time we visit. On my return home to Kilglass near Strokestown, the hills were ablaze with bonfires of welcome. However, when I returned to my local Sinn Féin Company meeting, I saw new members there, people from Rooskey and the surrounding countryside. People who had spied on the North Roscommon Brigade Old IRA. Some of those spies had caused the arrest of myself and my brothers, but had now jumped on the new political bandwagon! I walked out of that Sinn Féin meeting in disgust and did not return! I did not return. Have you that underlined, love?'

'Yes, Dad. I'll type this out and you can check it tomorrow.'

'Thank you, daughter.' Dad looks very sad.

I know he's remembering the death of his hero, Michael Collins, at Béal na Bláth.

Addendum

My Dad became a pacifist. He said many times that the Civil War was the greatest tragedy in the history of Ireland.

A local nurse, who was friendly with a Black and Tan, was one of a number of spies who lived in and around Rooskey. She may have sent that false message which caused the arrest of Dad and my uncles and the attack on my grandparents.

I met that nurse in Rooskey after Dad died. A Mrs. Reynolds introduced me, saying that I was the daughter of Mary O'Beirne and Joesph Phelim Burke. Her attitude to the Burke brothers was full of hatred. After their arrest, she probably had her hair shaved off by members of Dad's Brigade.

Above Kilglass Lake

A short time after Dad's death, we decide to honour him by revisiting his home place. Fom Galway City we drive past the restored De Burgo tower house in Claregalway, along by the richly textured Esker Riada, through Moylough, Mountbellew, Newbridge, Ballygar, Roscommon town and Elphin.

In Carrick–on-Shannon I say, 'Dad attended the Presentation Brothers' Secondary School here in Carrick before he joined North Roscommon Brigade, Old IRA. We stop to gaze at the school building.

With sadness in our hearts, we drive on to Scramogue, the scene of that famous ambush. 'This is where North Roscommon Brigade flying column lay in wait for Captain Peek and his Auxiliaries on 23rd March 1921.' I point to the turn on the road.We then continue on our way. We cross over the bridge of Rooskey along by the river Shannon and on up to visit the church on the hill above Kilglass Lake.

'Dad was baptized and confirmed in this church,' I say as we leave the car and stand outside the church gate.

'Brigit Burke, Dad's mother, presented this church with a monstrance for Benediction,' Philomena says. I go to the main doorway and to the sidedoor of the church, but fail to open either of them.

'We must arrange to see that monstrance on our next visit.' Philomena wipes tears from her eyes.

'His old home next,' I decide as we drive towards the hill of Mullagh.

'Such a wonderful view,' Teresa exclaims. We then pull in at the old farmhouse.

'Here are the remains of a Penal Church,' I whisper as, holding hands, we stand in a circle on the lawn in front of the house. 'Eternal rest to all who have passed over this doorstep. May they rest in peace,' we pray in unison, our heads bowed.

In my mind's eye, I see the Black and Tans arrest Dad, Uncle James and Uncle Pakie, then kick and chain them before throwing them into camouflaged Crossley tenders.

'Forgive those Auxiliaries, forgive them,' I whisper.

While my sisters take photographs, I make a number of charcoal sketches.

'Now we must visit Dad's cousin, John Burke. His farm runs along by the Boyle River,' I announce.

'The Boyle River is a tributary of the River Shannon,' Teresa adds.

'Do you know that John Burke's glebe house, Riversdale, was once the residence of film star Maureen O'Sullivan?' Philomena says as we turn to drive towards Boyle.

When we arrive at Riverhaven, we admire the ornate gates and the long curve of the avenue leading to Riversdale House. John's wife, Martina, serves us afternoon tea in a sittingroom overlooking the river.

'This is a photograph of our daughter Una, the up-and-coming fashion designer.' John takes a framed photograph from the sideboard.

'Her work has been commissioned by Madonna, by Lady Gaga and many others,' he adds. 'I must Google Una Burke's latest exhibition of leather jewellery. I hear it's magnificent,' says my sister Claire.

'She was always gathering old pieces of cow hide and tanning them with vegetable dyes, then twisting them into strange ornaments and now her work is exhibited in London, Paris, New York, Tokyo – all over the world,' John remarks.

'Congratulations to both of you! She's very talented,' says Teresa.

'I'll tell her that her Galway cousins called,' John replies.

'Before we leave, we'd love to see the new discovery on your land, John. That excavated multi-period site mentioned in the *National Geographic* documentary.'

'Of course, Patricia. I'll take all of you over the fields. It's only a short distance.'

As we walk through glistening grasses, he informs us, 'This complex Neolithic, Bronze Age and Medieval ecclesiastical site is frequently mentioned in The Annals during the 13th century and is of very high status. It's directly associated with the O'Connors, the kings of Connacht.'

Myself, Teresa and Philomena with Mimi and Fleur

When we arrive at the site, he points with both hands and continues, 'You can see here the ruins of a small fortified building and a possible Hall House, which have been explored. According to that documentary, these ruins may be the remains of the Bishop's Palace, built in 1253 AD.' We stand in awe as plainchant echoes through ancient cloisters away across the Boyle River and on towards the River Shannon.

He consults a small book. 'This site was already established as an

Early Medieval enclosed settlement. More than 120 skeletons have been excavated here from what was once a well-ordered cemetery dating from the 7th to the 14th centuries AD.'

Holding his arms wide open, he quotes, 'Here a huge number of prehistoric artifacts have been recovered dating from all the medieval contexts and field-walking strategies. These artifacts show the intensive use of this site during prehistory.' We make the Sign of the Cross again and bow our heads in prayer. We then return to John's glebe house above the River Boyle.

Voice

I move from the school in Briarhill to St. Brendan's, which is on the edge of Galway City. As a result of the growth of suburbia nearby, there are sixty-eight pupils in the junior division.

'Why do you stay on teaching junior classes?' friends ask.

'Because I enjoy leading children into a world of wonder, instead of stuffing their minds with stunted ideas. I'm privileged to join in their magical imaginative thoughts. I've developed methods of teaching to which they respond. It's the most important time in their lives.'

'How can you put up with the repetition?'

'What repetition? I learn more from the juniors' unspoilt creativity than I do from the senior classes. Pablo Picasso himself said that he wished he could paint like a five-year-old child! It amazes me that teaching juniors is still considered *infra dig*. There is a *caste* system, nose-upturning by some. In fact, the children's foundation is laid down in the junior departments.'

I continue to teach in spite of a very bad cold, which becomes a chest infection. Suddenly no vocal sound comes except a strange croak. My GP sends me to hospital for Xrays and then to see an ear, nose and throat consultant at The Crescent. The consultant covers my ears with thick muffs and asks me to count aloud. He then examines my opened throat and vocal chords by probing with steel implements.

I'm afraid of the haughty consultant to ask if there's a tumour.

He tells me not to use my voice for six weeks, to write down what I have to say. I'm cut off from my social life. A substitute teacher takes over my work.

In a grocery on Shop Street, I write my list in a notebook and I show it to the shop assistant behind the counter.

'Is it real honey you want?' she shouts back at me. I write again and point to my list.

'I'm not deaf', I write. 'Comb honey, if you please', I write again and point to my list. She glares at me, turns her eyes to heaven, then shuffles off to collect my order of butter, comb honey, brown bread and milk.

I join a Transcendental Meditation course. For years I do not trust my voice.

I'm scared every time I try to speak.

On the advice of a friend, I take lessons in the Alexander Technique from Richard Brennan. Sessions of acupuncture also help. Gradually I regain vocal sounds and learn to trust those sounds.

Listening to music

Return

Through Burren grykes and turloughs, we drive southwards to honour memories.

In Ennis, Eamon says, 'Look, love! There's the signpost for Killadysert!'

Turning right at the junction, we journey along twisty roads towards the mouth of the River Shannon. Small birds, skylarks and thrushes, rise from thorntrees and sing for us.

River air from the Shannon welcomes us. I have returned to my birthplace.

The house is big and solid, an Old RIC Barracks, built by the British. A young Garda, his dark hair brushed back from a wide forehead, greets us.

As I climb upstairs, I wonder which is my birth room.

I stand in a doorway and know that this is where my spirit mourned that other place of happiness. Birth-cry of my mother. My first gasp for air.

I close my eyes, rock myself in folded arms to the rhythm of river-mouth waters.

Downstairs, I ask the Garda if any books belonging to my father are still here.

'A few months ago, most of the written material was sent back to the Depot in the Phoenix Park. But we'll look in the old office.' With a special key, he opens a door near the Day Room. He takes a bundle of ledgers from a top shelf and we begin our search. Dust rises on sunbeams as we open and close neatly written reports.

'Dad, please help us to find even a small trace of your work here.'

We search and search.

'Yes! Yes! Here's my Dad's signature!'

His name is written in black ink.

'But look at this! Your scribble in blue crayon beside his! Your first signature!' Eamon smiles.

With my finger I trace over my father's perfectly formed letters, then I touch my blue scribble.

'Thank you, Dad. Thank you.'

Gárda Barracks, Killadysert, Co Clare

Etching

Under the direction of Laura Vecchi Ford, the Italian artist, an Extra-Mural Etching course is set up in University College, Galway.

Positioned near tall windows in the converted studio is a printing press from Urbino. Double-imaged glass shelves hold tins of inks, Orient Blue, Terracotta, Warm Sepia, Crimson Alizarin, Cerulean from Laurence of Bleeding Heart Yard, London, from Charbonnel, Quai Montebello, Paris and Via Sasso, Urbino, Italia.

When the course is over, I continue to work with these intriguing techniques.

Gauze-masked, alone among acid baths,
I grapple with images on zinc or copper.
Incense of melting resin rises
from etched plates on a wire-meshed stove.

Some areas of copper I protect with opaque bitumen as I develop new techniques in soft ground. Textures, delicate or coarse, pressed into soft wax, I watch the acid eat into unprotected metal.

From bundles of soft hand-woven paper, Fabriano, Arches, Saunders, I choose and dampen ivory sheets. Acid washed away in clear water, I take a burin and cut into tawny metal. I burnish other areas on the plate, then ink-up the relief.

The printing-press shrieks
as, pushed between huge cylinder
and bed of the press,
forced between etched lines
and open-bite spaces,
the damp paper
takes up the relief image.

That moment, when I lift the paper from the inked plate, is full of excitement.

Success, failure?

Sometimes I see an image forming and I work again with burin and burnisher. I put the plate into the acid bath for a short while, take it out, wash and proof it, protect areas with bitumen, then back into the acid bath and wash and proof it again. I'm never satisfied. I write Beckett's words, 'To be an artist is to fail as no other dare fail,' on white card and pin it high above the wastepaper bin. Evening after evening, week after week, year after year, I search for images. I follow a vision.

At last a torso forms in turquoise bubbles as *Gaillimh, daughter of Breasail*, raises her etched arms from the River Corrib.

My etchings are included in selected Annual and International Biennale Exhibitions during Listowel Writers' Week. The exhibitions tour to The Arts Council Gallery, Belfast, The Arts Society Gallery, Cork and The Douglas Hyde Gallery, Trinity College, Dublin.

My work is awarded a Prize at The Listowel Third Biennale by Herman Hebler, Patrick Murphy, Coilin Murray and Geoff Steiner Scott, the 1982 Jury. It's exciting to see my name beside famous artists, *Wolfgang Troschke. Akira Kurosaki, Sophie Aghajanian*, David Barker and *Maria De La Paz Jaramillo*.

I'm invited to exhibit at the 1982 *Fredrikstad Print Biennale*, Norway.

My works are included in the EVA, Limerick, Claremorris Fine Art and I'm shortlisted for the *Alice Berger Hammerschlag* Award in 1979.

Smaller etchings of mine are selected and exhibited annually by a gallery in Cadaques, Barcelona and tour to Madrid, Andorra, Paris, Hawaii and Japan.

Ceól, an etching of jazz musicians, is selected for the *oireachtas* exhibition in the Municipal Gallery, Parnell Square, Dublin. I'm delighted too when the Irish Arts Council purchases three of my *Tús* etchings. They are included in an exhibition which tours Ireland and are also exhibited at Dublin Airport.

Other works are included in The Exhibition of Visual Arts, Limerick 1978, The Third National Fine Arts Exhibition,

Claremorris 1980, Galway Arts Festival Exhibition 1978, Group Exhibitions at the Project Gallery, Dublin 1980 and 1984.

I continue to hold solo exhibitions in Galway City, Dublin's United Arts Club and *An Damhlann* in Spiddal and Galway City.

In between I work on a *Petrushka* image. I've always been fascinated by this folk-story from Russia. As I work, I listen to Stravinsky's forward-thinking ballet music.

I do not know that during the 2013 Galway Arts Festival, I'd watch in wonderment as Fabulous Beast Theatre perform Stravinsky's *Petrushka* in the Black Box Theatre.

Now and again, painters visit the etching workshop in UCG. Some develop skills in etching. Apprentice printmaker Neil Finn from Cork is in charge of the materials. Painters Cormac O'Neill and Chris Jolley visit the workshop regularly. Chris prefers to paint his Biblical portraits in his own studio above Middle Street.

We are shocked by news of Chris's sudden death. His funeral Mass in Kinvara is attended by his wife, his stepdaughter Victoria, his young children and his brothers and sister. Galway artists and writers read stanzas from St. John of the Cross, Chris's favourite saint.

Afterwards I wrote the following poem. It's included in my first published collection.

Above the Waves' Calligraphy.
High into the tower he climbed.
He carried Christ on his back.
For the last time he twisted upwards
towards the April night.

When he fell amongst cobalts
and ultramarines,
the Christ-bones offset
on his ivory shroud.

For three days he floated
in his sky tomb,
as his blood congealed on stretched boards.
We did not hear the keening of the Magdalenes.
We did not hear the breaking of the bones,
We did not hear the bursting of the heart.
Nor see the lonely flutter of the scarecrow.
They closed him into a pale wooden box
and wedged him under a slabbed hill.

That stony cell is now his cold cloister.
His painted shrouds are hanging in the tower.

Ceól Soft ground colour etching

Exhibitions

During a solo exhibition of paintings, etchings and mono-prints in the Gallery of University College, Galway, I'm invited to put on a solo show in the Bridge Mills.

My work, with its textures and vivid colours, looks different, but exciting against the stone walls and wooden beams. Outside the swollen River Corrib hurries with excitement to meet the Atlantic ocean. One of my etchings, 'Gaillimh, daughter of Breasail', is based on a story which fascinates me. Breasail's daughter drowned in the River Corrib and gave her name to Gaillimh, Galway. Here is my poem based on that story.

Daughter of Breasail
The woman moves towards the river
to cool her pregnant body.
She steps on limestone
honeycombed by rain.
She lifts her garment
and floats to the Atlantic.
We name her new-born city, Gaillimh.

On the opening night of the exhibition, I'm delighted to meet Brian Keenan. He has just been released from captivity in Beirut. We have a long conversation about light and colour. Held in darkness for so long, he spoke of how his sudden coming into intense light affected his whole being. We smile for photographers. Sales are made.

Michael D. Higgins, with his artistic flair, opens an exhibition of my paintings at The Tavern Bar and Restaurant in Eyre Square. Two of my portraits entitled 'A Galway Girl' are bought by the Abbey actor Pat Layde.

'These portraits remind me of my darling wife. She's from the Aran Islands,' he says as we chat in the famous Tavern Bar.

'Eamon and I are fans of yours,' I tell him.

He's delighted when I add, 'We've watched you in many stage productions in Dublin and in London.'

Years later I hear that his Galway wife had died. At a course in Liberty Hall, I meet his second wife, who mentions that my 'Galway Girl' portraits reminded him of her too. After Pat Layde's death, she puts the portraits up for auction. They are bought by a man who is also married to a Galway girl!

On many occasions, I'm invited to exhibit my work in The United Arts Club at 3 Upper Fitzwilliam Street, Dublin. All are successful solo shows.

With Brian Keenan at my exhibition in Bridge Mills Gallery.

Michael D. Higgins, guest speaker at opening of my first art exhibition in the Tavern Bar, Eyre Sq. Galway, late 1960s.

Stage Play

At a Theatre Workshop during Listowel Writers' Week in the early 1980s, I'm told by theatre critic Fintan O'Toole that my one act stage play, set in a fictional Magdalen Laundry, shows great promise and that I should develop it into a full-length play.

Back in Galway, I reread *The Gospels*, *The Book of Job*, *Dante's Purgatorio*, *In Memory of Her* by Elizabeth Schussler Fiorenza and Mary Condren's *The Serpent and the Goddess (Women, Religion and Power in Celtic Ireland)*. I do not read play-scripts by other writers.

There are many rewrites of the play. It now has the title, *Eclipsed*.

I do not use stories about the women I met in the Galway Magdalen Laundry. Luckily, I do not find it difficult to create fictional characters.

With great care, I choose the contralto aria, 'He was despised' from Handel's *Oratorio*, *Messiah*, sung by Kathleen Ferrier for the opening and closing scenes.

Plain chant, *Credo* and *Magnificat* sung by a soprano will be recorded locally and I include rock 'n' roll songs by Elvis Presley, also country tunes.

During Passion Week and Holy Week before Easter Sunday, statues and crucifixes in Roman Catholic churches are covered with purple fabric. This custom is echoed by my use of purple muslin drapes, which conceal the set at the opening and closing of each performance. This adds to the mystical quality of the play.

I set the main section of the play in 1963 during the Second Vatican Council. It was also the year when President John F. Kennedy visited Ireland. Elvis Presley's rock 'n' roll singing was also having an effect on this side of the Atlantic.

For another special reason, I name the fictional laundry, St. Paul's Laundry, Killmacha. I've always believed that St. Paul promoted patriarchy in the early church.

Killmacha is a combination of pagan and Christian words – kill (cill) is the anglicisation of Gaelic for church or cell/oratory of the early church. Macha, a sun goddess, a life-giving image, a fertility goddess, was one of the most important goddesses of ancient Ireland.

In 1990, I watch as bulldozers move in and demolish our local Magdalen Laundry. There are no photographers present, no onlookers. A notice with the words, NO DUMPING, is erected amongst the rubble. Alone and tearful, I take numerous photographs. At home later, I write this poem.

Make Visible the Tree

This is the Place of Betrayal.
Roll back the stones
behind Madonna blue walls.
Make visible the tree.

Above percussion of engines
from gloom of catacombs,
through a glaze of prayer,
scumble of chanting,
make visible the tree,
its branches ragged
withwashed-out linens
of a bleached shroud.

In this shattered landscape,
sharpened tongues
of sulphur-yellow bulldozers
slice through wombs
of blood-soaked generations.

This is the place
where Veronica,
forsaken,
stares and stares
at a blank shroud.

Four lines from the second stanza are inscribed on a limestone plaque as part of a memorial sculpture to The Magdalen Women in Galway City. Unveiled on International Women's Day 2009, it is set on the original site of the Laundry. In March 2011 a limestone slab inscribed with the entire poem, *Make Visible the Tree*, is erected beside the memorial sculpture.

The memorial sculpture to the Magdalen Women.

The Tyrone Guthrie Centre for the Arts

It's Holy Week. The weather has turned cold and snow covers this historic residence and gardens once owned by Tyrone Guthrie. During a week-long workshop we gather around the writer John McGahern. We read from our work and listen to his criticism.

'A writer should be everywhere, but nowhere visible,' John says.

Each morning after breakfast, we concentrate on our creative work. At midday we stop for lunch followed by a walk in the gardens or along by the lake. Then it's back to editing and rewriting.

One afternoon we gather in the music room and I read two scenes from my stage play, *Eclipsed*. They are very well received.

After a communal dinner, some of the artists in the house usually go to the local pub for a nightcap. The pub is within walking distance.

'Now that the snow has cleared from the roads, I'll drive there in my new Renault Parisienne!' I take car keys from my handbag. 'Anyone want a lift?'

John sits in the passenger seat and acts as guide. Two other writers, Ciarán and Seamus, sit in the back of the car. We wave to other artists as they stride along the avenue.

'Take the first right at the thorntree,' John directs.

I drive for a few miles.

'Shouldn't we be near that pub?' I ask.

'It only takes ten minutes on foot.' Seamus is uneasy.

'Take the next left, then right again,' John answers.

No sign of the pub and closing time looms.

'I'll ask at the next house,' says Ciarán.

I pull into a gateway and wait as Ciarán runs along a stony pathway and knocks at the farmhouse door.

'No reply here,' Ciarán shouts and he hurries away from the dark doorway and back to the car.

'We must have crossed the border into the North and your car has a southern registration, Patricia!' declares Seamus. 'This is bandit country! People are afraid to answer the door, especially at night. The UDA, the UVF, the UDF!'

I shiver as a visit to St. Louis Convent, Monaghan in 1972 comes to mind. We had taken Aunt Clara for a drive and had accidentally crossed the border. Dressed in her nun's head-dress and habit, she sat in the passenger seat of the Ford Cortina beside my newly ordained brother, Father Brendan. Rounding a corner, we were surrounded by a group of B. Specials who had jumped from a lorry. When they saw the clerical collar and the nun's coif and veil, they mouthed obscenities and spat at us before ordering us to get back without delay to the South.

'We'd better move away from here,' I say to John as I try to reverse from the dark gateway, but the car stalls. Ciarán and Seamus get out and push, push on slippery gravel. Eventually the engine hiccups, starts and we drive away from the shadowy entrance.

'The next right,' John says.

'The next left,' Ciarán contradicts.

'No. The next right,' John repeats.

In the distance the lights of the pub glow. We arrive just in time for one drink before closing time. The other writers laugh at our story.

'A car holding the brightest brains in this country and ye go astray on the few yards down to the local!' Andrew, a painter, dressed in a designer smock, raises his pint of Guinness to John.

'Ye must have driven over the *féar gortach*!' the barman says with a puzzled look.

'On yer way back be sure to take the first right.' He signals to us as we leave.

Outside the pub, we turn right and wave to the walkers who follow.

'Next left,' John directs.

'I hope you've enough petrol, Patricia!' Seamus says.

I drive for miles and miles through obsidian of thorntree hedges punctuated by filigree of larch trees. Their dark lives of meshed roots are still in winter sleep, but are dreaming of spring.

Road edges sparkle with snow drifts instead of meadowsweet, buttercups and bluebells. A badger's wondrous markings glow as it scuttles away from my car headlights.

'This is your kind of country, John,' says Seamus.

'We've a multitude of small lakes in Leitrim. They make our landscape luminous.'

'Look! There's a shooting star!' I say in delight.

'And there's another and another.' John points to the south.

'We're lost again! The *féar gortach* has hijacked this car,' Seamus says.

'We call it the *fóidín marbh*. If you step on the *fóidín marbh*, you keep going round and round in circles and you cannot escape. That's what we believe in Conamara,' Ciarán says and makes the sign of the cross.

'We should turn our coats inside out if it's the *fóidín marbh*. But isn't it really about magic, a magical world,' I observe.

'Yes, a magical world,' Seamus says softly.

'Isn't it just like writing, John? Rewriting and rewriting and then some of the time it works!' I say and John nods in agreement.

'Rewriting and rewriting,' we say in chorus.

At two-thirty in the morning we arrive in a small town called Rockcorry. A country market is being set up by farmers, their dark shapes move under tawny street lights.

'Ye're lost indeed! Guthrie's place is "way over in that direction!"' one farmer, his breath misted by the cold, points to the northwest.

'This'll warm ye up after crossing that *féar gortach*!' He hands us mugs of hot soup.

'Thanks a thousand times, we're starving.' I smell the soup's delicious aroma.

He moves away and speaks to a man who is loading a stall with cabbages and potatoes..

'My cousin Jamsie will be driving back near Annaghmakerrig in about ten minutes. He'll lead you to the front gate. But put this bread in your pocket in case you drive across that *féar gorta*ch again.' He gives me a wedge of buttered bread.

I wrap the bread in a tissue before I push it deep into the pocket of my waxed raincoat.

The soup finished, we thank the farmer and follow Jamsie's lorry into darkness. Snowflakes begin to fall again as we reach the high walls of Annaghmakerrig.

I beep a 'Thank you' to Jamsie, swing through the gates and up along the avenue.

'From now on we'd better walk to the pub!' says John.

'But with bread in our pockets and coats inside out,' I insist as I lock the car and we enter the great house.

'Tomorrow is Holy Thursday! Only two days left to write our masterpieces,' Seamus says sleepily.

'The day after is Good Friday, Good Friday in Annaghmakerrig!' I'm pensive.

'They're all gone to bed! Even that famous ghost,' Ciarán remarks as we walk into the warm kitchen.

'I'm more afraid of some of the living out there,' I shiver.

'Goodnight, my friends, and goodnight to our resident ghost too!' I stifle a yawn.

Suddenly the telephone shrills through the night.

'At this hour, who could it be?' Seamus is now wide awake.

'It's probably Tony beyond in New York, checking on his girlfriend. Should I answer it?' asks Ciarán.

'Let it ring.' Seamus takes off his anorak. He turns it inside out and wraps it around his shoulders.

I move towards the stairs. The dissonance of the telephone triggers uneasy memories. Images return of my distress when I was held up at the border on my way to Enniskillen.

Camouflaged machine-guns pierced viridian hedges. British soldiers in my own country demanded to see my passport, then questioned me for what seemed like two hours.

Unable to sleep, I switch on my bedside lamp and work on the following poem.

'Where do you come from?
Where are you going?
Where? Where? Why?'
Soldiers, heavy with guns, circle a checkpoint.

Dry throat silent. Snow-bullets crimsoned,
carmine of rhododendron stains the green.
Dark voices barter for a seamless vest
here, where flesh explodes and that bruised head looms
between the trees.
Snow deepens
its white winding sheet
on Rockcorry, Newbliss
and Annaghmakerrig.
The sun splinters.
Forsaken,
that pierced heart dies,
Day is Night.

With the title, 'Good Friday, Co. Monaghan, 1989', I include it in my published collection, *Above the Waves' Calligraphy.*

Eclipsed

During Listowel Writers' Week, Fintan O'Toole, an eminent theatre critic, advises me to send *Eclipsed*, now a full-length play, to the Abbey Theatre and to all of the other Irish theatres.

Rejections arrive. One well-known theatre director asks if I realise what I am saying in my script. He suggests that I change the dialogue of the Magdalen characters. His mother, who had worked in a Magdalen Laundry, told him that the women wouldn't speak like that. Of course, I do not change the dialogue. It's not a documentary, it's a play. A letter-writer advises me to send *Eclipsed* to European theatres, as it could never be produced in Ireland.

Field Day Theatre Company, very important in Northern Ireland, replies that it is giving *Eclipsed* another reading and will be in touch. I wait for nine months. Later, I hear that Field Day Theatre Company has dissolved.

At the end of 1991, Punchbag, an emerging theatre company, are looking for new plays. From the number submitted, three plays are chosen: *Eclipsed*, *Face-licker Come Home* by Rita Ann Higgins and another play by Gerry Forken. All three are performed in an old garage. *Eclipsed*, directed by Rebecca Bartlett, is chosen for promotion but, after that trial performance in November 1991 a change of directors is announced. With a new cast, *Eclipsed* opens on 14th February 1992 in that converted garage near the Spanish Arch in Galway City.

During rehearsals I write a fictional name, Cillnamona, for Brigit Murphy's home place. Later I discover that there's a real Kilnamona near Ennis in Co. Clare.

At times I'm obliged to object to certain drifts in the production process.

Grykes in Burren limestone grow deeper.

Seeing my fictional characters on stage is a terrifying experience.

During a radio inrerview for RTÉ, Julian Vignoles questions me about my experiences as a novice in the local Magdalen Laundry. That interview is included in his *Magdalen Laundry Documentary* and is short listed for the *Prix Italia*. Sections from the interview are repeated on RTÉ at Easter for many years.

During Galway Bay FM's program on *Eclipsed*, my poem, *Make Visible The Tree*, is read by an actor. I lack the courage to read my own work on radio.

A protest is organised outside the theatre, because *Eclipsed* is set in a laundry run by nuns. The protesters' objection is that the nuns are depicted in a bad light. For me *Eclipsed* is becoming a minefield.

Other theatre companies suddenly show interest.

When asked to sign a two-year contract with Punchbag, I refuse because two years seem too long. However, before one preview, while the rain-soaked audience gathers outside, I'm ordered, 'Sign now, or else the audience will not be allowed in!' Reluctantly, I sign.

On opening night the theatre company presents me with a bouquet of flowers. As I chat with members of the audience after the show, I leave the bouquet on a nearby seat. Later, when I turn to take up my flowers, they have disappeared. It's St. Valentine's night and some girl has been presented with a stolen bouquet! An omen for *Eclipsed* ?

People who normally do not go to the theatre travel in busloads from Co. Clare, Co. Galway and Co. Mayo to see the play. Burly men shed tears and try to come to terms with the treatment of pregnant unmarried mothers.

Punchbag develops a strong PR system.

One night as I stand in the foyer during the interval, I overhear two over-coated farmers talking.

'They say the girl who wrote it was an inmate!'

'Sure, she was an inmate, the poor girl!'

I'm about to correct their story, when I suddenly realise that this is a wonderful compliment, the best review I could hope for.

Another night during the long run to full houses at Spanish Arch, Galway City, I'm ordered by a theatre employee to stand and give my seat to a member of the audience.

'You haven't paid for your seat,' he says.

I do not reply, but I move out into the foyer.

Eclipsed tours Ireland to critical acclaim. Another change in the cast is announced.

In April 1992 a major crisis occurs in our diocese. Our bishop, a patron of the theatre, resigns in controversial circumstances and leaves for the USA. The story of his affair with Annie Murphy and the existence of his son is discovered by the media.

When I wrote Brigit's dialogue in 1988, I did not know the bishop's story, though now I'm accused of using it in my play.

Edinburgh Theatre Festival

In preparation for the Edinburgh Theatre Festival, another play, *Fine Day For A Hunt*, by Tom McIntyre, goes into rehearsal at the same theatre near the Spanish Arch. Excitement grows backstage.

Before *Eclipsed* opens at the *Demarco Gallery Theatre* in Edinburgh, the directors announce that Sister Virginia's crisis of faith, the entire Credo Scene, is to be cut for the Edinburgh run. I object strongly, explaining that the Credo Scene is the heart of the play.

Fortunately, I succeed in convincing the directors and the scene stays.

During one of the performances, I notice eleven reviewers in the audience, notebooks and pens in hand.

Eclipsed is awarded a *Scotsman* Fringe First and Critics' Choice.

The Guardian, *The Glasgow Herald*, *The List*, *The Irish Times* and many other newspapers give wonderful reviews. There are more interviews, more photographs.

I share an uncomfortable attic bedroom with two of the women actors. Except for a cup of tea at breakfast, I eat all of my meals in small cafés and restaurants. One morning a work list is pinned to the kitchen wall of our spartan apartment.

CLEANERS FOR TODAY

My name is at the top of the list.

I'm not in the novitiate now! I've written this important play. Why should I take on this extra work? I walk down the stone stairs and out into clean Edinburgh air.

Another morning as I walk towards the *Demarco Gallery Theatre*, I'm confronted by a billboard for *The Evening News*. In large black lettering beside a photograph of Eamon Casey, Bishop of Galway, Kilmacduagh and Kilfenora are the words

BISHOP ON THE FRINGE: LOVE-CHILD PLAY BACKED BY CLERIC

Shocked and in tears, I retreat to kneel at the back of the Roman Catholic Cathedral.

Later I hear that some of the actors, knowing that I'd be deeply upset by this type of commercialism, had tried to prevent me from seeing the billboard. But Edinburgh is a small place even during Theatre Festival time.

When interviewed in Edinburgh by Myles Dungan for RTÉ, I insist that the nuns did not go out with grappling hooks to capture the Magdalen women. Society and the State colluded with the sisters-in-charge of the Laundries in order to rid themselves of those outcasts, those unmarried Irish mothers.

Unknown to me, the theatre directors arrange a telephone recording of the struggle scene between Brigit and Sister Virginia with Radio Canada.

When I return from lunch, I hear the following excerpt being recorded in the small bathroom. I decide to wait and listen.

Brigit: Chocolates! Hhh! Keep your bloody chocolates! The keys, Pasty Face! Give me the keys!

Sister Virginia: I – I can't. You know I can't give you the keys, Brigit. I'll pray for you, Brigit!

Brigit: (*Imitating Sister*) You know I can't give you the keys, Sister! I'll pray for you, Brigit. Pretending to help. You're just like the rest of them! You think if you keep us locked up, that we'll forget about living. About being alive. Don't you? That our heads will go soft and mushy from hymns and prayers! You think that we won't see what your crowd is up to! Well, Pasty Face, Brigit Murphy here sees through you! Sees through the whole lot of you! Mother Superiors, Bishops, Popes and all!

There's the rattle of Sister Virginia's rosary beads.

Brigit: Look at youself, Pasty Face. You're a woman. Aren't you? Did you ever have a lover? Tell us that now, Sister. Ha! Would you like a bit o' lipstick, Sister? You don't know anything. Never had a lover. Never had a baby! So you're white and shining, Sister. Not the same as us, are you? Whose side are you on anyways? Why aren't our lover boys locked up too? One law for them and another for us! Scab! Spy! I'll daub it on the walls of Hell! I'll daub it on your baldy skull. Scab! Spy! Informer!

I hear a thump as a body falls.

Brigit, All sweet smiles and 'Here's chocolates!' But you're as bad as the rest. You're young and you keep the keys! Stiff and starched you go back every night to your nice white bed in your nice white cell. You say your nice sweet prayers to your Nice Clean God. Prayers and Hymns and heaven when we die! No! No! No! Now is what matters! We're alive now! It's no use when we're dead. We want to live now!

Sister Virginia: But I want to help, Brigit! I am on your side!

Brigit: No! You're not! I'd kill you, but you're not worth it!

There's the sound of items falling, click of the recorder and a voice interrupts as the bathroom door opens and I'm handed the telephone. The Canadian interviewer asks, 'Why didn't you write a novel instead of a play, Patricia?'

I'm astonished by this question. Am I being told what genre I should use?

Of course, a novel would have been easier to manage business-wise, but in spite of so many painful experiences, I love writing for stage.

Joni Mitchell, a Canadian singer-composer, hears the programme and is inspired to write a song about an unmarried mother called Brigit.

I'm warned by the actors that the company directors want to take the award for themselves and exclude me, the author, from the presentation of the Fringe First Award. I'm determined to walk on stage along with the two directors. I accept the award, a bronze plaque with *Eclipsed* and my own name inscribed above that of the company.

The BBC Scotland reporter Andrea Miller tells me that, though most actors are egoists and grab every success to themselves, she was surprised to see each actor come and thank me sincerely for writing *Eclipsed*.

BBC Scotland Television broadcasts an interview with me, which includes excerpts from the play.

On my return home to Galway, I hear that *Eclipsed* is shortlisted for The London Independent Theatre Award 1992.

In this blaze of publicity, my quiet lifestyle has changed forever. I'm battered in spirit and body. Reluctantly, I agree to take part in a documentary on the Magdalen question.

Immediately Magdalen songs are composed and recorded, newspaper articles are published. A Magdalen Industry has begun.

Telephone call after telephone calls come from other writers: 'I'm writing a novel about the Magdalens.'

'What time did the women rise in the morning? Their bedtime?'

'Recreation time? Describe their diet. Did their families visit them?'

'How were the women dressed? Did they ever see their babies again?'

It's relentless.

Questions from adults asking if I had met their birth mothers are heart-rending. If only I could answer.

When one of my telephone-caller's novel is published, she says in an RTÉ interview that she's the only person who could or should have or had written about Magdalen Laundries. I had seen her take notes during a performance of *Eclipsed* in Andrew's Lane Theatre.

On a dark morning I collect our post before preparing breakfast. When I open a letter with the Blackpool postmark visible, a brown envelope is enclosed. On opening this envelope, I find my photograph cut from our local newspaper. Horns and devil's symbols in black ink adorn my image. Shocked, I realise that somebody out there hates me and hates my writing. Eamon and my sisters comfort me and eventually they trace the origin of the letter.

One male telephone caller has an East Galway accent.

'I never knew you wrote poetry! I was interested in poetry at secondary school, but it was beaten out of me by a teacher!' His voice has a strange excitement when I answer. His frequent calls make my skin crawl.

Eamon advises me to question him. Each time I ask for his name and address, he gives me different information.

'I know where you live. I'm going to call on you soon,' he insists as he describes the location of our home. Whenever that phone rings, my hands tremble.

One night as I switch off downstairs lights, the phone rings. 'I'm coming to see you!' I instinctively know that he 's across the road.

By chance I have pressed 'Record' on my answering machine. Next morning Eamon calls in the Gardaí.

A male and female Garda listen to the recording. I tell them about the caller's various names, addresses and eccentricities. Notes taken and calls made to other Gardaí, they try to reassure me that he will not call again. Eamon attaches a caller display-box to our telephone. Still afraid, I check that box when there are calls at unusual times.

We install a house alarm.

The local theatre directors wish to tour *Eclipsed* to New York and other cities in the USA. The two-year contract with the local theatre company has run out and new contracts are offered. There are many long phone calls from San Francisco, where one of the local directors has made contact with wealthy business men.

I decide not to sign, because my play now deserves a new production company and a new director. New blood, new ears, new eyes with imagination would be best for *Eclipsed*. From now on, I'll insist on short-term contracts.

I fly Shannon-Boston to attend the American premiere at the Forum Theater in Worcester, Mass. USA in March 1994. My cousin, Carol Ann Moroney, meets me at the airport and packs my luggage into her car. We drive in a snowstorm to Worcester, where I've been booked into a multi-storey hotel.

I ring Kenny's Galleries-Bookshops in Galway City to congratulate John O'Donohue at the launch of his published collection of poems, *Echoes of Memory*. I had been delighted when he requested my permission to include some of my black and white etchings with his published poems. *Benedictus* is the title of my first drypoint-etching in his collection. He also chose a colour etching for the cover. This colour etching is part of a diptych, which had been praised by the *Irish Times* reviewer of Listowel National Graphics Exhibition.

On the phone from across the Atlantic, I hear the musical Clare laughter resonate in the Gallery.

In spite of a heavy snowfall, which closed the airport, shops and schools, the premiere of *Eclipsed* plays to full houses and wins the *USA Moss Hart Award for Theatre 1994*.

Carol Ann is of wonderful assistance to me during my stay in the USA.

I do not know then that she would pass away suddenly in the Spring of 2012.

I hear that other Boston theatre companies who had been to Galway City for the Arts Festival had been told by a member of my local theatre company that I had no contact number.

Truth disappeared like water from turloughs in Burren limestone.

Black Dream

Trapped in my black habit, coif and veil, I try to climb up over
stained-glass walls.

I slither and slide, slither and slide. No escape. No escape.
Rattle of rosary beads in a black cloister.
The faceless Superior repeats,
'No vocation, Sister! No! No vocation? Are you sure? Are you sure?
You must wait for permission from Rome.
I put you under Obedience.
A Mortal Sin if you tell.'
I slither and slide, slither and slide.
'Not back here again! No. No. No!'
I hear the scrape
of scissors cold on my skull,
as that dark-voiced Superior
shears my hair.
Waxed corridors. Silent shapes.
Incense-drenched Magnificat.
Again. Again.

Drenched in sweat. Again, again.
I wake up.
I'm at home. I'm in my own bed.

No starched coif-tapes cut into my neck.
No starched half-circle covers my heart.
No rosary beads rattle in a black cloister.
It's a black dream.

I've written and published the script of *Eclipsed*. It's being produced in theatres around the world. In Spring 2013, Professor Charlotte Headrick of Oregon University, on a Moore Institute Visiting Fellowship to NUIG, compiles the production history of *Eclipsed*. I fold my black dream and leave it in that convent parlour.

Eclissate

Associazione Teatro Firenze and the actor Ciara Santagostina succeed in contacting me through Edinburgh Theatre Festival.

Eclipsed/Eclissate, is translated into Italian at the University of Florence.

The Italian premiere opens in Teatro Tredici, Via Nicolodi, Florence, the City of Flowers.

Reluctantly leaving our dog, Brambles, in kennels near Moycullen, Eamon and I fly to Rome, where we stay overnight in a small hostel near the ancient *Via Aurelia Antigua*. Two nuns run this sparse and spotless accommodation.

On that first afternoon, we make a short visit to Vatican City, which is within walking distance of the hostel. Dazed by the splendour of St. Peter's Basilica, the Loggia of the Benedictions and St. Peter's Square, we go astray on exiting the gates of the Vatican.

We hail a taxi, but the driver brings us around and around what must be the seven hills of Rome, as he tries to find our hostel.

'It's my first time on this route,' he informs us as we stare at unfamiliar buildings.

Eventually we arrive at our hostel doorway.

'I do not speak English!' the younger nun replies to our requests for directions.

'But you're speaking English now!' Eamon says sharply.

Exhausted, we drink a nightcap in the foyer and climb upstairs to our spartan bedroom.

Next morning on our way to catch the train to Florence, we pass that slaughter house, the Colosseum.

'It still reeks of blood!' I say and turn away.

'Raphael, Bernini, Michelangelo, the Sistine Chapel! We'll have more time on our return from Florence,' Eamon consoles me.

Leaving the tumult of Rome, the train takes us through the sun-ochred peace of Tuscany.

Florence, the City of Flowers

The Uffizi Gallery, the Ponte Vecchio and Dante's house are close to our small hotel.

From the shadows of Brunelleschi's Duomo, the great spirits of Cosimo de' Medici, Lorenzo, the Magnificent, followed by Leonardo Da Vinci, Dante Alighieri, Beatrice, Raphael, Michelangelo, Fra Angelico and many artists of the Early and High Renaissance pass by as I cross the Arno on the Ponte Vecchio.

On the first night of *Eclissate*, every woman receives a rose as she enters the marble-adorned foyer of Teatro Tredici. Sitting in this strange audience, my shoulder muscles are tense until the voice of contralto Kathleen Ferrier echoes through Teatro Tredici and out through Via Nicolodi into the Florentine night.

'He was despised, despised and rejected, A Man of Sorrows and acquainted with grief.'

Nellie-Nora and Rosa appear on stage in the Firenze-Killmacha Magdalen laundry.

Though I do not speak Italian, I'm delighted by the cadences of the translated dialogue. The choreography of the actors, who are mostly professional dancers, adds to my happiness.

After that first night's performance I'm interviewed on stage by members of the Florentine Press. A translator is provided. One reviewer remarks, 'This is a story from the Dark Ages, nothing like this could happen in Italy!'

Truth disappears like water from turloughs in Burren limestone.

A young Italian woman, who helps backstage, comes forward and announces, 'My mother was locked away in a laundry and I was reared in an orphanage.'

'Where was that?' the reviewer asks, taken aback.

'In Sicily,' she replies.

'Ah, Sicily! The South! Not here in this part of our country!'

At the University of Florence, I meet academics from Urbino, Bologna and Rome, who question me about *Eclissate*. They had attended the first night of my play.

Also present is the Irish Ambassador and his assistant. I speak of the Irish Potato Famine and the setting up of shelters for women who came to Irish cities seeking food. These shelters were eventually taken over by nuns.

In *Eclipsed*, set in 1963, I focussed on unmarried mothers and nuns in a fictional laundry called Killmacha. Killmacha is a combination of Kill = *Cill* = Cell or Church and Macha, pagan goddess of fertility. The St. Brigit's Cross, which is a constant part of the set design, shows the Christian cross superimposed on the pagan fertility symbol.

There are more interviews on Florentine radio, receptions, photographs, bouquets and many tears.

Michelangelo's magnificent Carrara marble sculpture of David is being restored and is hidden behind scaffolding.

We visit the Museo di San Marco, where Savonarola, who led the expulsion of the Medicis, was Prior. Through a glass screen, I view 'relics' in his cell.

On the luminous side of this dark story is the sublime Annunciation by Fra Angelico.

In the Uffizi's collection I'm amazed by the spatial depth in Giotto's *Ognissanti Madonna*, by Botticelli's use of new pigments in his Birth of Venus and by the richness of Raphael's Madonna of the Goldfinch.

Promising to return, I move to the Museo dell' Opera del Duomo to see the original panels of Ghiberti's Baptistry Doors. I stand in awe before Donatello's Maddalena sculpture and, like her, join my hands in prayer.

We buy food from street stalls and eat as we walk from museums to galleries. But after each performance of *Eclissate* we relax at dinner in a city-centre Trattoria. The Tuscan menus offer *acqua nocca* or bean soup, roast pork and different pastas. After dinner, I do some window-shopping. I admire beautiful Oltrarno shoes, Madova gloves and handbags of finest leathers made by master craftsmen. I buy notebooks and address books covered with marbled paper, which echo the warm ochres and siennas of this city.

On a visit to a hairdresser, I notice young black men entering and leaving through steel doorways at the side of the salon.

'Topping up their skin-tans, Signora,' the hairdresser remarks as she twirls her brush and comb.

'But they're already black,' I reply.

'Male models must be perfectly tanned for our great Firenze fashion shows.'

The spirits of Michelangelo and Leonardo, carrying large sketchbooks, disappear through the salon walls.

With poster for *Eclissate* in Florence.

Siena

By coach we travel through burnt umbers and ochres of the Tuscan countryside and arrive in Siena. Though the *Piazza del Campo* surrounded by *Palazzi* is central to this elegant city, our first visit is to the *Casa di Santa Caterina*.

In her father's workshop once filled with dyed fabrics and vats of colour, we see the metal lantern Santa Caterina carried to visit lepers, also her scent bottle, which helped comfort rotting casualties of the plague.

A caretaker nun, Sister Dominic, answers my questions about Caterina's death. She mimes slicing her hand through her own neck and putting her disembodied head in a bag.

Back in Florence later, I write:

Now Caterina's skull lies bandaged
in a golden tabernacle
under these lacquered ceilings,
her body in Rome near headless sibyls
of the Forum.
Women should keep their heads, not ask questions.

Before rejoining the coach to Florence, I gaze at the celebrated *Piazza del Campo*, where the *Palio*, the Bareback Horseracing Festival, takes place in July and August. My thoughts go back to our own Galway Races and I whisper my poem:

Race Cards, Race Cards, Official Race Cards.
Three-card-trick men,
live-on-their wits men.
Tanned ladies clutch tipsy hats
in hope for Press and RTÉ.

Jackpot tickets –
Twenty thousand pounds guaranteed.
P. A. crackle, crushed plastic,
reek of horse-dung, armpits, urine, chips and Guinness.
Giant balloons only one pound!

Swing-boats and chair-o-planes curve
above littered meadows of our Norman castle.
'The horses are about to leave the Parade Ring!'
Swinging binoculars and reserved stand labels,
punters, angling at 45 degrees,
rush to the greedy Tote.
Jockeys in royal blue epaulettes, diamond hoops,
quartered caps, scarlet chevrons and emerald sleeves,
whips and spurs at the ready.
The white flag is raised!
They're off! –
In the Champagne Bar bookies celebrate.

Later in the coach on its way back to Florence, I close my eyes and imagine the colourful *Palio* Festival in *the Piazza del Campo of Siena.*

Apuan Marble

Adolf and Miriam Legner, parents of Marcus, one of the theatre directors, take me by car to visit Pisa. The Leaning Tower is really leaning and is closed for safety reasons.

As we exit the motorway, I see a line of parked cars. Beside each car a young woman displays her body.

'Ladies For Sale. Pimps traffic them in from Eastern Europe and make them work in this way,' Adolf Legner explains.

'A new form of slavery,' I remark. Miriam nods in agreement.

We drive away and on towards the brightness of Carrara marble quarries in the Apuan Alps. Bones of a sea-world crushed and laid down millions of years ago, fired in earth's cauldron, spewed out by volcanoes, are transformed, made luminous.

This extraordinary landscape is now being ravaged by monstrous machines, which carve gigantic whitenesses for Eastern palaces.

At a small café we lunch on *lardo di colonnata*, fat bacon salted in marble baths, with freshly baked bread and espressos. Skin and blood of millions of human slaves must have been absorbed by this marble as they hacked into these mountains. I pretend to eat the lardo, but I dump it in a paper napkin. Does that marble bath-dust contain human flesh?

By special permission we are allowed to climb in a creaking lift, which zig-zags up to a small oratory high above snow-clouds. Kneeling before the tabernacle, I light a candle for those girl-slaves on the roadside. I light another candle in memory of millions of slave-ghosts, who move from sculpted caves through thousands of years.

Obedient to Caesar,
to lust for white marble,
they cut and push

cubed ocean beds
metamorphosed in white heat.
Scumbles of marble dust
layer their blood-sweat,
mosquitos feast on their skins.
Their heart-arteries implode.

I'm amazed to see that I'm the first Irish person to sign the visitors' book in this oratory above the clouds.

Below this snow-line Dante pursues Beatrice. Michelangelo, the divine sculptor, in old clothes and smelly goatskin boots, returns to release his angels from blocks of pure white marble.

We leave this gleaming paradise of iced rock and we zig-zag down to warmth of clay and sand in the Etruscan Riviera.

I applaud Puccini's Mimi, as her voice echoes along the coast of the Golfo di Genoa. The poems of Byron and Shelley are woven into a calligraphy of turquoise waters.

At a farewell dinner in Florence I say goodbye to Ciara Santagostina, who played Brigit Murphy in *Eclissate*, and to Markus and Massimo, our directors from Associazione Teatro Firenze.

'We promise to visit you in Galway later on in the year,' they say.

'And we promise to return for your new production of *Eclissate* during the

Firenze-Napoli Festival.'

'*Ciao!*'

As we return to Rome by train, I had planned to visit the catacombs and take a trip to Pompeii. But instead, I go from basilica to basilica and stare at the preserved bodies of ancient saints. In the crypt of St. Peter's one red rose lies on the tomb of the human-hearted Pope John the twenty-third.

On the *Via Appia Antica*, the oldest road leading to Rome, I take off my shoes and feel ancient cobbled textures under my bare feet. Ghosts walk with me. Romulus and Remus, Hannibal blinded by

Alpine snow, Mark Anthony, Brutus, Caesar Augustus, Virgil, St. Peter in bloodied chains. Irish monks sing *Alleluia, Alleluia!* Broken-hearted, Hugh O'Neill and Rory O'Donnell arrive from Ireland.

Wars, wars, wars. Blood, blood, blood. Death-smells.

I hear the agonised cries of defeated rebel-slaves from the Third Servile War as they are paraded between 6,000 crosses on which captured rebels are executed.

I hear the clash of Caesar's armoured chariots returning, triumphant, from Gaul.

I hear the crash of an earthly Empire.

Eddie with Adolf and Miriam Legner at Carrara marble quarries in the Apuan Alps.

Sight

In the summer of 1990 I become allergic to preservatives in the eye-drops prescribed for my glaucoma. I'm confronted with the horror of darkness, of not being able to see the glory of human faces, the textures of landscape, the wonders of sky and ocean, not being able to paint, not being able to read. Darkness. Darkness forever.

I visit a consultant ophthalmic surgeon in Dublin. To save my sight, surgery on both eyes seems to be the only choice.

A letter from my friend, poet-philosopher John O'Donohue, says that he has returned to Ireland from Tubingen. Conferred there with a PhD in philosophical theology, he is now in his native Burren with his mother and family. I ring John and tell him my story. He invites me to his home in Fermoyle valley above Fanore.

I'm delighted to meet John, his mother Josie and his sister Mary again.

In the Burren there are many holy wells. Some are dedicated to St. Brigit. People with eye trouble in Co. Clare make pilgrimages to these wells and take home bottles of the healing waters.

John and I walk from the valley and visit a holy well high up in sculpted limestone.

A river from the well rushes downhill towards Black Head. John blesses me, then takes water from the well and anoints my eyes. We pray together. I imagine my worries, netted in sparkling turquoise and amber light, flow down through lilac-tinted grykes and out into the Atlantic.

As I drive back to Galway, my thoughts are on ultramarine gentians, cream-carpeted mountain avens, fragrant bee-orchids, grass of Parnassus. Now asleep in earth-darkness, they prepare to transfigure this karst landscape in Spring. Exotic butterflies will emerge from their wintry cocoons. Butter-coloured brimstone, small tortoiseshell, pearl-bordered fritillary, grayling butterfly will glorify grykes and turloughs.

The surgical precedures on my eyes, one in early October, the other in early November, are successful. On leaving the hospital, eyes now uncovered, I'm once more astonished by November sunlight on Adelaide Road, by the richness of fallen leaves.

From darkness, light and colour now have an extra intensity.

I no longer need eye-drops. Thank you, St. Brigit, blessed healer and patroness of poets. Thank you, John, for your *beannachtaí* and for what you call your 'blast of prayers.'

In October 2012, I visit Mr. Eamonn O'Donoghue, Consultant Ophthalmic Surgeon at the Galway Clinic. He arranges an appointment for the removal of a cataract from my right eye. Surgery is performed under local anaesthetic rather than the usual general anaesthetic.

I beseech St. Brigit again for help as a sculpting tool with pulses of sound burns away the dense cataract, which is scarred from previous surgery. My body squirms.

There's the sensation that my eye is being drilled out in preparation for a filling.

A new lens now replaces the original. For some weeks afterwards there is discomfort, but no pain. The procedure is a success.

Light and colour again transfigure turloughs and grykes in Burren limestone.

Thank you, St. Brigit and thank you, Mr. Eamonn O'Donoghue.

Solo

I present a solo exhibition of paintings and etchings, delayed because of my eye surgery, in the Art Gallery of University College, Galway. The guest speaker is Colm ÓhEocha, President of UCG.

I'm invited to hold another solo exhibition in the Bridge Mills' Art Gallery. The opening of the exhibition is attended by Brian Keenan, who had recently been released from imprisonment in Beirut.

I then concentrate on rewriting my stage play, *Eclipsed.*

But every other week I meet Anne Kennedy, a poet friend from Galway Writers' Workshop and, over coffee, we discuss my poems.

At one stage I'm next on Salmon Poetry's list for publication, but suddenly another poet's name replaces mine on that list. I wait and wait.

Eventually, the script of *Eclipsed* and my collection of poetry, *Above the Waves Calligraphy,* are published together in 1994.

On the day parcels with published copies of *Eclipsed* and *Above the Waves Calligraphy* arrive, I sit with my friend, poet-philosopher John O'Donohue, in a coffee shop in Middle Street. Excitedly I open the parcels and we clap hands as my first books emerge into Galway daylight. I present signed copies to John. Though deeply involved in the Save Mullaghmore controversy, he had found time to read and discuss my poems before I sent the final manuscript to Salmon Poetry Ltd. I recall that one evening as we sat beside the fire in my home, he read his own poem about a coffin. I was astonished by the words he chose and I said, 'But you are down in the grave with this coffin!'

He read on:

'From the net of soil insects creep, amazed …

I'm honoured when Michael D. Higgins, TD, Minister for Arts and

Culture and the Gaeltacht, writes a wonderful introduction for my collection of poetry.

Etchings in both black and white and colour are included. My dream of combining my visual art with my poetry in a book has come true. However, because colour is so expensive to print, only four colour etchings are included. Though the titles were clearly written below the images, there are errors with some of the titles, so my happiness is short-lived.

The covers of both books are also based on etchings of mine.

Eclipsed and *Above the Waves' Calligraphy* are launched together in the Kenny Art Galleries-Bookshops. Minister Michael D, Higgins, TD is guest speaker.

The Minister says, 'Patricia I recall as the first person in Galway to be totally committed to the Arts. It was the early 1960s … There's a lovely formation behind this work. It is beautifully honed.'

He continues, 'Eclipsed changed everything. It's a play that is as faithful to the lives of the characters represented as it is to the hidden stories and could almost not have any other author.'

The Kenny Gallery is filled with friends and well-wishers, who listen as I read one of my poems. Sales are made and I sign copies of both books.

Eclipsed is reprinted in 1997 by Salmon Poetry Ltd. but a statement on the inside cover is changed to, 'All rights whatsoever in this play are strictly reserved and application for performance etc. should be made in writing to the author and publisher.'

I ask Salmon Poetry Ltd. to correct this and exclude the word publisher from application for performance rights. This is done in the next edition.

On 24th September 1997 I sign a ten-year contract with Salmon Publishing Ltd.

A third edition of *Eclipsed* is printed in 2001. Later this sold-out edition is added to by extra reprints.

Early in 1999, Charlotte Headrick, an American academic, visits me here in Galway City. Before she leaves, we discuss the possibility of a production of *Eclipsed* in the USA. I agree to give performance rights.

Charlotte emails her thanks to me. 'You helped me so much when I directed the production of *Eclipsed* for Western Kentucky Theatre Company at the Russell H. Miller Theatre in April. It went on to be produced at Indiana University Theatre as part of the National Endowment for the Humanities', she says.

The Pleiades Theatre Company's production at Mex Theatre, Kentucky Centre moves on to the Womens' Prison of Louisville, where it is subsequently studied.

In November 1999 Ciaran O'Reilly and Charlotte Moore ask permission to produce *Eclipsed* in the Off-Broadway Irish Repertory Theatre, NY. This production receives excellent reviews from *The New York Times, Curtain Up, The Irish Voice* and *The Internet Magazine of Reviews*.

The West Coast premiere of *Eclipsed* by Theatre Banshee in Burbank, Los Angeles, 1995 wins Critics' Choice and Best of the Weekend from the *Los Angeles Times*. It also wins four nominations in the *Los Angeles Theatre Area Awards* and three awards from *Dramalogue*, the premier USA theatre magazine.

Eclipsed Tour

I'm very pleased when, in Spring 1998, Michael Diskin, Manager of the Town Hall Theatre, Galway City, contacts me about a new Irish production of *Eclipsed*.

This will be the first Irish production since the original in 1992.

I meet him in his office beside the theatre's Green Room.

Michael sits at his desk and reads from his diary. 'Our production will run here from 22nd June to 5th July and I hope to tour it to Cork Opera House, Watergate Theatre in Kilkenny, Hawkswell Theatre in Sligo and Andrew's Lane Theatre, Dublin.' I sit opposite him as he marks his diary and hands me a contract, which I'm delighted to sign.

'Who would you like as director?' he asks.

'My first choice is Caroline FitzGerald, who directed a rehearsed reading of my three-act play, *Clarenda's Mirror*, during the 4th International Women Playwrights' Conference here in 1997,' I reply.

'Yes! She was Resident Director and Assistant Artistic Director at the Abbey Theatre,' Michael smiles as he dials her phone number and speaks with her.

'Caroline agrees and I'll arrange a meeting.' He checks his diary.

'She directed many new plays, including *Boss Grady's Boys, Prayers of Sherkin* and *White Woman Street* by Sebastian Barry,' I read aloud from her bio.

'And recently she directed plays by Beckett, Brian Friel, Jennifer Johnston and Ulick O'Connor,' Michael continues.

When I meet Caroline at the Town Hall Theatre, auditions are arranged and a cast is chosen.

A week later Tomás Fitzpatrick arrives from Berlin to design the set.

A Vermeer-like photograph of Síle Ní Chonaonaigh by London photographer Sarah FitzGerald becomes the publicity poster. Yards and yards of muslin are dyed purple for the set drapes.

Costumes for the nuns, coifs, veils, guimpes, black habits are designed and sewn up. For the penitents' costumes we buy dark grey overalls and off-white aprons with pockets. In second-hand shops we buy thick stockings and rough-looking shoes.

When interviewed by a local journalist, I insist, 'Eclipsed is not a documentary! It's a play.' This statement annoys some people, who question my use of 'penitent women for public entertainment.'

'My characters are works of fiction. I do not use stories about the Magdalen women who worked with me in the Galway Laundry!' I repeat.

While Eclipsed is on tour to Andrew's Lane Theatre in Dublin, I'm told that Brigid O'Hara-Forster, Associate Editor, Time Magazine, Brettenham House, London wishes to see my play and to interview me afterwards.

We sit in the theatre office as Brigid questions me about my own experience as a novice in a Magdalen Laundry.

'Your play has a mystical quality,' she remarks as she looks at the published script. 'Today I visited the National Gallery, where I spent time with Nicholas Poussin's painting of women weeping in The Lamentation over the Dead Christ. Christ too was despised and rejected like the penitent women in your play.'

'Yes, thank you, Brigid. The purple drapes of the set design add to that mystical quality. And I chose the Contralto Aria He was Despised from Handel's Messiah for the opening and closing scenes. Sister Virginia's Credo Scene, her crisis of faith and crisis of vocation, is the heart of the play.

Brigid looks up from her note-taking and repeats, 'Crisis of faith, crisis of vocation?'

'Sister Virginia's faith is tested, as is her vocation. Her insistence that the women are our sisters in Christ offends Mother Victoria,' I add.

'One of the women characters is called Brigit. Why did you choose that name?' she asks.

'I chose each character's name carefully. Brigit Murphy is named after St. Brigit, but there was an earlier Brigit, a pagan fertility sun goddess.' I show her a St. Brigit's Cross.

'I give a St. Brigit's Cross to the director of every new production. The Christian cross is superimposed on a pagan fertility symbol.'

'Brigit. Pagan fertility sun goddess and Christian saint,' she writes.

'And patron of poets,' I add.

'Tell me about the Brigit resonances in *Eclipsed*, Patricia.'

'St. Brigit was ordained Bishop of *Cill Dara* by St. Mel. She was the first and only Woman Bishop of the Irish Church! In Act 1, Scene 3, Brigit Murphy puts on the bishop's surplice, holds up a mop-crozier and blesses the women. In Act 1 Scene 6, the Mandy and Elvis ceremony, dressed in bishop's robes and mitre, she says. "Remember I'm the Bishop! I'll do this important wedding!"'

'You chose Sister Virginia's name to show her renunciation of the flesh,' she writes.

'And I chose Mother Victoria's name because Victorian England and French Jansenism had more of an effect than Rome on attitudes to sex in Ireland,' I say. Her interest in the deeper levels of *Eclipsed* pleases me and makes this a very happy interview. I give her the postal address of writer John O'Donohue in Camus, Conamara, Ireland.

'Camus! Another Camus, but this time the name of a place in Ireland.' She writes the address. She has heard of John's best-seller, *Anam Cara*. When I return to Galway, I telephone John and apologise for giving his address without his permission.

He's delighted and says, 'To be mentioned in *Time Magazine* is every writer's dream!'

A few weeks after the interview, Caroline FitzGerald calls unexpectedly.

'It's about Brigid O'Hara-Forster!'

'Is it Brigid from *Time Magazine*?' I ask.

'Yes. Brigid collapsed in London,' Caroline sobs.

'No! Not Brigid O'Hara-Forster! She's such a strong woman, so full of life. I promised to send her a copy of Séamus Ó Catháin's *Festival of Brigit, Celtic Goddess and Holy Woman,* but it's out of print.'

'Brigid died instantly.'

'No! No! Brigit – dead? No! Now it's too late to tell her that I'm searching for a used copy.' My voice is full of tears.

'Her notes from your *Eclipsed* interview are still on her desk in Brettenham House, Patricia. I'm worried,' says Caroline.

Síle Nic Chonaonaigh on publicity poster.

Eclipsed Film

Tristan Gribbin was cast as Cathy in the first presentation of my stage play, *Eclipsed*, in Galway City in 1992, but wasn't cast in the Edinburgh production. I meet her at the bus station as she leaves to visit her fiancé in Iceland.

'I've a letter here from the Head of Drama at BBC Northern Ireland asking if I'm interested in a film adaptation of *Eclipsed*, Tristan!'

'That's very good news, Patricia,' she smiles.

'But there are enquiries from San Francisco and Los Angeles too. I'm new to this film business!'

'Listen to all of them. You need legal advice before you make a decision, especially before you sign any agreement about film rights. I'll call on you when I come back to Ireland.' Tristan waves goodbye as she climbs into the bus for Shannon Airport.

After some time, I decide to trust BBC Northern Ireland.

Another letter from the BBC informs me that Samson Films Production Company has been appointed to produce the *Eclipsed* film. This is followed by many phone calls.

In order to get some fresh air and to clear my head, I bring our dog, Brambles, for a walk along *Loch an tSáile*. Suddenly a greyhound breaks away from his owner, crosses the road and attacks us. Brambles slips his lead. Both dogs tumble into the water as they fight. My screams, together with snarls and high-pitched barks, echo from *Loch an tSáile* to Renmore. The owner of the greyhound, armed with a walking stick, arrives. He joins in the fight. The greyhound jumps out of the lake followed by his out-of-breath owner. Smells of wet human and wet dogs hit my nostrils.

Brambles barks in victory as we return through our garden gate, along by the rose bushes and into our house. I sing his praises while I shampoo and dry him.

But the phone rings.

'It's David Collins from Samson Films for you,' Eamon says as he takes the hairdryer from my hand and gives me the phone.

'Hello, Patricia! David Collins here. Our company is composed of my wife, Jackie, Solicitor James Hickey and myself. We in Samson Films are represented by Matheson Ormsby Prentice Solicitors, Burlington Road, Dublin,' David Collins informs me.

'Hello, David! I'm represented by Mason Hayes and Curran, Solicitors, Fitzwilliam Square, Dublin,' I reply.

'I've posted you copies of a Screenplay Agreement and a Film-Television Rights Option Agreement. Read them and I'll meet you in Galway next week. For signatures,' David Collins adds.

When I go back to the kitchen, Brambles comes close and looks up at me as if he wants me to help him.

'Brambles has breathing problems.' Eamon has a worried look.

'To the vet immediately,' I say and fasten the lead to Brambles' collar.

The phone rings again, but we hurry to the car and drive to the veterinary clinic.

'I see he has been in the wars.' Michael, the vet, lifts a shivering Brambles on to the examination table.

'There's lake water in his lungs and he has one smashed tooth.'

I look away as pieces of broken tooth are extracted and suitable injections are given.

When we arrive home, I wrap Brambles in a blanket. The doorbell rings.

I open the door to a headscarved woman.

'That vicious dog of yours has injured our highly valuable greyhound. He'll miss the most important race of the season because of that attack. My husband suffers from heart trouble and he had to jump into the lake to rescue our famous greyhound,' she announces.

'Our Brambles is not vicious. He was attacked by your greyhound, Madam.'

'You'll be hearing from us!' She points her right hand towards me and stamps her feet on her way towards our gateway steps.

'I'll ring Michael, the vet, and inquire about that so-called valuable greyhound,' Eamon says. I join Brambles in the kitchen and wait.

'That greyhound is neither famous nor valuable according to Michael,' Eamon reports in a relieved voice. He pats Brambles, then lights a cigarette and inhales.

'No more doorbells or phonecalls for today. I need a cup of strong tea.' I collapse into an armchair. But that phone rings again.

'Please answer it, Eamon.' I close my eyes and curl up among the cushions.

Eamon returns to the kitchen. 'David Collins will meet you in Jury's Hotel, Spanish Arch, at three o'clock next Friday.'

'I'll read those film documents when they arrive in tomorrow's post. Then I'll consult my solicitors,' I say.

Thunder crashes and lightning blazes as I arrive at Jury's Hotel to meet David Collins. We both hold plastic-bound red-edged copies of the Screenplay Agreement and of the Film-Television Rights Option Agreement. We shake hands.

'Tea and biscuits, Patricia?'

I nod and he gives the order to the waiter. He admires an antique locket I'm wearing.

'My solicitors have amended Clause 4d of the Assignment, which is essentially a gagging clause when talking to the media,' I say.

'Why?' He's surprised.

'They say, and I quote, "it is amended so that the word *probable* replaces the word *possible* in the third line and the word *will* replaces the word *may* also in the same line. This is because the Clause as it was drafted is too speculative in that anything anyone might say to any person concerning any matter may be reproduced or reported in the public media."'

The waiter bows graciously and places the tray with tea and biscuits on the small table.

'Thank you. A slice of lemon instead of milk, please,' I smile.

'No problem, Madam.' The waiter bows again.

'My solicitors also question the paucity of the money offered for the film rights, David.'

'I've been to the Bord Scannán office up the street and they have joined the financiers for this film,' he answers.

'That's good news. I'm pleased.'

'By the way, I've arranged for a BBC script editor, an Armagh woman now living in London, to visit you while you write the treatment and the first draft, Patricia.'

Before he leaves Jury's Hotel to return to Dublin, I sign both documents. He admires my handwriting and he too signs with a flourish.

'Today is the 7th of September 1994,' I say. He nods as he returns the signed documents to his portfolio. I keep my own signed copies.

After each visit the script editor from the BBC reports on my work to David Collins.

At the same time I'm working on a new stage play, *Clarenda's Mirror*.

My treatment script is accepted by Samson Film Limited and by the BBC.

A creative writer finds it difficult to be told what to put on paper. When I suddenly realise that I've lost control of my story, I write my own screenplay, *Seen and Unseen*.

This script is locked away in my filing cabinet and hasn't been read by anyone.

'You shouldn't be working on a stage play when you're working on this screenplay,' the script editor warns when I tell her that the Abbey Theatre says that my submitted play-script of *Clarenda's Mirror* shows great promise. I don't mention my *Seen and Unseen* script.

After a few months, David Collins and I meet again in Jury's Hotel.

'BBC says that your first draft isn't viable. We've appointed a new writer, Peter Sheridan,' David Collins announces. I want to ask him if Peter Sheridan will also be reported on by this script editor, but I'm so angry that I'm unable to speak. I leave Jury's Hotel in tears and walk home.

Later, when I'm given Peter Sheridan's script to evaluate, I inform the BBC that I object to the title, *The Maggies*, a term used to pour scorn on the Magdalen women. I object to the fact that it's set in a mental hospital instead of in a Magdalen Laundry. I also object to certain references to Fr. Peyton of the Rosary Crusade. Otherwise the writing is good.

However, I agree that the Film-Television Rights Option Agreement can be extended from 1st July 1996 for another two years.

When, after what are now four years, the planned film is not made, I expect that the film rights will return to me on the first day of July 1998. But on the last day of June 1998, the day the agreement expires, an unsigned letter arrives from David Collins which says that it 'exercises the agreement' and encloses a cheque for £5,000. On that same day I return the cheque by registered post. However, the fact that I opened that letter and returned the cheque means that the Film Rights Option Agreement has been legally exercised.

I've lost my film rights forever. Infuriated at this treatment my work, I shout, 'Cannibalism! Cannibalism!'

I then shower and shower to cleanse my whole being of contamination.

Consequences

'We intend to proceed towards production of our own Magdalen Laundry film,' BBC informs me by letter. I do not reply. After some time the BBC television film *Sinners* goes out on the channels.

Tears fill grykes and turloughs in Burren limestone.

'We need more Cardiovet tabs for Brambles' angina, Eamon. Only three left. Order some from the vet's clinic, please. I'll collect them on my way from the shops.'

'We'll have to make sure that he swallows the tabs. I found one in his basket yesterday,' says Eamon.

'This knob of butter should help. Over to me, Brambles! Good boy. Down the hatch. That's a good boy!' Brambles gobbles the butter-covered tablet from my hand.

The phone rings.

'It's a journalist from *The Glasgow Herald*,' Eamon says. 'Will you take it?'

'Tell him to hold on, Eamon.'

I pray for patience before I pick up the phone.

'Hello! This is Patricia here in Galway,' I say guardedly.

'I'd like to talk with you about Peter Mullan's film, *The Magdalene Sisters*. First day of photography is in June 2001. Vanessa Redgrave will play the principal character,' the journalist announces.

'I'd like to remind you about an infamous laundry run by lay people on Peter Mullan's own doorstep in Glasgow!' I reply.

'A laundry here in Glasgow?' He's surprised.

'Shortly after *Eclipsed* won the Fringe First at Edinburgh Theatre Festival, *Washing away the Stain*, a documentary about that Glasgow laundry with excerpts from *Eclipsed*, went out on BBC Scotland.'

'When was that?'

'In 1993 and directed by Andrea Miller. Peter Mullan sees the mote in our Irish eyes and doesn't see the plank in his Scottish eyes. Why has Peter Mullan decided to make the film in Scotland, when it's grant-aided by Bord Scannán's head office in Galway, and set in an Irish Magdalen laundry?' I ask.

'Bord Scannán?' he queries.

'That's our Irish Film Board. I'd also like to tell you this –The actresses cast in Eclipsed decided not to audition for that film. I really am in a hurry. Goodbye and thank you,' I conclude.

A Galway writer tells me that she'll write to Vanessa Redgrave, who is a human rights activist, and object to her taking part in his film.

Eventually, Geraldine McEwan instead of Vanessa Redgrave plays the principal character of Sr. Brigit in *The Magdalene Sisters*.

In an issue of *Time Magazine* in 2003 I see a photograph of Glaswegian Peter Mullan beside a report on his film about an Irish Magdalen Laundry. Caroline FitzGerald's words come back to me: 'Brigit's notes are still on her desk in Brettenham House, Patricia! From your interview with Brigit O'Hara-Foster of *Time Magazine*.'

There are telephone calls from theatre people in Ireland, Europe and the USA.

'This film is so like *Eclipsed*. But why is your name not in the credits?'

'Copyright! Intellectual copyright! You must do something, Patricia!'

'I've read the film-script and it's very close to your play-script!'

'I'll put you in touch with the top Copyright Attorney in New York City, Patricia!'

On the afternoon of June 18, 2003, a phone call from the Writers' Centre in Dublin says, 'Miramax Films of New York City have requested your contact number. Have we your permission to give it?'

'Yes, but tell Miramax to write to me as we're about to leave for a short break,' I reply in amazement.

As I pack our luggage, I notice that we need toothpaste and I run to the corner shop. On my return my voice-mail contains the following message from Frank Lomento of Miramax Films, New York City: 'We have your book, your play here, Patricia. Would you like to come to New York and appear on TV to promote our film, *The Magdalene Sisters?*'

I've never used 'street language', but I now feel like using a torrent of swear words.

I decide to sleep overnight on this audacious request.

If I hadn't entered the Novitiate in Galway City and hadn't been sent to work in the local Magdalen Laundry, I wonder what form the Magdalen women's story would have taken, if any.

Before leaving home the following day, I leave a message during USA night-hours for Miramax Films, New York City, saying, 'My stage play, *Eclipsed*, has already given a voice to the Magdalen women. Their story has already been told on three continents. But I have another stage play, *Stained Glass at Samhain*, which looks at that story from a nun's point of view.'

So far there has been no reply from Miramax Films.

I write the following poem.

Deep in the dark
of her soul-story,
she swims.

His shadow looms.

See him circle,
blind her with camera-eyes.

His jaws open.

Listen to her moan-song.
Unable to digest her soul.
he vomits.

But keeps her story.

With four main penitent characters, as in *Eclipsed*, Peter Mullan set the film in 1964. I had set my play in 1963 for the following very special reasons:

Vatican 2, taking place in Rome, was causing an 'opening of windows' in the institution of the Roman Catholic Church.

John F. Kennedy, the first Catholic Irish-American President of the United States, attractively tanned and white-toothed, visited Ireland. The influence of Elvis Presley and Rock 'n' Roll music had reached our island.

From London the swinging sixties sent many messages of liberation.

During Ciara Dwyer's interview with Peter Mullan in the *Sunday Independent*, he replies to her questions, 'I couldn't have made it up. I'm not that good a dramatist. What disappoints me is the attitude of those who say nothing like this ever happened.'

Ciara writes, 'I have one problem with the film. All the nuns are monsters. … There is not a shred of humanity to be seen. The film is a bit too black and white with the nuns playing the hundred-per-cent baddie roles. When I put this to Peter he tells me that there are some scenes where we see glimpses of the nuns being humane. I am hard pressed to remember them. He defends the angle he took. "It's a diary of these four girls. If one wants to see the nuns' perspective, fine. I don't give a f**k." …'

Ciara continues, '… But what I find hard to stomach is the imbalance of Mullan's film. If you want to see the story of the Magdalene laundries, find a production of Patricia Burke Brogan's play, *Eclipsed*. It, too, is a work of fiction. But, unlike Mullan's film, *Eclipsed* gives a fair account of an unfair time.'

Similarly in an interview with Fintan O'Toole, Peter Brook, renowned international director, says that his objection to Hollywood and to theatre conducted on a purely commercial enterprise is that it tells lies. 'The responsibility of anyone in the arts is to look, which is more difficult, for the other side of the coin. The moment you see a black side, your obligation is to look for the luminous side. The role of the arts is to see what more there is behind the surface.'

My anger grows. Should I take on the film industry? Should I waste the rest of my life listening to attorneys making orations in stuffy courtrooms? I decide to turn my thoughts towards the thousands of Magdalen women, to the darkness of their great wounding. Though those women gave birth, created new lives, the art in which woman is most like God, they were used and rejected by lovers, by their families and by the Irish State. The Church colluded. Their names and the names of their babies were obliterated from the history of humankind. What has happened me and to my play *Eclipsed* brings me closer to them in their despised and rejected lives. With them I too am eclipsed.

I'm consoled by James M. Smith's words. I quote from pages 91-92 of his volume:

Several works have explored the Magdalen Laundries in depth, but two dramas by Patricia Burke Brogan proved especially important for rupturing the secrecy that shrouded this aspect of Ireland's past. *Eclipsed* and *Stained Glass at Samhain* ...

Burke Brogan's *Eclipsed* rescues Ireland's Magdalen women from the amnesia at the center of the nation's nativist's history. ... *Eclipsed* transcends mere dramatic fiction and assumes the status of ritualized commemoration. Burke Brogan's play performs rather than fossilizes history ...

Although rarely acknowledged as such, *Eclipsed* first introduced the tropes by which other contemporary retellings have narrativised the Magdalen experience ...

Patricia's play is the fundamental text that provided Irish society with a narrative by which to discuss, and thus know, this aspect of our past. [1]

---

1 James M. Smith's *Ireland's Magdalen Laundries and the Nation's Architecture of Containment*. University of Notre Dame Press, University of Notre Dame, Indiana, USA, 2007.

2. Mika Funahashi's *Contemporary Irish Theatre in Context Symposium*, Shiga University, Hikone Campus, Japan, October 2009.

The scholar Mika Funahashi of the International Association for the Study of Irish Literature (IASIL) writes about *Eclipsed* and also mentions the shame attached to sufferers from Hansen's Disease (leprosy). In Japan, lepers too were treated as outcasts of society. 'Unclean.' Some survivors, though cured of leprosy, never left the sanatoria because they were 'the shamed.' At one time there were about 5,700 leprosy survivors living in fifteen sanatoria throughout Japan. Their average age was seventy. That stigma remained even if some survivors managed to leave the sanatoria. [2].

In many areas of the Third World, i.e. across India, Nepal, Indonesia, sub-Saharan Africa, Madagascar, Mozambique, Brazil and Venezuela, the incidence of the disease remains constant as does the stigma.

On a background of a multi-coloured *Doras* painting, I collage torn-up pieces of my published poems. My dog, Brambles, and I walk across this collage.

Pilgrimage (A poem in my studio)

Canvases flat on terracotta tiles,
I scatter torn-up poems
over layers of cloisters, altars,
dark doorways of my journey.
Bare feet soaked in blood-colours,
crimsons and magentas,
I walk across this huge collage.
Our dog, Brambles,
stronger after years of Cardiovet
concealed in butter
pushes forward
and walks with me.
He barks as I sing
to celebrate
his victory
over a greyhound
in Loch an tSáile.

We make paw-prints, footprints.
When Brambles' heart stops,
I lift his body
and find his death-sweat
imprinted
on terracotta tiles.

Brambles

This collaged diptych hangs in the foyer of Galway Education Centre.

The Director of the Centre, Bernard Kirk, decides to dedicate one of the rooms to Irish writers.

Framed photographs of a number of writers from Joe O'Shaughnessy's portfolio now hang on the walls of The Writers' Room.

Easter in Paris

'Paris! Paris! I'm delighted to be here again, Eamon,' I say as we arrive at Charles De Gaulle airport. We pick up our luggage from the carousel, go through Customs and take a taxi to our small hotel. Squashed into a tiny lift with our luggage, we ascend to our bedroom on the third floor. The only window looks down on an enclosed patio.

On my return to the main entrance, I say, 'Where is the fire escape,' to the receptionist.

'Fire escape, Madame! You are not in Ireland now,' he replies.

'But if … I always ask,' I say. In my mind's eye, I see flames enveloping that third floor.

'You are in Paris, Madame! Continental breakfast from 7.30 to 9.00 am,' he continues. I decide to leave our safety in the care of the Lord.

Later that evening our guide announces, 'Be ready at 9 am. tomorrow, Holy Saturday. I've arranged tickets for St. Denis and La Sainte-Chapelle.'

Next morning, with our group, we wait outside for our minibus. I watch an apricot mist unwrap the sun above Sacre Coeur de Montmartre.

'Deo Gratias,' I whisper as we drive towards the Basilica of St. Denis.

'This was a place of pilgrimage in medieval times, a powerful Benedictine monastery. It is the first monumental masterpiece of Gothic art, a model for French cathedrals including Chartres,' our guide says as we gaze skywards in admiration.

We then enter, genuflect and kneel in prayer.

'Attention! We now go to visit another treasure of our city,' the guide announces and checks us into the waiting minibus. I take a last look at the extraordinary architecture of St. Denis as we drive on our way.

'La Sainte-Chapelle!' she announces. 'Tickets and papers ready! Security! Be careful!' Outside the palace courtyard gendarmes frisk-search and question all who enter.

'La Sainte-Chapelle with this Concergerie were the seat of power and the residence of French Kings from the 10th to the 14th centuries,' our guide says as we enter,

'Built in six years, La Sainte-Chapelle was the personal undertaking of King Louis, Saint Louis. It was designed to house the relics of Christ's passion, especially His Crown of Thorns and a section of the True Cross. This put France in the forefront of Latin Christendom. King Louis accepted the relics from Emperor Baudouin. After about two years, other relics were brought from Byzantium and more were brought two years later. The relics were kept in a special reliquary in the palace until they were transferred to the apse of the newly built La Sainte-Chapelle.'

Hands joined, I pray with my eyes.

'Here in the upper chapel, you can see 6,458 square feet of stained glass,' our guide continues. 'Notice how this elegant structure seems to fade away leaving only those magnificent windows! They tell the story from Creation to Redemption through Christ. You may stay for another ten minutes, then please return to your taxi. Thank you.'

Overcome with emotion, still spinning in a paradise of colour, I write this poem on my return to that claustrophobic hotel bedroom.

In Sainte Chapelle on Ile de la Cité
walls of stained glass off-set royal purples
over sculpted apostles and marble floors.
Lancet windows vault like ballet dancers
as stone mullions dissolve in arpeggios of light.

Centuries ago, master glaziers
were dreaming up new colours for this huge reliquary.

Above a crystal tabernacle
blood-stained medallions and fleurs-de-lys
glow with his crown of thorns, his splintered cross
carried from Golgotha and Constantinople
to King Louis and Blanche of Castille.

Within this luminous tomb,
a trinity of mysteries,
we'll keep watch for Easter morning.

At home in Galway, inspired by my visit to La Sainte-Chapelle, I work on a new play. It takes place at that otherworldly time of *Samhain* and is located in Killmacha Magdalen Laundry. There are many rewrites. Eventually, with the title of *Stained Glass at Samhain*, I submit my script to Michael Diskin at Town Hall Theatre.

Stained Glass at Samhain

My excitement grows when Michael Diskin, Manager of the Town Hall Theatre, announces that my play, *Stained Glass at Samhain*, will be premiered on the main stage of the theatre on October 31ˢᵗ 2002.

The fictional location of this play is St. Paul's Convent and Novitiate attached to the Mother House and Magdalen Laundry at Killmacha. The buildings are being demolished during the performance. The play is set during *Samhain* (Halloween) when the boundaries between the living and the dead dissolve.

I have chosen the music for the production with great care. I bring my selected CDs to the Town Hall Theatre.

The director, Caroline FitzGerald, arrives from Dublin.

Geraldine Plunkett and her daughter are coming from Carraroe by car and will arrive in about ten minutes, Caroline tells me.

I take CDs from my portfolio.

'This is my favourite recording of Mozart's *Requiem in D. Minor*. The *Benedictus qui venit in nomine Domini* for pre-lights-up and repeated at the end of the performance. The *Agnus Dei* from the *Requiem* for the end of Act 1 Scene 2.'

'Very good! Which recording of *I Dreamt I Dwelt in Marble Halls* have you chosen for Katie as she sings to the convent cows?' Caroline asks as she checks my script.

'I failed to find my favourite Margaret Burke Sheridan recording, but this one by Méav is really good.' I give her the CD.

'Here is the Nóirín Ní Riain solo *Kyrie Eleison* with shruti box for the end of Act 2, Scene 2, just before Sister Luke's Mass story,' I add.

'And this is *The Limestone Rock* by Micho Russell for Act 2 Scene 3. *Lux Aeterna* is also from *Mozart's Requiem* for Act 2 Scene 6, as in my script.'

'Wonderful! Peter Ashton will test the CDs and put them all on one CD for the show,' Caroline says as she checks the time.

'Darina Ní Dhonnchú, Fred McCloskey and Máire Hastings are in the Green Room,' Des Braiden, now dressed in bishop's magenta robes, reports.

'Money is very scarce and rehearsal time is cut back. Normally we should have six weeks instead of six days for rehearsal. But now the preview and opening night will coincide!' Peter Ashton says as he takes the CDs.

'Only five days left,' Caroline FitzGerald announces from the main stage.

I had made a number of penitent-puppets from pieces of fabric, cast-off tights, netting, scraps of wool and white acrylic paint. In a small trolley, I had pushed rolls of off-white netted fabric, bought for €40 in Ryan's sale, home to College Road. Later, the fabric along with my penitent-puppets are transferred by van to the Town Hall Theatre.

'What are these dolls for?' The van driver is puzzled.

'These puppets represent the consecrated penitents, the Magdalen women, who became institutionalised, spent most of their lives locked away in the laundry and are buried in nameless graves,' I answer him as we carry the puppets backstage.

Caroline and I had created the stage design on paper. Now with the help of a drama student from NUIG, we paint the netting to resemble cloister columns of stone.

'We need a deep trough downstage to resemble a demolition site! A few hard hats, a shovel, bricks and gravel!' Caroline tells Arthur Bell, who is constructing the set. I show him my photographs of the demolition of the local Magdalen Laundry.

Into this deep trough we pack various articles connected with a convent and laundry: old aprons, cardigans, worn-out boots, canvas shoes, linens, starched coifs and guimpes.

'Lighting is absolutely important for my *Stained Glass at Samhain!*' I tell Paul Noble, the lighting designer.

'This is the main image in the play!' I point to a tall painted flat, which resembles a stained glass window showing the *Lamentation over the dead Christ.*

We place it at an angle downstage left.

'It'll be shattered towards the end of the performance,' I add.

'But how will that be done?' Arthur Bell raises his hands.

'We'll put sections of coloured plastic to resemble broken stained glass in a drop-box high above the stage,' Caroline indicates.

I arrange the penitent-puppets on a long bench downstage left. I then attach a number of cardboard guimpes to a carver chair (Sister Luke's chair-copter).

'Three days to go!' Caroline FitzGerald, script in hand, walks quickly across the stage. I hold up a single guimpe.

'Sister Luke will write NO DUMPING with soot on this guimpe. I need a tall wooden post, Arthur. Sister Luke will attach her guimpe-notice to this post and erect it in that trough.'

We cut a supply of cardboard guimpes and position them with a mug of soot beside the copter-chair.

'Place them just here for Sister Luke's handwritten manuscript,' I tell Jane Talbot, the stage manager. The dissonance of timber being sawn and shaped can be heard as Arthur Bell works on the set.

'Where will we put the small table for His Lordship's breakfast?' Jane asks.

'Put it behind that cloister column, Jane. And, Sister Benedict, you'll carry it onstage after Act 1 Scene 7,' Caroline directs.

Rehearsal. Rehearsal. Rehearsal.

'Two days to go!' Jane's voice is stressed.

We put a low bier-chair for the shrouded figure of Sister Luke downstage right at the edge of the stage. Stiff shapes of painted netting resemble fragments of the convent-laundry walls.

'Sounds! Demolition sounds! Check now! We'll have a full technical rehearsal later,' Caroline announces.

Michael Diskin, Manager of the Town Hall Theatre, is pleased when he sees the finished stage design,

'Some theatre companies spend thousands on a fireplace for just the corner of a set!' a stage hand declares from the stalls. We take a bow.

As Mozart's *Requiem in D Minor* fills the theatre, we smile as the sound is adjusted and the transparent netted cloisters echo Magdalena Hajossyova, Jaroslava Horska, Josef Kundlak and Peter Mikolas with the Slovak Philharmonic Orchestra in *Benedictus qui venit in nomine Domini.*

In the Green Room Sister Luke and Maura Ber practise their duet, *Seothín Seó*. Maura Ber is a young penitent, who, having escaped from the laundry, had been invited to Boston by her Aunt Nora and has now arrived back from Harvard to do research for her thesis on Magdalen Women.

Caroline directs Sister Luke, an elderly nun played by Geraldine Plunkett, whose shrouded spirit-body returns at *Samhain* to tell her own life story. Darina Ní Dhonnchú, as Sister Benedict, a white-veiled novice in charge of the sacristy, rehearses her lines and swings a thurible to and fro.

'Remember it's Sound Up for *Kyrie Eleison* by Noirín Ní Riain with shruti box! Sister Luke, you'll rehearse your description of Father James's special Mass. Attended, of course, by all your saints and thousands of angels!' Caroline says as Geraldine Plunkett and Peter Ashton nod in agreement.

'One day to go!' Tension rises higher and higher.

The stained glass window-flat falls across the stage, missing Maura Ber by inches.

'No! No! Don't say break a leg!' she exclaims and hurries offstage.

'I'll see that it's absolutely secure,' Arthur says and walks on with hammer and nails.

In the afternoon, Caroline directs Máire Hastings as Mother Victoire, who fusses over the Bishop of Killmacha's breakfast. Mother Victoire orders the Sister in the kitchen: 'Have three brown eggs ready to place in the enamel saucepan! – The special saucepan for His Lordship's boiled eggs! – Three, Sister Perpetuo – Three brown eggs! Not too small and not too big! The toast? The toast evenly cooked! Remember one boiled egg, the best and the brownest must go on a linen napkin beside the eggcup. – Ready? Now the eggs! In they go. Two minutes and five seconds before you take them out! – Your watch has stopped? Then count, I say. One, two, three. Count! Count! Count!'

'That scene in the sacristy between Sister Benedict and Father James, we'll run it again,' Caroline decides.

Holding his breviary, Fred McCloskey as Father James turns to Sister Benedict, who is polishing the thurible, and says, 'But wait until I tell you this story, Sister! When the builders were preparing the foundations for a new Cathedral on the site of the bombed Cathedral of Nagasaki, what did they find amidst the rubble and nuclear waste? They found a charred, but otherwise perfect, thurible. Devastation. Desecration. 70,000 humans incinerated, many thousand sickened with radiation and one small thurible survived the plutonium horror. And that thurible is still being used for ceremonies in the new Cathedral of Nagasaki! The ways of war to the ways of peace. *Deo Gratias*.'

'Sister Benedict, you'll turn and, eyes downcast, question him with the words, "70,000 humans incinerated, many thousand sickened with radiation and one small thurible survived the plutonium horror." – Now, look straight at Father James as you repeat *Deo Gratias*,' Caroline directs Sister Benedict.

'Highlight the thurible and Sister Benedict's face during this scene, ' she directs Paul Noble.

'Good! Rehearsal! Rehearsal! Nuns' habits must be ironed, no creases! Back here at 2 pm. sharp.'

The angelic sounds of *Benedictus in nomine Domini* float around us and inspire us as we lunch in the Green Room.

'Tomorrow is the day!' we say excitedly.

'And we're booked out for all of next week!' Michael Diskin smiles as he arrives from the reception desk.

'*Alleluia, Alleluia!*' we clap hands.

In 2003 the script *of Stained Glass at Samhain* is published by

Salmon Poetry Ltd.

Later, in an interview with Victoria Amanda of Edinburgh University, she asks me about my use of stained glass in the play-script I reply:

This stained glass window with the image of the dead Christ is the main image in my play. There are many layers of meaning here. Apart from the obvious stained image of the church, the window allows light in, must have light coming through to show its glorious colours. Light from light. Though destroyed during the performance of the play, the window is a symbol of Hope. Sister Luke in Act 2, Scene 7, as she picks up the stained glass, now shattered during the demolition of convent and laundry, says,

'For Father James when he returns from Paris. Together we'll make a Resurrection window from these broken pieces. My Angels and Archangels promise to help us.'

It's a symbol of Love and Hope. Note the fragility of the glass, the fragility of human beings, I continue. In Act 1 Scene 2, Father James in his defence of Sister Luke's mental health, says, 'Sister Luke is saner than most of us, Mother Victoire! We miss the many splendoured thing.' He holds up a mug, looks towards the stained glass window and says, 'All made of clay, whether it's china or rough pottery. All come from the earth like glass, clear or stained. But now, O Lord, Thou art our Father. We are the clay and Thou our Potter and we all are the work of Thy hand.'

Launch of Published Script

On 2nd October 2003, the guest speaker at the launch in the Town Hall Theatre, Galway City is the eminent dramatist Tom Kilroy. I'm delighted by his words of praise.

'It gives me particular pleasure to celebrate Patricia's play. A lot of contemporary plays nowadays are very grim and harsh. They would have their own authenticity – "street cred" – I believe is what it's called.

It's a wonderful thing to come across a truly visionary play, a poetic play and a play which uses the stage in a very interesting way.

It's visionary and at the heart of it is the quite original character of Sister Luke. The play itself is, as Patricia tells us in her notes, about the time of *Samhain*, when the boundaries between the living and the dead evaporate.

To write a play like this, which is a ghostly play, a play where you have mysterious things happening and you have a genuine sense of the spirit world, you actually need a medium on stage. You need some kind of a figure which is going to bring the audience into that other world and Patricia has created this wonderful character of Sister Luke.

Now when I say that the play is visionary and poetic, I don't mean anything airy-fairy, because this is a playwright who has a very pragmatic sense of staging and she has a very strong sense of the sweaty business of putting a play on stage and what is required to make the machine work. We have here that combination, which is a very good one.

The work itself is dominated by an image of demolition, clearly a companion piece to *Eclipsed*, a marvellous earlier play, but with a significant difference, the difference being that it is written out of the immediate present, so that looking at the Magdalen phenomenon, she is looking at it from a point in time as close to us as Joe Duffy's [radio] programme this afternoon. If you heard that program, you heard those moving voices of women who actually suffered this particular experience. I found it very moving and I was even more moved by the silence, the fact that they were talking about those unknown, unrecognised, unmarked graves. So that behind the actual voices of living people, you have this sense of the great silence permeating the whole thing.

Now what is particularly forceful about this play is that that ugly, horrible part of our history is looked at not from the point of view of the victim, but from the point of the nuns and that Patricia creates with great detail, a detail a director would have great fun and excitement with in recreating on stage.

Patricia creates in great detail the whole ritual of the Church, which is now history. All of the sacred objects and the sacred rituals of the rather strange patriarchal church, that at least some of us grew up with, she approaches from the point of view of the women who were in fact members of the order, the women who were responsible for running these institutions.

What is gratifying to me is that she makes those figures entirely human, because one of the things about looking back on a part of history like this is that you see it in terms of victims and victimisers, abusers and abused. This of course is the most natural way to think about it and we now attend very closely to the victims and to the abused.

We are inclined to forget that the people in this story are also human and the great strength of this play is that Patricia has given a human heart to these women, particularly to Sister Luke, who in addition to being a reverent, ghostly presence is a fully fleshed human being. She's a crazy nun, a *duine le Dia*. But in point of fact, as is the case with many crazy people, she is far saner than those around her.

She has a wonderful presence. There's a kind of seer-like quality about her, beyond the institution she sees into the future with some kind of hope. Remarkable! A remarkable achievement! Because what we're talking about, of course, is rescuing spirituality from the institutions that in some respect destroyed it.

This play rescues spirituality and in that way and for that reason, the play goes beyond the theatre. I couldn't pay a higher tribute to a play by saying that.

I'm delighted to launch your book. Thank you.'

When my turn comes to thank Tom Kilroy, I'm so overcome with emotion that I can only whisper, 'Thank you.'

Balla

Mom prepares my trousseau for boarding school. White cotton sheets and pillow cases, Foxford-wool blankets, a pink Foxford-wool dressing gown, chocolate-brown moccasin slippers, fluffy hand towels, bath sheets and blue laundry bags are bought in Galway City. Two navy gymslips, a royal blue blazer with crest, two royal blue jumpers and a matching tie-belt for everyday wear are ordered. Mom places lavender-scented tissue paper between folds of my black velvet best-wear dress. I help by sewing my name in Cash's marks on every item before packing my trunk. I smile at my reflection in my new black patent buckled shoes.

In navy-blue gabardine coat and felt hat, I hug Mom, my sisters, my brother and our dog, Daisy. Dad gives me his Waterman fountainpen-and-pencil set. Silver-grey with bronze speckles, they rest in a presentation box lined with crimson velvet.

'I'll take care of them, Dad,' I promise as I stroke and kiss the gold nib, then twist the cap back on.

Dad comes with me on my journey to *Ard Scoil Naomh Lughaidh* and to my new life. Having passed through Tuam and Claremorris, we arrive in a small village, drive up a leafy avenue and stop at a conservatory, which shelters a huge oak door. My Aunt Clara, a St. Louis Sister, welcomes us. She serves us afternoon tea in the convent parlour.

I try not to show my loneliness to Dad as he hugs me and returns to the car. Half-blinded by tears, I watch that car as it moves down the beech and lime-tree avenue, passes the gate lodge, turns into the small village and disappears. Aunt Clara takes my hand and leads me upstairs to Holy Angels' dormitory. As she makes my bed, she consoles me, 'You'll be going home for Christmas holidays, love.'

And I'll stay at home with Mom and Dad, Aunt Clara. I'm not coming back here ever! I can study at home and practise for my piano exams. I don't want that stupid scholarship,' I sob.

'I'll look after you, love. You'll make lots of new friends. Still snuffling and wiping my eyes, I notice many tearful faces as we walk along the school corridor to the assembly hall.

'See, those little girls are lonely for home too,' Aunt Clara says. 'Centuries ago St. Mochua blessed this place and named it *Ball Áluinn.*

The Sister Superior addresses us from her lectern. 'Let us praise St. Mochua and St. Louis.Wear your school badge proudly with its *fleur de lis* and St. Louis motto, *Dieu le Veult.* In the refectory do not hold your cutlery, especially knives and forks, like pencils. Eat soup from the side of your soup spoon. Elbows should never be propped on dining tables. Keep your hats on when out for walks and do not link one another.'

Lonely for home, lonely, lonely. Every night in Holy Angels dormitory, I shed tears into my lavender-scented bed linen. Aunt Clara tries to comfort me by leaving small gifts under my pillow, an apple, a chocolate biscuit or a crochet handkerchief.

Every week a letter from home arrives. Dad writes that our dog, Daisy, is recovering from a slight collision with a car. He also gives some international news.

Mom sends a parcel of fruit, tinned beans and nuts for Halloween. I share the parcel with the other boarders at our Round Table in the refectory. Dad writes that honeycombs from our beehives could not be sent by post, but that a good supply would be kept for Christmas. The bees are healthy and are settling down for winter. I miss their music and their coloured-pollen stockings as they arrive home from honey-collecting excursions.

In black velvet dresses edged with Clones lace, royal blue blazers and wearing our buckled patent shoes, we walk in single file to the Blue Hall. On the terrace above the tennis courts, tulips, flaming braziers, are a foreground to a green cumulus of beech and elm below *Cnoc Spolgadáin.*

Gradually I settle into the school routine. But when we are out for autumnal walks, I glimpse through village windows the glow of home fires. I long for the loving shelter of my own family, for my

Mom and Dad.

I imagine that I hear Dad sing *My Dark Rosaleen* in our sittingroom with its plush high-backed chairs and armchairs bought in Kitty Kiernan's shop in Granard. He then takes *The Book of the All-Round Angler* from bookshelves beside the fireplace. Mom is preparing sweetbreads in the kitchette. Jars of nutmegs and exotic spices glow on a shelf above her worktable. My new dress of *Broderie Anglaise* is folded across her Singer sewing machine. The scent of brown bread, which is baking in the kitchen range, fills the air.

In my own armchair, I'm reading *Portrait of the Artist*. Dad checks my book.

'She's reading James Joyce,' he tells Mom. They confer.

'I want to be an artist too,' I announce. Dad continues to read and Mom continues to prepare dinner.

But here in the village of Balla, I drag my legs and hang my head. My eyes are full of tears as we turn from the street into the dark avenue which leads to our school buildings.

'Tell Patricia to walk properly,' a message is passed from the two Sisters who chaperone us.

On Saturdays, I sit at the piano in the Blue Hall and play notes to tune viola, violins, cellos, double bass. We wait until Sister Caecilia raises her baton for rehearsal of *Ballet Music from Rosamunde*. 'We must prepare for the annual school-orchestra examination,' she announces.

Every evening I leave study to practise arpeggios, chromatic scales, Schubert Impromptus, Chopin Nocturnes in preparation for piano and violin exams. My Latin homework is crushed between Shakespeare's *King Lear*, French grammar and trigonometry. Moira, who shares a desk with me, helps with Latin homework whenever I overstay at music practice. My love of Latin also helps me absorb Horace's Odes and Virgil's pastoral poems.

The Pleasure Grounds full of exotic trees and oriental shrubs surround the walled garden. Cedars of Lebanon, Persian Ironwoods,

Japanese Snowballs, Chinese Hawthorn trees brought back from his world travels by Sir Robert Blosse Lynch flourish among native flora.

In the English class, Sister Phelim says, 'I'd like you to write an essay. This evening go out into the Pleasure Grounds. Look closely at trees. Let me have your essays on Tuesday morning.'

I touch textured barks and examine leaf shapes. I put my arms around enormous tree trunks, smell their greenness and admire the filigree pattern of branches against the sky.

'Yes, your essay is good. Now read it out for the class,' Sister Phelim instructs me.

As I read with reluctance, I notice that Dolores, who sits in a desk near me, has pushed her fingers into her ears.

School orchestra St Louis Covent, Balla,
Myself, pianist, sitting centre.

This historic house is haunted. According to our teenage stories, the ghost of Sir Robert Blosse Lynch tumbles down the wide staircase and breaks his neck at least once a week. Before dawn his wife pirouettes on the tennis courts, picnics on strawberries from the walled garden.

Because I'm *ciotóg*, I develop a skill for lawn tennis. I show off my left-handed service with pride.

Then bespectacled Dolores humiliates me. 'You're like a sack tied in the middle. You're so broad, you'd have no problem stopping goals at camogie! That red hair of yours makes me sick! Show-off, carrot-head *ciotóg*! Why don't you use a scrubbing brush on your freckly face? Look here! This is how tennis should be played!' She sends the tennis ball close to my ears. I want to answer that my hair is auburn and that my Mom says my freckles will disappear when I grow up. But taking my tennis racket, I walk towards my special beech tree and sit in its shelter.

Aunt Clara notices my sadness. 'Hold your head high, love,' she advises. 'You have important ancestors, writers of note. An ancestor of yours, Thomas Lewis O'Beirne, and his brother Denis studied for the priesthood in Saint Omer.

'Saint Omer! Why in Saint Omer, Aunt Clara?'

'During Penal Times priests were persecuted here in Ireland, so students for the priesthood went to seminaries in Europe. However, Thomas Lewis did not persevere as a Roman Catholic clergyman. Later as a Protestant rector in London, but also an ordained Catholic Deacon, he was accepted by Mrs. Fitzherbert, a Roman Catholic, to officiate at her marriage to the Prince of Wales. That was in 1785.'

'But that's so long ago in 1785, Aunt Clara!' I protest.

'The Prince of Wales became George the Fourth of England in 1820. At one time Thomas Lewis was Protestant Rector of Templemichael in Longford town and his brother Denis was Roman Catholic Parish Priest in the same town. Isn't that unusual?'

'Yes, but my hair!' I interrupt and hold out one of my plaits.

'In 1789 Thomas Lewis was ordained Protestant Bishop of Meath. His long poem *Crucifixion* is in the National Library as are scripts of his stage plays,' she says proudly.

'Eugene Francis O'Beirne, your mother's great uncle, was a famous author and adventurer. With Dr. Cheade and Lord Milton, he was first to cross the Rocky Mountains on foot. Mount O'Beirne in the Yellowhead Pass region of Alberta is named after him. I'll tell you more about him and about another ancestor of ours next week.'

'Yes. But I'm too fat! Look at me! And my hair, my freckles, Aunt Clara,' I interrupt again.

'Chin up, love! Freckles are beauty spots.' She pats my cheek.

Years later I discover that Eugene Francis O'Beirne was unjustly expelled from Maynooth College. He then gave up his Roman Catholicism and published a volume, *An Impartial View of the Internal Economy and Discipline of Maynooth College*, which criticised the discipline in that seminary. According to the O'Beirne family tradition, he met his wife, Jane Cooper of Markree Castle, in Canada.

In 2008 my sister and I stay overnight at Markree Castle. We are booked into the en-suite bedroom in which Johnny Cash stayed when he visited Ireland.

Next morning we listen to a guide, who speaks of the Castle's history.

'Since the invasion of Cromwell, except for a short period after the Battle of the Boyne, Jane Cooper's family lived here in Markree Castle, Co. Sligo. Cromwell didn't have money to pay his officers. Instead he gave them large portions of land.

He gave Markree Castle and the surrounding grounds to Edward Cooper. Edward Cooper's army defeated the great O'Brien Clan. Chieftain O'Brien lost his life in battle. Edward married his widow, Máire Rua, and he went to live with her in Leamanah Castle, Co. Clare. She had her two sons take the name of Cooper as protection from the English invaders. Her first son inherited Limerick Castle and her second son inherited Markree Castle. It was occupied by the Free State Army during the Civil War in the 1920s,' the guide informs us.

'The great oak staircase in Markree Castle is overlooked by a huge stained-glass window, which traces the Cooper family tree back to the time of King John of England. Jane Cooper's name is visible among the glorious colours. But in Markree Castle there is no acknowledgment of the marriage between adventurer Eugene Francis O'Beirne and Jane,' the guide continues.

Aunt Clara is moved to the order's Mother House, St. Louis Convent in Monaghan.

'Now you've to stand on your own two feet, carrot-head!' Dolores teases.

When I win an award for Inter Cert results, my friends carry me, my plaits flying, on their shoulders. But Dolores, racket in hand, runs out to the tennis courts.

'Hitch your chariot to a star!' Sister Dympna advises me.

I put on an exhibiton of my drawings and paintings in aid of the foreign missions. I'm delighted when it's almost a sell-out.

Preparation for the annual school operetta begins after *Samhain* (Halloween).

During recreation, under the direction of Sister Borromeo, our art teacher, we paint flats, suitable backdrops and illusions for *The Gondoliers*. The music of Gilbert and Sullivan envelops us as we mix colours and apply paint with large brushes.

I think of my Dad who, as a teenager, designed and painted stage sets for his local theatre group on the Hill of Mullagh above Kilglass Lake.

'When I joined Strokestown Sinn Féin *Cumann*, my stage sets and equipment were set on fire and destroyed by British sympathisers,' my Dad had told me when I questioned him about his stage sets.

Dad with his medals.

Fish

In the science lab. we, now in *rang a cúig*, stare at wall charts showing human skeletons.

'My Dad says that we are the descendants of monkeys and apes!' announces Dolores as she hops and hobbles on hunched legs.

'No. No. Not apes! Not monkeys!' Fiona insists and makes the sign of the cross.

'God made us in his own image and likeness.'

'Gorillas and chimpanzees and orangutans,' Dolores twists and pulls out her lips

'From clay. He made us from clay!' Mary Alice tosses her blonde ringlets.

'From whales. We're the descendants of dolphins, whales and fishes,' Pearl argues.

'I'd prefer to come from birds. Then I could fly high into the sky and go home every evening,' I sing-song my declaration, as I extend my neck and fling out my arms.

'Make a model of the middle ear.' Sister Isidore, our physiology teacher, interrupts our newly discovered version of Darwin's Theory of Evolution.

'The middle ear,' she repeats and points to me.

'Yes, Sister Isidore,' I answer.

I gather pieces of paper, rubber bands, adhesive, string. I make drawings for a papier-maché model. My confidence wanes a little as I begin to realise how extraordinary the architecture of the human body is, but I don't give up on my middle ear project.

'Don't you realise that only God himself can make us,' Fiona whispers, as I struggle with my model of the tympanic cavity, the eustachian tube and the ossicles, the incus, malleus and stapes.

'They resemble a hammer, anvil and stirrup,' Sister Isidore explains.

It's Friday, but an omelette, the usual alternative to fish, is not a choice to-day.

'We are descended from dolphins, whales, mermaids and big fishes,'
Pearl's voice echoes in my mind. A fish, headless, but with fins and
tail attached, rests on my lunch plate. My stomach heaves and I turn
away.

'You'll stay here until you eat this fish!' the Sister in charge of the
refectory warns.

'What would your Aunt Clara say if she heard you were so
disobedient!'

Alone and in tears, I sit for what seems like hours at the Round
Table. Eventually, Sister orders me back to study. I then comfort
myself by reading Shelley's *To a Skylark*.

In a daydream, I hope that we have evolved from skylarks and
swallows.

My middle ear project, in spite of so much effort, isn't successful. I
decide to ask my Guardian Angel to finish it for me.

Faith can move mountains. In primary school, I hid my school
knitting in our antique cheese dish and asked my Guardian Angel to
finish the heel of my sock. I hated knitting with those steel needles
and their tuneless sounds. I pray over and over again, 'Angel of God,
my guardian dear, to whom God's love commits me here.

Ever this day be at my side to light and guard, to rule and guide
and please, please, make Sr. Isidore forget about my middle ear effort.'

To make things worse, I've lost Dad's fountainpen. I pray and pray
to St. Anthony, but my lovely gold-nibbed pen has disappeared from
my desk. Is this because I disobeyed Sister in the refectory?

After Christmas the weather turns very cold. I take my well-worn
hot-water bottle to the kitchen hatch. Having filled it, I rush upstairs
to St. Mary's dormitory, but the rubber hot-water bottle bursts and
scalding water pours on to my left arm. I'm rushed to the infirmary,
where Sister Ella peels off the sleeve of my jumper. I'm in deep shock,
as skin comes away with the sleeve. Raw flesh, raw, raw.

Confined to bed, blisters form and cover my inside forearm from
elbow to wrist.

Sister Ella arrives with scissors and an enamel basin. She cuts open the blisters, drains the liquid into the basin, then wraps my arm in thick bandages.

In a short time the raw flesh becomes septic. Sick with pain, I plan a structure, which would replace my left arm for violin practice. My right hand would then play the strings. But a one-handed pianist is certinly out of the question.

The piano examinations take place before the end of term. Pain, pain.

My future as a musician is now in doubt. So is my life, though I do not realise it

Leaving Cert results arrive. I just scrape through honours in written and oral Irish, but get an average of 90% in other subjects and 100% in oral English. A call to Training arrives. As I've been awarded Third Place in Ireland in Open Competition to Teacher Training College, this call must not be refused.

Carysfort

The College, a brick building, three-storeys high, is a contrast to that country residence in *Ball Aluinn, County Mayo*. A tornado of *Gaelic* hits me. Some students speak Donegal *Gaelic*, others Munster *Gaelic* and a few the familiar Conamara.

In the study hall I share a desk with Bríd, a student from the midlands. As we open our books and settle down to work, she says, 'Watch out, a Phadraigín! The nuns at home warned me that the nuns in this training college were devils dressed in nuns' habits!'

'Your nuns said that about the nuns here? Devils dressed in nuns' habits! With horns and cloven feet? Don't be silly!' I reply.

'The horns and cloven feet are all covered over. Disguised. Look at the special shoes they wear. Clumpy and twisted up to suit their foot-shapes! Sure the devil himself can do what he likes, even with nuns' habits! Remember what Lucifer did in Paradise!'

'What about their horns?' I'm smiling to myself.

'They keep cutting one another's horns back. We must pull off Siúr Susanah's veil and have a look,' she giggles.

No! That'd be real trouble, a Bhríd. There's always one good nun, even if the others are bad.' I shake my head. When we see a dark side, we must look underneath for the luminous.

'Believe it or not, that's what the nuns at home told us! Devils in nuns' habits.'

She makes the sign of the cross on both our foreheads.

On Saturday afternoons, I take a bus to visit my Aunt Lucy, who lives near the Navan Road. She comforts me with a meal of homemade brown bread, bacon, sausages and black pudding. Her husband, Bernard Carroll, who teaches in a school nearby, questions me about my studies.

Instead of continuing with my study of the piano, I'm ordered to take church organ lessons. When I was ten years of age, I had played the church harmonium for *Benediction*. My legs were barely able to reach and push the pedals. Now I'm faced with large wooden keyboard pedals, three manuals and an array of control buttons.

Gradually I learn to work the pedals, heel-toe, heel-toe. I adapt my finger-touch to suit the organ keyboard. Because I love the music of Johann Sebastian Bach, I concentrate on his *Preludes and Fugues for Organ*.

One October day, I sit in a lecture hall where a nun talks about *Oideachas* in a monotonous tone. I gaze in admiration through a nearby window at a young beech tree, its leaves now multiple shades of copper.

Suddenly my name is called. *'Tusa! Tar anseo!'* I stand up and walk towards the nun as a barrage of spittle-laden Dublin-Gaelic echoes through the hall. My hair stands on end. The warning words of Máire, another student from the midlands, come back to me. 'If that snakey devil of a nun gets a set on you, you'll suffer!'

From that day until I finish in college, that nun makes sure to punish me. My written work comes back regularly with the note, *'Labhair liom, le do thoil!'* which means a call to her office for another torrent of angry words.

I spend every spare minute in the college library with its great art books, but at times I wish that the spitfire nun would arrange to have me expelled.

By designing illustrations for teaching practice, my confidence grows. My images are more powerful than words. The pupils are fascinated as they watch.

That glorious tree still shines out in my mind beside that dark *Oideachas* figure.

I survive and become a teacher.

When I see that income tax has been deducted from my salary, I grumble to my father, 'Income tax! But, I've only begun to work as a teacher, Dad.'

'It's the least you might do for your country, love,' he replies.

I do not grumble that every dinner served in my South Galway digs is tinned salmon mixed with white breadcrumbs.

At a college ball.

As a student in Carysfort
Teacher Training College.

My first visit to Listowel Writers' Week

Eamon and I take the train from Galway to Limerick, then the bus to Listowel for Writers' Week. Mafra, one of my friends from our Choral Society, sits in the front seat. She takes a bottle of brandy from her handbag, puts it to her lips and swallows a great mouthful. She begins to sing *Beidh Aonach Amárach i gCondae an Chláir*, then offers the brandy to the driver, the conductor and the passengers. We join her in song as we cross the River Shannon.

I turn my head westwards towards Killadysert, my birthplace, where the river meets the Atlantic. Shannon air raises my spirits as I remember my Dad and myself in that small squeaky boat. I'd shouted, 'Daddy, Daddy, the River Shannon is coming into our boat.' Dad scooped up the water with a tin and emptied it with a splash beside the dolphins.

Dad and I didn't know then that archaeologists would discover a long boat which had been embedded in this estuary for hundreds of years.

My eyes on the river, I whisper one of my poems.

Rhythm of water
pleats and folds
on river-mouth
at Labasheeda.

Pulse of jet-planes
from Moscow, from Boston
shudder above Ardnacrusha.

Rhythm of stone axe
on straight-grained poplar
shaped and carved this canoe
seven hundred years ago.

Heartbeat of a child
swells from a womb-canoe
below Saint's Island.

In Killadysert
the child plays
with mud-patterns
from the estuary.

With a blue crayon
she makes word-patterns,
finds a river poem.

Mafra passes the bottle of brandy around again and again as the songs get louder and we drive through the furze-stained bogs of north Kerry. A head-scarved woman, pioneer pin shining on her coat lapel, closes her eyes and fingers her rosary beads.

The conductor, cap now sideways on his scrunchy red hair, insists that there would be a return bus from Listowel to Limerick the following Monday, bank holiday or not. Mafra offers him another swig of brandy. The driver refuses, but raises his voice with,

The pale moon was shining above the green mountain,
The sun was declining beneath the blue sea,
As I strayed with my love by the pure crystal fountain
That stands in the beautiful vale of Tralee.

Mafra uses the empty bottle as a baton. Tenors, baritones, sopranos, altos, basses, crows, even the woman with the pioneer pin join the driver with,

Oh no 'twas the truth in her eyes ever shining that made me love
Mary, the Rose of Thraawlee.

In Listowel, we're welcomed by John B. Keane's literary agent,

Londoner June Blizz, who directs us straight to a nearby pub. Mafra and June had often socialised together in the Drury Lane area of London.

Not used to the endless rounds of alcohol, Eamon and I leave the pub and find Stack's Hotel, where we have booked Bed and Breakfast.

I wash away the stench of cigarette smoke and whiskey from my hair, hands and face, then I go for a walk around the writer-crowded streets. A tweed-suited man, manuscript under his oxter, a faraway look in his eyes, passes a group of women poets.

The Dublin bus arrives, and stops beside St. John's Church in the Square.

From the bus rushes a group of lady writers wrapped in ponchos and long skirts, their new portfolios bulging with Dublin romances. I admire their courage as I think of my own poems and stories hidden behind bookshelves.

Next evening, John B. invites us to a show in the local theatre, featuring Rosaleen Linehan and Des Keogh. During the interval he treats us to gins and tonics in a nearby hostelry.

It's Saturday night and we're in Stack's small smoke-filled bar. June Blizz has gone on another date with another twenty-year-old Kerryman.

'June's own bed hasn't been used since we arrived in Listowel!' Mafra announces as she sits on writer Ben Kiely's knees and together they sing 'I dreamt I dwelt in Marble Halls'. John-Joe, a local fiddle player, Tony Cronin, the bespectacled Dublin poet and ourselves applaud and shout, 'Encore!'

A couple of Dublin women poets look in, swing their blonde curls and decide to hurry to the pub next door.

Ben orders another round of drinks, but the skinny barman refuses to cash Ben's personal cheque. Ben leaves for John B's pub, saying in his exquisite Omagh voice, 'Don't move! I'll be back before John-Joe finishes that hornpipe.'

On Ben's smiling return, the concert continues until we move to the dining room.

Still singing, Mafra takes Ben's knife and fork and tries to cut his steak into bite-size pieces. 'A steak knife, please! This great writer must eat!' she shouts in frustration.

Between peals of laughter, we chew and chew our own steaks.

On Monday morning, having discovered that there was no bus service from Listowel on bank holidays, we succeed in hiring a taxi. On our way to drop June Blizz at Shannon Airport, we stop the taxi at least twice. June throws up on Kerry furze bushes.

'See you in London next week!', Mafra waves to June as we drive away from Departures to catch the train to Galway.

Mafra has mislaid her return ticket, so she packs a bundle under her dress, twists a signet ring around her third left-hand finger and pretends to be asleep when the ticket-collector announces, 'Tickets, please!'

'Always works in Catholic Ireland', she says, patting her bundle, when the collector moves to the next carriage.

'Now, listen to this!' she adds. 'After a late night party in Dublin, me and one of my famous journalist boyfriends were speeding through Fitzwilliam Street, when I spotted a Garda check point. I pushed a cushion under my coat, and groaned in pain. A young Garda stood at the half-open window.

'Holles Street, Holles Street! I'm about to give birth, officer! Help! Hurry! Holles Street! Holles Street!' I screamed.

The young Garda signalled us straight on. We made sure to drive up to Holles Street Maternity Hospital. We then returned to the party for another few brandies.

'Your ticket, Mam!' the ticket-collector comes out of the shadows, where he had overheard Mafra's story.

'But, my darling, I lost my return ticket. Pregnancy makes me forgetful', Mafra explains.

'Your fare, Mam!' he insists as he rattles his money bag.

'Catholic Ireland is dead and gone!' Mafra sighs as she searches that hidden bundle for her purse.

Other Visits to Writers' Week

A group of art enthusiasts in Listowel arrange a series of National and International Graphics Exhibitions to run in conjunction with Writers' Week.

I'm delighted when my etchings are selected for both the National and Biennale International Exhibitions. Each year, I'm invited to the exhibition openings.

We drive through Ennis and southwards to Kerry. My spirit is again netted in memories of my childhood as we cross the River Shannon by ferry.

I'm awarded a prize at The Listowel third International Biennale 1982 for my etching, *Gaillimh, Daughter of Breasail* and I'm invited to exhibit in *Fredrikstadt Print Biennale* in Norway.

My next visit to Writers' Week is to a short-story workshop given by novelist, Julia O'Faolain. We meet in the kitchen of Listowel College. She had requested a kitchen space, because she believes story-writing is very like cooking.

She speaks of her father's book *Short Stories* and also recommends the work of other prose writers.

Even though I've been awarded first prize for my short story, *Sunflowers*, in *The Connacht Tribune's Writing in the West*, I'm too timid to read it to the group. Julia reads my story aloud and says it has a lovely shape.

A writer from Australia is annoyed when Julia calls his stories 'yarns'. He storms out as he shouts, 'I have already published more books than you'll ever publish in your lifetime, Julia O'Faolain!' She continues with the workshop as if nothing strange has happened.

Bed and Breakfast in Stacks' beautiful thatched house on the river is so comfortable that I'm tempted to relax there instead of attending the workshops.

From the back garden I walk towards the fast-flowing River Feale.

Suddenly a river-rock moves,
raises a curved neck,
forms long legs stealthily,
freezes.
The heron stabs the river.

Amazed, I promise myself that I'd return later in the year.

I drive across the bridge and into the literary town for another literary session.

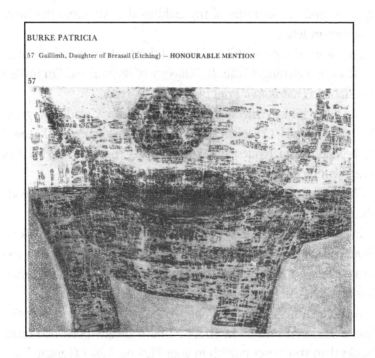

BURKE PATRICIA

57 Gaillimh, Daughter of Breasail (Etching) — HONOURABLE MENTION

57

Corcomroe Paschal Night

I drive through darkness to Corcomroe Abbey for the annual Dawn Mass.

Away from light-polluted skies, I hope to see the comet Hale-Bopp, but not one star shines on my journey through Clarinbridge, Kilcolgan, Ballinderreen and Kinvara.

Unseen too along the Coast Road, the Atlantic moans a requiem.

As I approach *Béal a Clogga*, the glow of a Paschal bonfire rises outside the monastery's twelfth-century ruins.

'*Fáilte róibh go léir!*' Local people welcome visitors from Europe. Christians and Non-Christians, Agnostics, Atheists and Pagans gather in the textured Burren. Here and there faces are high lighted by the amber bonfire, their bodies lost in darkness. Spirits of Cistercian monks mingle again with the living.

Incised on the sanctuary wall, but almost invisible now, eroded by wind and rain, is an image of a fisherman in his boat full of fishes.

Eyes closed, I whisper my poem.

Paschal Night
A monk cuts into blessed plaster
to reveal this fishing boat,
this fisherman.
Flash of fish-scales from his nets
beyond our seeing.
Before dawn
the monk begins
to sculpt harebells
for the altar.
Through this roofless,
doorless abbey,
matins and lauds echo
from ice-scraped grykes
above our hearing.

When the first streak of light silvers the east, poet-philosopher John O'Donohue, with Cistercian monks, celebrates Easter Mass within these ancient ruins.

Glory to God in the highest and peace to his people on earth.

Plain chant, accompanied by the dawn chorus, resonates through fire, earth and water, as light transforms glacial erratics and grykes on this, the youngest landscape in Europe.

Benedictus qui venit in nomine Domini.

Benedictus, medium: drypoint.

The stone has been rolled back. The tomb is empty. *Alleluia.*
Alleluia from Corcomroe to Jerusalem, from Calvary to Fermoyle.

Bread from cracked fields,
Wine from stone pockets.
Invisible Credo
on the road to Emmaus.

Beyond a wall of night-cloud
Hale-Bopp drags its sparkling net.
I reach up and search-scrape
into that darkness
to reveal this fire-wound
millions of years old.

The sun rises,
begins to dance.

I am netted
in the invisible.

'Paschal Night' from *Décollage, New and Selected Poems*

Millennium Celebration

Tom Kenny of Kenny's Bookshops and Galleries telephones.

'We'd like to commission you for a painting or etching to celebrate the Arts in Galway in the Millennium, Patricia.'

'Thank you, Tom. Great news. I'm honoured.'

'A poem by John O'Donohue and an image by you. This will be a limited edition, signed and numbered by John and yourself,' he continues.

John O'Donohue and I confer. He sends me his chosen poem, *The Transparent Border.*

Because John loves blue above all other colours, I choose *Night Beach* one of soft-ground relief etchings with many tones of blue.

'This image from a small edition printed by myself was included in International Exhibitions in Barcelona, Paris and Japan,' I tell him.

He's delighted with my choice.

I do not know then that John, while on a visit to Avignon, will slip quietly across life's transparent border in early January 2008.

The limited edition print commissioned by Kennys, signed and numbered on back by John O'Donohue and myself.

Before his death John had been writing a thesis on the works of the German philosopher, theologian and mystic, Meister Eckhart von Hochheim O. P.

Meister Eckhart was declared a heretic by Pope John the Twenty-Second during the Avignon Papacy.

No record of Meister Eckhart's death or burial site has ever been discovered.

(He probably died in Cologne c. 1320.)

Eclipsées in Paris

Early in 2007, I receive a letter from Aurelie Harp and Aude Saintier of Sun Act Theatre Company in Paris.

'We'd be honoured to produce *Eclipsed* here in Paris,' they write.

Luckily, the play had been translated into French. Emails and letters are exchanged.

A contract is drawn up and signed by both Sun Act Theatre Company and myself.

The play is to be produced in *L'Article*, a small theatre in Paris. Aude and Aurelie email me again to say that they have been contacted by Pierre-Loic Monfroy, another theatre director.

'We'll arrange a meeting in September with Pierre-Loic, the director of *Theatre Coté Cour*, when he returns from a summer tour in Avignon. He too loves *Eclipsed*.'

Before the play goes into rehearsal, the actors change their company's name, Sun Act Theatre Company, to Ag Baile Theatre Company. A new contract is signed and the production will run at weekends for three months at *Theatre Coté Cour*, 12 *Rue Eduard Lockroy*, 75017.

Aurelie and Aude notify *L'Article* about their change of plans.

'*Theatre Coté Cour* is situated near *Place de la Republique*, a great theatre-centred location in the 11th district, a very lively neighbourhood. *Pierre-Loic Monfroy* will direct,' Aude emails me.

Aurelie is to play Sister Virginia, but after four weeks of rehearsals, she finds she is pregnant. Another actor is auditioned and cast as Sister Virginia. In 1995 Theater Banshee's Leslie Baldwin, who played Sister Virginia in *Eclipsed*, also found she was pregnant, but went ahead with rehearsals because she was still in the early stages. The actor who played Brigit Murphy had to be very careful in Act 2 Scene 3, where she punches Sister Virginia and throws her to the ground.

Theater Banshee's production won many awards including Critic's Choice from *The Los Angeles Times* and Critic's Award from *Dramalogue.*

In 2006 another production of *Eclipsed* by Theater Banshee, to celebrate ten years of its work in theatre, was awarded Critic's Pick, Pick of the Week and Triple Crown.

My sister Philomena and I fly Air France from Dublin to Charles de Gaulle Airport and take a taxi to Hotel Tourisme in Avenue de la Motte-Picquet near the Eiffel Tower.

A few years earlier we had spent Easter week here in this city. Afterwards I wrote a series of poems about my visit. *Spy Wednesday, Paris; Maundy Thursday, Paris* and *Holy Saturday, Paris.*

Maundy Thursday, Paris

Latecomers, we stand barred
outside the congregation in Notre Dame.
From the vestibule
we peer into stained glass shadows.

With a crash the organ exults from the gallery,
radiance floods the nave.
Vested in white, a multitude of priests
place candles along linen-covered tables
in celebration of Christ's last supper.

The Bishop of Paris begins his homily

A spirit-woman in long robes
slips through those narrow door-bars.
Alizarin crimsons and ultramarines
glow on her white gown
as she glides past startled ministers
and places a jar of spikenard
low on the marble altar.

The Bishop is silent while the woman chants the Magnificat.

Outside, near the Metro,
a lavender-seller intones the Marseillaise.

After showering and changing from our travel clothes, we call a taxi.

Our excitement is intense as we sit with the First Night audience in *Theatre Coté Cour.* My heart beats faster as the voice of Kathleen Ferrier floats forth during the opening of the purple drapes. *He was despised, despised and rejected, rejected of men.*

The actors play their ensemble roles with passion. The audience responds sometimes with laughter, sometimes with tears. The rhythm of the dialogue in French delights me. Each 'penitent' wears a small rosary beads on her wrist.

'The rosaries were given to us by a contemplative nun from a convent beside *Sacré Coeur,*' Aude, who plays Brigit Murphy, tells me when she comes to meet us through the applauding audience.

When she introduces me to Jack Garfein, a survivor of the Holocaust, my eyes fill with tears. He is now world famous for his work in theatre and film.

He congratulates me for giving a strong voice to the Magdalen women.

Aurelie, who is in the late stages of pregnancy, cannot attend, but sends me a special bouquet of roses.

As we leave the theatre and walk out into the crowded street, we and the actors are showered with flowers. There are songs, hugs and more flowers as we make our way to a special restaurant for supper.

The Paris newspaper *Le Figaro* gives *Eclipsées* a very good review under the title of '*Le triste destin des magdalenes, filles perdues et oubliées.*'

Thank you to all at Ag Baile Theatre to Aurelie Harp, Aude Saintier, Muriel Michaux, Alexandra Bienvenu, Marine Jouhet, Helene Pivette, Natalie Guillemain and Regine Mondion and to Pierre-Loic Monfroy and all at Theatre Coté Cour.

Grykes grow richer in Burren limestone.

On our way back to the airport, I look towards *Sacré Coeur* and think of the hours spent on that height, making pastel sketches of Paris. Surrounded by other artists, who were speaking in different languages, I worked under the shade of multicoloured umbrellas. I resolve to develop those sketches for a series of Paris Paintings.

In the Pompidou Centre, I'm moved and excited to find an exhibition of twelve paintings by Rouault. Stained-glass colours glow from darkly textured contours. Clowns, prostitutes, judges and self-portraits hang side by side with his *Homo Homini Lupus.* Man is a wolf to man. Painted after two world wars, Rouault's Man is hoist on a gallows, head sideways, neck broken, hands open, a figure acquainted with grief. His *Man of Sorrows* hangs twisted in agony on a cross. His *Ecce Homo* insists, 'They do not know what they do'. I resolve to visit the library in NUIG on my return to Galway and view again Rouault's *Miserere et Guerre* etchings donated by the late Monsignor Pádraig De Brún.

In Charles de Gaulle airport as we wait for our Air France flight home, we meet a young woman from China. During our conversation she tells us that before she escaped to Paris, she was tortured for being a member of Falun Gong.

She gives me a bundle of papers showing the injustices perpetrated in that once highly cultured country.

Mika Funahashi, an academic from Waseda University, Japan, flies to London and takes the Eurostar to Paris to attend the last night of *Eclipsées*. Afterwards she tells me how much she enjoyed the performance and the end-of-production party. She said that it was the best night she ever had in Paris.

2009. At a conference in Japan, Dr. Riana O'Dwyer from NUIG reviews essays on Irish Drama. Included is one by Mika Funahashi on *Eclipsed.*

A Theatrical Challenge of the Magdalen Laundries, International

Institute for Education and Research in Theatre and Film Arts Global COE Programme.

Theatre and Film Studies 2009. Vol. 3.

In 2010, Mika Funahashi interviews me here at my home in Galway City. From Tokyo she sends me a CD and tape of that interview.

Pastel sketch Sacré Coeur, Montmartre.

Human Rights

When I was seven years old my mother told me that her first cousin, Nan O'Beirne, who was married to Dr. Joseph Faul, lived in the village of Louth with their seven children. 'There's a hiding place in Castle Plunkett which is on their land. Blessed Oliver Plunkett took refuge there while on the run,' my mother said.

'Our own Blessed Oliver living in a hidden place? Had he no real home?' I asked.

'Yes, love. Blessed Oliver had to hide during the Confederate Wars just after the Cromwellian invasion. Priests were ordered by the Viceroy to leave Ireland immediately and all Catholic churches, convents and monasteries to be closed down. But Blessed Oliver stayed in Ireland.. He was eventually captured, brought first to Dublin Castle and then to Tyburn in London, where he was hanged, drawn and quartered on 1st July 1681,' my mother said hesitantly.

'Horrible! Awful! Poor Blessed Oliver!'

'His head is kept in a glass shrine in St. Peter's Church in Drogheda. We'll visit and pray there when you're a little older,' she promised.

In Galway City I attend a lecture by Father Denis Faul, son of Nan and Dr. Joseph Faul. Years later he will be promoted and given the title of Monsignor by the Vatican.

During his lecture he shows slides of the tortured bodies of prisoners in Northern jails. We here in this Southern audience are shocked by what human beings have done to other human beings across the border.

When the lecture is over, I introduce myself. 'I'm Mary O'Beirne's daughter, Father Denis. Mary O'Beirne from Clooneen near Rooskey.'

'A daughter of one of the O'Beirnes from that farmhouse beside the river Shannon', he says with a smile and shakes my hand. He gives me a publication, which contains photographs of the scarred limbs of Republican prisoners.

'Please sign it for me, Father Denis.' I offer him my pen.

Some time afterwards, I read this report in an Irish newspaper:

'Father Denis Faul, son of Nan and Dr, Joseph Faul, is acclaimed internationally for his work for human rights. He says daily Mass in Long Kesh, the Maze Prison. British soldiers, who guard the gates shout, "Here comes f---ing Faul!" as he drives past into the prison.'

'He'll never be made a bishop. He speaks out too much!' a friend remarks.

I do not know then that, years later, at an O'Beirne family gathering in Longford town, two of his sisters, both medical doctors, will ask me, 'Were the Magdalen Laundries as awful as you show them in your play, *Eclipsed*, Patricia?' I'm taken aback, but tears fill their eyes when, instead of using words, I nod.

I should have remembered that the Faul and O'Beirne families had always worked for human rights.

The night before I had been interviewed by Pat Kenny on his RTÉ show. Advice on what to say had been offered by many people. I made up my mind to talk about my play rather than about my work in the Galway Magdalen Laundry.

'In an enclosed theatre space I imagined and wrote dialogue for four unmarried mothers, a Mother Superior, a white-veiled novice, and two orphans. I chose the contralto aria *He was Despised* from Handel's *Messiah* sung by Kathleen Ferrier for the opening and closing music,' I say.

Pat Kenny does not seem pleased because I refuse to say that I had locked the women away. Afterwards, in the hospitality room of RTÉ, he tells me that he had not heard of or seen *Eclipsed*.

'My play says everything,' I inform him.

After breakfast next morning, my cousin Bernadette and her husband drive me from Dublin to Longford town, where we join our cousins, the O'Beirnes.

Family Gathering

From the O'Beirne meeting place, the Longford Arms Hotel, we drive in convoy to Bornacoola Church. Mass is concelebrated there by my brother, Father Brendan, and Monsignor Denis Faul. This is the church in which my mother and father were married.

I can see them as they stood at that marble altar and pledged their lives to one another.

After Mass we visit Cloonmorris graveyard. Inside the iron gates stands a large white marble monument on which the names of our ancestors are engraved: great-grandfather John, great-aunts Mary, Lucy, Clare, great-uncles Denis, Stephen, Terence, Eugene, Charles, Thomas, grandfather John and grandmother Mary Ann.

My sister Philomena reads my poem written in memory of Clarenda, who is buried here with generations of O'Beirnes.

Your name, Clarenda O'Beirne,
died November 26, 1889, aged 54,
Your life-story carved on white marble
in Cloonmorris graveyard.
Your bone-dust mingles with clay colours
between the old monastery and Qenuven's Ogham Stone.

Beside the graveyard gate stands that Ogham Stone dedicated to Qenuven, a pagan goddess. Beyond the O'Beirne monument are the ruins of an ancient monastery.

There are layers of history here in this small area.

As I leave the graveyard, I look towards the O'Beirne monument and then look back towards the O'Farrell headstone. I imagine the sweaty efforts of grand-uncle-in-law John O'Farrell as he tried to disinter his dead wife, grand-aunt Clare, in order to re-bury her remains with his own family, the O'Farrells.

From Cloonmorris, we drive along by the River Shannon to the farmhouse in Clooneen. I open the side gate for cousin Gerite Woods and myself. We walk up into the high garden with its glory of flowering shrubs.

As I inhale their fragrance, I say a thank you to my own mother, who planted them.

On holiday here as a child, my father had told me that when the old moons died they fell down into this high garden and became big bowls of yellow jelly.

The Flankers, Drumsna, residence of grand-uncle Bernard O'Beirne J.P.

I had searched and searched between rose bushes, pampas grasses, sunflowers and forsythia. Should I continue my search?

We drive a short distance to the preserved ruins of Shannon View at Bun-an-Eas, where my grand-aunt Clare and her husband John O'Farrell had lived and died.

'At the beginning of the nineteenth century, our ancestors, the ex-seminarian, writer and explorer Eugene Francis O'Beirne, Thomas O'Beirne, surgeon to the British Army in the Curragh, and the adventurer Robert O'Beirne were born here in this stone house. Another cousin, Brigadier-General James O'Beirne, often visited here,' Mary O'Beirne tells us.[2]

We walk through the gateway and stand close to the walls.

'Did you hear about Charles O'Beirne, who returned from his world travels to Shannon View?' Gertie Woods says.

'No, but I'd like to hear that story.' I turn towards her.

'Charles arrived here with a trunk, which was double-locked. He kept it beside his bed. He always kept the keys on his person. Until the day he died, he was served the best of food, his clothes were laundered, shoes polished, socks darned. After his burial in Cloonmorris graveyard, they gathered here in Shannon View for the usual family meal.'

'But his trunk! Who opened it? What happened, Gertie?' another cousin interrupts.

'They all stood around the trunk, while my great-uncle John twisted the keys and–'

'What was in it? Tell me!' I say.

'It was full to the brim with …'

'With money!' a cousin exclaims.

'No! With old newspapers!' says Gertie.

'Only old newspapers! Oh! What happened then, Gertie?' another cousin asks.

'That night there was a bonfire, which could be seen from

---

[2] **Eugene Francis O'Beirne's** first book, *An Impartial View of the Internal Economy and Discipline of Maynooth College*, is reviewed and criticised in Jeremiah Newman's volume, *Maynooth and Georgian Ireland*.

Another cousin, **Brigadier-General James O'Beirne** (1840 – 1917) born Ballagh, Elphin, Co. Roscommon, with a Law Degree from St. John's College, played prominent part in American Civil War. He was awarded the Congressonial Medal for Bravery. He was also in charge of Lincoln's deathbed and was involved in the pursuit of Lincoln's assassin, John Wilkes Booth. He was active in Republican politics and he headed the immigration depot at Ellis Island.

Clooneen to Rooskey and across to the Hill of Mullagh!

'A bonfire of old newspapers! But that's a pity. They were probably his archives from all those countries he visited,' I insist. 'Yes. A great pity,' Gertie nods in agreement.

During our journey from Longford to Bornacoola, to Cloonmorris, to Clooneen and back again to Longford, we glimpse the silver of the River Shannon edged with stately reeds. We hear the music of its waters and breathe in its river smells, as it runs southwards towards Ardnacrusha, Labasheeda and Killadysert to meet the Atlantic Ocean.

In my mind's eye, I see Dad watch over my brother Brendan and myself at the shore of the River Shannon. Holding our small fishing rods, we wait and wait for a catch.

'We'll whisper ten Hail Marys and the fish will bite,' Brendan says softly.

'But we'll have to count the Hail Marys on our toes, because our fingers are holding our fishing rods,' I whisper.

Dad joins us in prayer.

'A fish, a fish!' shouts Brendan.

He draws in the line. We bend down to examine the little fish.

'It's only a baby fish!' I say.

'We should put this little trout back into the river. Its mother will be sad if we don't,' says Dad.

'Yes, Dad. Its mother will cry for her baby.' I nod my head.

'Tomorrow we'll try again and we might catch a big trout,' Dad says, as he carefully returns the fish to the viridian water.

I wave *Slán* to my River Shannon, then I close my eyes in silent prayer.

Back in the Longford Arms Hotel for lunch, members of the family stand at a rostrum and tell family stories. John O'Beirne presents our cousin, Gertie Woods, with an O'Beirne Coat of Arms crest.

After many congratulatory speeches, we say *Slán abhaile* and drive away to Galway. Others drive to their homes in Dublin, Dungannon, Lisnaskea, Drogheda, Sligo and Cork.

Grykes have grown richer in Burren limestone.

My sister, Philomena, at Cloonmorris
Graveyard.   Photo by Stephen Faul

Inquisition

A letter from the USA requests permission to produce *Eclipsed*. I'm shocked when I read the address; Salem

'That word, Salem, resonates with Puritan hysteria,' Eamon observes.

'Salem! Isn't that the place where, in 1692, people were accused of practising witchcraft. They were found guilty, brought to Gallows Hill and hanged. A Puritan Inquisition!' I say to Eamon.

My thoughts go back to that letter posted to me from Blackpool in England. Enclosed in a smaller envelope was my photograph graffitied with horns and witch symbols. I shiver as images of witches being burned to death in Europe come to me.

'As the smell of burning flesh fills my nostrils, I read aloud from one of Dad's encyclopedia. 'Five hundred women accused of witchcraft were burned at the stake in Geneva in 1515!'

I see Joan of Arc's body engulfed in flames outside the Cathedral of Rouen.

Later, I find out that the production of *Eclipsed* will go on in Salem, Oregon, not in Salem, Massachusetts, where the witchcraft hangings took place.

Eamon's Illness

The white-coated consultant reads paper files, then turns towards me and says, 'Your husband has a brain tumour.'
'A brain tumour? No. No!' I'm shocked.
'His brain is rotting away,' he continues as he shuffles the files.
I decide to visit the office of the Alzheimer's Society in Eglinton Street. There I'm given good advice.
For more than ten years since that diagnosis in February 1999, I take care of Eamon as his health worsens. During those years invitations to the opening nights of my stage play, *Eclipsed*, in Los Angeles, San Francisco, Miami, Tubingen, Ghent, Brussels, London, off-Broadway etc. are turned down without questioning.
Because of his loss of balance, he falls backwards frequently. If he falls on his way to the bathroom, I either keep him wrapped in duvets until morning, or, reluctantly, call our good neighbours for help.

During sleepless nights, I write this poem.

Sounds.
What words
can tell the pain
in the eyes,
in the face,
in the way
the body moves?
Make new sounds,
sounds never heard
before the first human
stood upright
and all words were pure.

Search for vowels, consonants
to lift and pull
against the force of gravity,
to draw up the skull,
the spinal column,
the long bones.
Find blessed sounds
to banish
that dark shape
waiting
at the foot
of the stairs.

I'm advised by other carers to take whatever help is offered to us. A fortnight's hospital respite is arranged for Eamon. If I had known then what was to come, I'd have refused all contact with the HSE.

On Eamon's return home, a HSE official calls. This is my first encounter with the HSE. Who asked them to call? Eamon is interviewed on his own. Why aren't we interviewed together? Before leaving, the HSE official turns to me and says, 'Your husband has certain rights. He could bring you to the Court of Human Rights in *Strasbourg*, if you place him in a nursing home against his will!'

Nursing home care has never been mentioned by me during the years I looked after Eamon. This has brought darkness into our home.

A few months later another respite arrangement is made for Eamon. Eamon objects to taking respite, but eventually agrees. He has his own room and is treated well by the nurses.

While I take this short break, our good neighbours, Frank and Joan Meagher, Ann and Gabe Walshe and their son, Neil, visit him. They bring him the usual supply of Players' un-tipped cigarettes, Tullamore Dew whiskey, cream crackers and his favourite juicy oranges with thin skins.

Midway during this respite period, I'm called to a meeting at the hospital. Have the medical staff discovered something more ominous in Eamon's deteriorating health? In case I'd be upset by bad news, I leave my car at home in College Road and ring for a taxi. The official meets me in the foyer and tells me to wait in the office until I'm called. The person responsible for older people and another official speak with Eamon on his own.

The official then accompanies me to a small room at the end of a corridor, where the two officials and Eamon are gathered. I give Eamon his favourite Werther's sweets and Players cigarettes.

The officials announce that they'll set up a package for Eamon.

'A package! But my husband mustn't be packaged! He's a human being!' I object.

'He can bring you to the court of human rights in Strasbourg if you put him in a nursing home against his will!' they repeat. Exhausted from years of caring for Eamon, I burst into tears. I sob and sob. I'm made to feel like a criminal. Haven't I read that similar tactics were used in Soviet Russia?

Eamon asks me to leave with him as he shuffles slowly out of the room. I'm too upset to move and I continue to sob.

'Look at him! He's able to move!' an official exclaims.

Eventually they stop their barrage of words and leave as if they hadn't inflicted any pain on another human being. Is this their usual method of working I wonder, as they hurry away to a hearty lunch.

Grykes are sharper and turloughs in Burren limestone are full of tears.

The official advises me to stay in the office until I've stopped sobbing. After approximately half an hour, she calls a taxi and I return home.

When a public health nurse calls to our house the following week, I tell her about my experience.

'Either myself or one of the other public health nurses should have been called to that meeting. We know both of you for a number of years and could have spoken on your behalf,' she insists.

'Why do I need someone to speak on my behalf? Why? I've done nothing wrong,' I protest.

My own health is damaged by that treatment. Some weeks later one of the public health nurses says that my cardiac troubles were intensified by that meeting. My GP, when I tell him I felt bullied, says, 'No. You were not bullied. You were tortured.'

Where were you, members of the HSE, during those years of broken sleep, when I sat up in bed and listened for Eamon's breathing?

Where were you, when the slightest noise made me fear he had fallen again on the bathroom stairs?

Where were you during those years of telephoning our neighbours to help me lift him back into bed?

Where were you during those calls for an ambulance to take him, as he moaned in pain, to hours of waiting in Accident and Emergency?

Where were you when Eamon left the hospital without permission on the evening before his surgery?

Who gave you permission to write a personal letter to my husband Eamon in his nursing home? Your letter instructed him to leave unaccompanied at 11am in a taxi booked by you. The HSE decrees that once Eamon leaves the nursing home that you have no further responsibility for his safety. The cause of an almost certain tragedy, how can you sleep at night?

Where were you when before visiting him in that special ward, having covered myself in protective overall and gloves, I ring a bell, and wait for permission to enter? Where were you then?

When I said, 'But he'll fall backwards down our stairs again', you answered, 'That's up to Eamon!'

On 18th January I visit Eamon in the nursing home. He promises to stay there until Easter, when the weather will have improved and he can sit under our laburnum tree in the garden and smoke his Players untipped cigarettes.

'You'll be like that famous painting by Paul Cezanne, *The Gardener Vallier*,' I say.

'Then I'll be able to sow lettuce and maybe a few potatoes instead of...

'Of course you will when your strength returns, Eamon. Don't let them annoy you.'

'No. They mix my head up. I'll have a little snooze now and then I'll have another few Players,' he replies.

As I walk to the door, I turn around and wave, but Eamon is fast asleep.

I find it too painful to focus on writing, except for a few broken sentences. My real diary notes will be stored in my archives.

Eamon is missing for forty-eight hours. Eventually, my sister, Philomena, discovers that he's in another nursing home. She takes me to visit him there. He's hospitalised on two occasions. In protective overall and gloves, I enter the special ward and try to console him. His condition does not improve and he returns to the nursing home.

We watch as Eamon receives the Last Rites. He passes away during the early hours of 1st March 2011.

Passing

1.10 am, Tuesday, 1ˢᵗ March
Bruised clouds wrap storm-black skies.
Loch an tSáile croons a requiem.

Our laburnum tree shivers,
gives a low moan,
crashes into our sleeping garden,
roots high in the air.

a phone-call splinters our lives.
On our maple tree
all through night-darkness,
a robin chants Alleluia, Alleluia.

Myself and Eamon in a snowy Galway.

April 2009: My Illness

'I cannot go to hospital! I've so much to do, I tell a doctor at the Medical Centre in Whitehall.

'You have no alternative', he replies. 'Your recent X-Ray shows that there's fluid in both of your lungs'. He draws two lung shapes on his writing pad and then fills in three-quarters of the left lung shape and half of the right lung shape.

'That's why you're so breathless'. He points to his drawings.

'No, no! I'm just very tired, very tired'.

'Do you smoke or did you ever smoke?'

'No. I've never smoked, but I'm a passive smoker. Eamon, my husband, smokes untipped Players cigarettes'.

'I see. Your heartbeat is racing. It's beating twice as fast as it should. You must go to hospital immediately'. He writes a note.

'I don't want to be left lying on a trolley for twenty-four hours in UCHG. I'd prefer to go to Doughiska Clinic', I tell him.

Having collected a travel bag from our home in College Road, Philomena drives me to Doughiska Clinic. I check in at the reception desk in the carpeted foyer, where a man plays a Beethoven Concerto on the grand piano. He switches on the pianola device and leaves for lunch in the first-floor-café.

'Yes. I have Voluntary Health Insurance', I answer as I sign forms. A plastic band with my name is put around my wrist, but I know who I am! This is my own body.

I'm wheeled through Accident and Emergency into a special area and placed in a corner bed. A nurse checks my blood pressure. She inserts an intra-venous drip into my left hand and attaches disks with wires to my chest. I hear loud throbbing.

'That's your own heartbeat', the nurse replies when I question her. Throb, throb.

Dr. Brendan O'Cochlain, cardiologist, tall and dressed in a white coat, stands beside my bed and informs me that my heart is struggling to clear my lungs.

'After about a month, we'll do a cardio-version on your heart and get it back to its normal rhythm,' he adds encouragingly.

Throb, throb, throb. Breathless.

More machines, more wires.

In a wheelchair, I'm moved to a two-bedded ward. From my bedside window, I watch cloud shapes move above swaying treetops.

Except for an occasional course of antibiotics for influenza, I've never had to take medication. My body is now bombarded by drugs. Cordarone, Warfarin, Lasix, Slow K. etc. Words new to my vocabulary are repeated by nurses.

'Sure, Patricia is never sick!' neighbours exclaim, when they hear that I'm in Doughiska Clinic.

'She's worn out from all those years of caring!' another neighbour remarks.

Blood samples taken from my arms are tested for INR, density of blood.

Discomfort of bed-linens on my limbs. I find the slightest pressure of sheets and coverlet intolerable. This is my own body. The body I have hardly been conscious of until now.

Nausea, nausea.

During the night I wake up to find the sheets under my left side are soaking in blood. Half-awake and instead of ringing my bell, I roll out of bed, shuffle to the door and call the night nurse.

'Is this blood coming from my left lung?' I ask.

'That blood has come from your left hand. The intra-venous drip has slipped,' she comforts me and secures it back in place.

She changes my bed linens, my pyjamas and dressing gown.

'Thank you, nurse.' I try to smile.

Throb, throb.

Nausea. Nausea.

'These disks are attached to machines, which register your heartbeat upstairs in the cardiologist's office.' She inserts new batteries into a small gadget attached to the wired disks.

'Your heart condition is under constant observation,' she continues as she checks my pulse, blood pressure and takes my temperature.

'Thank you, nurse.' My own body, my own heart. I've never taken time to be conscious of them. Days and nights merge.

Clatter of dishes on trays, trays on trolleys, hospital sounds. Breakfast, lunch and dinner are brought by outside caterers.

'Not more food! No thank you. No!' I turn my head away from tray after tray.

Thousands of starving children would survive for weeks on this rejected food, I say to myself.

Throb, throb. Nausea. The tall cardiologist arrives at my bedside. Now silhouetted against the moving clouds and swaying treetops, he checks my pulse and says, 'Your heart is still racing!'

'What kind of lifestyle will I have from now on, Doctor?'

'You can live a normal life, but you must have your blood checked twice weekly. That's a nuisance, I know. After about one month, we'll do that cardio-version to bring your heart back to its normal rhythm.'

'Will that be dangerous?' I look straight into his eyes.

'Not at all,' he replies.

'Will I be allowed a glass of wine with dinner when I go home?'

'Yes, you will.'

I do not know then that my sense of taste will be distorted and I'll find even the finest wine undrinkable.

'This is Cordarone for your heart.' A nurse, her blonde hair peeping from under her hairband, offers tablets in a plastic container.

'Cordarone? One of my favourite red wines is called Amarone, nurse,'

'This is Slow K to replace the potassium you lose because of the Lasix,' another nurse says as she offers me a large orange pill in a plastic container.

'You must drink plenty of water,' she adds as I try to swallow.

I cough and splutter, almost choking as the Slow K refuses to slide down my oesophagus. The nurse comes to my assistance.

'Thank you, nurse. Thank you. You are all very kind.'

I inhale oxygen through tubes inserted in my nostrils.

My mother holds me in her arms. My swollen throat hurts. I cannot swallow. The room sizzles.

'Her temperature is very high, much too high,' the doctor, his bushy eyebrows twirling over gold-framed spectacles, says as he prepares a syringe.

The injection is very painful, but I cannot scream because of my septic throat.

'Hot whiskeys, plenty of hot whiskeys,' the doctor continues. 'I'll call again tonight.'

'She's only four years old,' my Dad says. There are tears in his eyes.

'We'll keep her in isolation here at home,' the doctor puts the syringe away in his leather bag. Every time I open my eyes, it seems that this kind doctor and the special nurse are drinking hot whiskies too.

Sizzle, sizzle. My bed seems to float.

No mother to hold me now, no Dad to sing me to sleep.

Since that childhood illness, hot whiskey, its taste and smell, makes me nauseous.

Visitors come carrying bouquets of flowers and books. I'm too tired to read.

My ankles and feet swell, are now too big for my size-five shoes. An angry rash appears on my neck, chest, arms and legs. Size-six shoes and sandals are bought, but barely fit me. Throb, throb.

My G P checks my medication and asks if I have added anything new to my diet. He changes me from Cordarone X 200 mgs tablets and writes a prescription for Sotacor 80 mgs. He also prescribes Lasix 75 mgs and Slow K to reduce the swelling.

'You must continue to take Warfarin. Two mgs three times daily until your next blood test,' he adds as he prints out a prescription.

'Warfarin! But that's rat poison!' I object.

'Yes. But it's an anticoagulant. Your blood must be tested twice weekly. Keep this Anticoagulant Therapy Record with you at all times.' He hands me a booklet.

Nightmares continue to upset me. I wander through huge spaces surrounded by derelict buildings. Alone, I cannot find a way out or see another human being. I wake up drenched in sweat.

Nausea, nausea. All of my senses are distorted, my hearing, my sense of taste. Black spots drift before my eyes. My limbs are weak. The coughing persists.

Nausea. Rat poison, rat poison.

Kate, a visitor, remarks, 'That woman, the one who defaced your photograph with arrows and witches' symbols and got her cousin to post it to you from Blackpool, must be busy again. Maybe she stuck more arrows into your heart and lungs.'

Kate splashes holy water over my body. I make the Sign of the Cross with reverence.

'She could have made a manikin in your image and performed her black magic on it!'

'Oh, my God, that's a horrible thought, Kate. Pagan superstition! Please don't talk like that.' I turn away as I say, 'The line between superstition and religion is very thin.'

Day after day, night after night, I lie in bed, eyes closed and listen to Lyric FM.

Carl Jenkins' wonderful *Agnus Dei* drifts over my body.

Agnus Dei qui tollis peccata mundi, dona nobis pacem. Peace, peace, peace.

Benedictus from Mozart's *Requiem in D Minor*, the haunting wonder of Plain Chant sung by Cistercian monks, Pergolese's *Stabat Mater*, St. *Patrick's Breastplate, I arise today.*

In spite of the fact that she is recovering from breast cancer, my sister Philomena looks after me durng my first weeks at home. With help from my sister Theresa, she cooks meals, collects my medication from Eyre Square Pharmacy and stays over every night.

Eamon still insists that he is able to look after me himself, though he is assessed as being of a High Level of Dependency.

Throb, throb.

My other sister, Claire, comes from her home in Leitrim and takes over from Philomena. Eamon is not pleased. This situation is not helping me to recover.

A visiting nurse tells me that Parkinson's Disease is probably the cause of his moodiness.

Warfarin, nausea, rat poison, nausea.

Months earlier, I had promised to read for ACIL, an International Conference on Irish Literature, in Galway City Library. Not knowing now whether I'll collapse or not, I go there, stand up on my swollen feet and read an excerpt from my *Memoir with Grykes and Turloughs*.

That skin rash and swelling disappear and reappear.

Water appears and disappears from Turloughs in Burren limestone.

During my twice-weekly visits to the Medical Centre, Sarah O'Hara, a very pleasant and compassionate nurse, checks my blood by pricking my middle finger-tip with a needle-like instrument attached to a small machine.

'This Coaguchek machine registers the INR, the density of your blood. The result determines how many mgs of Warfarin you need to take until your next blood test', she answers my questions. 'We'll look after you', she smiles. I wish all of the HSE nurses and personnel who had advised me about Eamon were so caring, I say.

Rat poison, nausea, rat poison, nausea.

My cardiologist calls me to the Doughiska Clinic. My heart must be given a jump-start in order to bring it back to its normal rhythm.

At 10 a.m. and fasting from midnight, I'm brought to the Intensive Care Unit.

When the result of my blood test comes back, a nurse takes me to a special room for an Echocardiogram. I recognise the Filipino technician there.

'You tested me on my first day here in hospital.'

She nods and smiles as she covers my chest with a jelly-like substance, attaches disks to different areas, then moves a small machine over my heart and lungs.

I dress again and the nurse guides me back to Intensive Care, where there are a number of anxious-looking men with disks and wires attached to their chests.

The nurse leads me into a special cubicle.

'Please undress and lie on this bed,' she says.

Should I run away? There are a number of large machines around me, also a television-shaped machine above the bed. One nurse takes my blood pressure, another wires me up to the strange machines. Nurses come and go. I'm like an astronaut on my way into space, but I'm trapped in my sick body. Throb, throb.

Dr. O'Cochlain, cardiologist, a serious expression on his face, asks me to sign a consent form. 'Call the anaesthetist now, nurse.' He takes the signed form, checks the numbers on the machine above my head and leaves. Will I survive? Is it goodbye pain, goodbye rat poison? Is it goodbye nightmares?

Throb, throb.

The nurse telephones the anaesthetist and leaves the cubicle. On her return, she checks the machines. Suddenly, she exclaims, 'Your heart has returned to its normal rhythm!'

She leaves quickly to consult the cardiologist. He hurries in, checks the machines, smiles and says, 'You may get up, dress and go home now! Your heart rhythm is normal. You do not need this cardio-version!' There are smiles all around.

'It's a miracle! A miracle, thank you, God,' I say as I hurry back towards the reception area. Even the men who are waiting for cardio-versions in the other cubicles smile as I pass.

My sisters, thinking that I'd need to sleep for a number of hours after the anaesthetic, are not yet in the waiting area. I'm starving.

Upstairs in the restaurant, I devour toast covered in butter and marmalade and drink strong tea. My sisters arrive and are overjoyed by my good news.

'We must celebrate! *Sláinte!*' We lift our cups of tea.

Sculptures

'We're going to visit Granny O'Beirne in Longford,' Daddy says as he puts on his tweed overcoat.

'Oh, please, can I go and Brendan too?' I catch the end of his sleeve.

'Cáit will look after you, love.' Mammy hands us a Crunchie Chocolate Bar and a Flake Bar. 'Here are your favourites.'

'But I don't like that new *cailín aimsire*! She picks her nose and doesn't wash her hands! She's not as nice as Bríd,' I object.

'Be sure to offer Cáit some of your chocolate,' Mammy and Daddy say as they hug us. We watch them get into the hackney as we bite into the chocolate.

'I'm not giving Cáit any of my Crunchie,' I announce and, mouth full, I hurry into the sittingroom. I climb on an armchair beside the mahogany bookcase.

'Help me to take down one of Daddy's big books, Brendan!' I reach out unsteadily for a book.

'Which book? Aren't they all the same size?' He wipes melted chocolate from his hands.

'I don't know. Try the one at the end of that shelf first,' I point.

'It's very heavy.' He gasps for breath and pulls it down.

'They're all called en-cy-clop-ed-ias. That's what Daddy says.' I turn pages.

'Oh, look at those people! They've taken all their clothes off!'

We giggle as we point to the sculptures' body parts.

'Look! She has a big pimple!' I shout. 'And here's another big fat pimple!'

'No! I think it's a boil,' Brendan says.

'No! No! It's a very huge big fat pimple, silly!'

Cáit, who is washing cutlery in the kitchen, hears us. With a dishcloth in one hand, she comes in, peers over our shoulders and shouts, 'They're dirty pictures you is looking at! I'll tell ye're Mammy and Daddy, when they come back. It's a *Peaca Mór* to be lookin' at them. Ye'll have to tell that in confession, or ye'll burn in Hell forever and ever, the two o' ye!'

She covers the opened book with her dishcloth and closes her eyes.

'*Peaca Mór!*' she repeats, opens her eyes and puts the book back on a higher shelf.

Truth disappears like water from Turloughs in Burren limestone.

The following Saturday, I, a seven-year-old sinner, go into the dark confession box.

It smells of cigarettes and onions.

'Bless me, Father, for I have sinned,' I tell the shadowy Canon when he pulls back the shutter. 'It's two weeks since my last confession.' My voice is shaky.

'And what are your sins, my child?'

'I - I looked at bad pictures in a big book, Canon.'

'What did you say? Speak up, child!'

'I looked at bad pictures in a big book, Canon!'

'How many times did you look at those bad pictures, my child?'

'I don't know, Canon,' I answer through my tears.

'No absolution! I will not give you absolution unless you truly promise never to look at those pictures again. Do you promise?' he shouts.

'Yes, yes, Canon, I promise!'

'For your penance say two decades of the rosary. Now say a sincere Act of Contrition.'

While I whisper, 'O my God, I am heartily sorry for all my sins,' the Canon mumbles words like *absolvo* in Latin, then makes the sign of the cross and closes the shutter quickly.

I stumble out of darkness into candlelight. Mrs. McGurk, dressed in a black hat and belted coat, catches me by my plaits.

'What did you get for your penance, *a stóirín*?' Her white bushy eyebrows make rings around her spectacles.

'Two sincere decades of the rosary, Mrs. McGurk.'

'Run up there and say your two sincere decades this minute!' She pushes me towards the altar. I kneel on white marble and sob as I count the Hail Marys on my fingers.

At home later, Daddy notices my tear-stained face.

'What's wrong, love? There's great news about Granny O'Beirne. She's getting better and she'll be coming to see us soon.'

'But Daddy, Cáit told us it was a *Peaca Mór* to look at the statues without any clothes in your En-cyclo-ped-ias. And I had to tell the Canon in confession.' I sob again.

'A *Peaca Mór*! Such nonsense! I'll have a word with Cáit and with the Canon too! The Vatican is full of sculptures, statues without clothes!'

'And Mrs. McGurk listened outside the confession box. She'll tell everyone about my two decades of the rosary!'

'Nobody believes a word she says! Didn't you hear the story about herself and Maggie Ward, love?' He tries to make me smile. 'Maggie brought her message bag filled with bottles of draught Guinness into the confession-box. Just as she began to list out her sins, the paper corks of the bottles began to pop in the heat! The smell of Guinness filled the church. That was the end of confessions for that weekend. Then Mrs. McGurk told the others in the queue that they'd all get General Absolution. She took off her feathery hat, and sat with Maggie Ward in the side-aisle of the church. Together they drank what was left of the Guinness. The Canon was furious when they asked him to join them. 'Willful waste makes woeful want!' said Mrs. McGurk. She has more on her mind than your two decades of the rosary, love.'

'So, is that why Brendan told me he got General Absolution from the Canon, Daddy?'

'Yes, love – General Absolution according to Mrs. McGurk! I'm sure the Canon couldn't sit for hours in that smelly confession box. And he doesn't drink Guinness. Mrs. McGurk, if we can believe her, told me while flicking her mascara-thick eyelashes that he prefers a glass of Tullamore Dew. She blames him for dumping her feathery hat.'

London. The Sixth Day of My Week

Outside the main entrance to the Tate Gallery I stand in a half circle with four other would be sculptors. I wave goodbye to Eamon, who goes off to visit a friend in the Irish Club.

A denim-clad instructor comes out and presents each of us with an apron, a supply of modelling clay, a tub of water, a wooden stand, and an array of sculpting tools.

'You're free to experiment with this clay,' he announces.

The morning sun highlights our excited faces as we take fistfuls of moist clay and slap them on to the wooden stands. We close our minds to passing traffic.

Another denim-clad instructor arrives with wooden splints, which will enable us to support the modelling clay. He whistles tunelessly as he moves around. I try to work in a contemporary fashion, but gradually a classical head and shoulders insist on forming as I tweak and push clay.

'Have you worked with clay before?' the whistler asks as he stands beside me.

'Yes, some years ago.'

'It's difficult to work in public!' he remarks and walks to the next apron-clad modeller. The first instructor moves near and watches. I wince as a clay ear slips from my terracotta skull-shape.

'I can never work, while another person watches,' I say.

He moves away.

Images of sculptures from the Cyclades come to mind, primitive shapes formed by sculptors thousands of years ago, but now on display in the British Museum.

I build up more clay to form a forehead and scrape out hollows for eye-sockets.

'Last summer I spent a week at a Henry Moore Major Exhibition here,' I tell the whistler, who has returned. 'Great human shapes, his

Mother and Child bronzes, his carved Reclining Figures.'

'His King and Queen bronze from that exhibition now looks out over the moors in Scotland! Have you seen it?' he asks.

'I admired it when it was sited outside the Hayward, but I've never been to Scotland.'

'You should visit Glenkiln,' he advises.

'I'm from Ireland!' I say with pride. 'In County Clare, my native county, we have the natural sculpted landscape of the Burren. Extraordinary works called grykes were cut into rock by retreating ice caps as they moved out into the Atlantic Ocean. Huge boulders, called erratics, were dropped across the limestone landscape from melting glaciers. If your conscious control doesn't intrude, you may see an enormous Sphinx gazing out towards America, or sleeping limestone elephants wrapped in purple rain clouds or a gigantic tiger poised above Black Head!'

'Henry Moore would have enjoyed your country! He used natural, organic sources for his work.'

'Yes, I was fascinated by his studio collections, pebbles, shells, eroded rocks, bone fragments, vertebrae, flotsam and jetsam. Here and there were mounds of black plasticene.'

'You can now model your own Celtic Sphinx from that clay. I'll be back before lunch break,' he smiles and moves to the next modeller.

With my terracotta-coloured hands I form a clay nose, a clay chin and clay neck, but I cannot breathe a spirit into my creation. Instead of a Sphinx, another image insists on staying in my mind. It's of the tobacco-stained teeth and blue-rinsed hair of our local fortune-teller, as she walks through Galway's Saturday Market Mrs. Loftus, our coalman's mother, as she walks through Galway's Saturday Market, chain-smokes her Woodbines and says, 'We're here for the good time, not for the long time, *a stór!*'

It's the sixth day of my week. My clay model will one day become a layer of dust on the face of the earth.

Sidney Nolan in Ireland

We're gathered in the art gallery of University College, Galway during the Australia-Ireland Conference. When introduced to Sir Sidney Nolan, I say, 'I very much admired your Ned Kelly series of paintings, Sir Sidney. I was so lucky to see them and your screen-prints, etchings and lithographs in an international exhibition a few years ago.'

The great Australian painter is delighted, as he smiles, bows and shakes my hand.

On the walls of the art gallery his huge canvases glow with portraits of *The Wild Geese*, the Irish soldiers, under the command of Patrick Sarsfield, who fled to the Continent after the Treaty of Limerick. Professor T. P. O'Neill declares open this special exhibition: 'We welcome this giant of twentieth-century Australian artists, this visual mythmaker, whose Ned Kelly and Burke-and-Wills paintings express in extraordinary colour the outback history of Australia. Now we are privileged to see his Irish historical work, his Wild Geese Paintings.' As he finishes his speech, Professor O'Neill says, 'Before emigrating to Australia, the artist's great-grandfather had lived close to Ailwee Caves in Ballyvaughan, Co. Clare. Planning permission to build a new house near the site of the original farmhouse for Sir Sidney and Lady Nolan has been refused by Clare Planning Authorities. This causes great distress to him and indeed to all of us.'

'There's no welcome here for a returned Wild Goose!' an Australian Durack remarks.

Grykes and Turloughs will now fill with the tears of rejected emigrants.

Before we leave the art gallery a member of the Galway-Australia Committee makes the following announcement: 'Tomorrow,

Wednesday, is Burke Day of the Conference. His Excellency, Mr. Brian Burke, will lead us to St. Cleran's near Craughwell, the home of Robert O'Hara Burke. On our return to Galway City, there'll be a public showing of a film on the first crossing of the Australian Continent led by Robert O'Hara Burke.

Because Sir Sidney is very interested in horse racing, we're organising a group to travel with him to the Thursday Meeting in Ballinrobe. Will those interested please write their names on this clip-board.'

On Thursday morning Sir Sidney, in a grey gabardine and a tweed cap, sits with us on a bus, which is of an uncertain vintage. He autographs our race cards as we sing our way on stone-edged roads through Headford, Shrule and Kilmaine.

Once a jolly swagman camped by a billabong
Under the shade of a coolabah tree.
And he sang as he watched
and waited 'til his billy boiled
You'll come a Waltzing Matilda with me.
Waltzing Matilda. Waltzing Matilda,
You'll come a waltzing Matilda with me.

'Our bus is waltzing too!' the Australian Durack exclaims.

This humble man, this great Australian artist, joins us in singing 'The Wild Colonial Boy'.

'There was a Wild Colonial Boy,
Jack Duggan was his name.
He was born and raised in Ireland
In a place called Castlemaine ....'

'Folklore holds that Jack Duggan was a forerunner to Ned Kelly,' a local historian whispers in my ear.

At Ballinrobe Races, as Sidney Nolan studies form and places bets, we don't know that the race of his extraordinary life would shortly come to a finish.

Sidney Nolan died in London in 1992.

I search for my race card with his autograph. So far I've failed to find it.

UCG Gallery exhibition 'Wild Geese' by Sir Sidney Nolan.

Requiem of Love

I'm delighted when the Arts Council awards me a Bursary in Drama for my monologue, which has the title, *Requiem of Love*.

I use the voice of a male alcoholic, who has a slight resemblance to a granduncle-in-law of mine. The location is a graveyard near the remains of an ancient church at dawn of Good Friday.

John O'Kelly, the alcoholic, had brawled his way through Australia, sobering up on Good Friday each year to write letters, he never posted, to his wife, Nora. Instead he carries them around, wrapped in an Irish tricolour. He now stands at Nora's graveside. He'd left her many years before, after being accused of a hit-and-run death. Nora was left alone to raise their children, Jane and Bernard.

'Why Good Friday?' an academic emails from the USA.

'I see John O'Kelly as a Calvary-like figure, at one side of the Crucifed, repentant, and about to be redeemed', I reply.

When Michael Diskin, Manager of the Town Hall Theatre in Galway, phones to say he wishes to produce my monologue, I'm very excited. We ask Caroline FitzGerald to direct. Donncha Crowley is cast as John O'Kelly. I make a number of mourner-puppets, to represent the McAllister in-laws of John O'Kelly. Because of my lifelong interest in and love of the *Esker Riada*, we give the title *Esker Riada* to our new production company.

I book a rehearsal space in the United Arts Club, Dublin, where I meet Caroline and Donncha Crowley. Before rehearsal begins, I walk down the stairs, which has been washed, slip and twist my left ankle.

'Break a leg! I've come all the way from Galway by train and taxi without any trouble and now look at me!' I say as they cover my ankle with bags of ice cubes.

Back in Galway, on crutches and not allowed to drive, I take a taxi every morning to the Town Hall Theatre. Caroline and I design the set.

'I've brought along the remains of that muslin gauze we used for *Stained Glass at Samhain*. We'll drape some of it over a strong wooden frame for the McAllister monument,' I say.

'But first I'll print the list of deceased McAllisters on it.' I prepare black paint and use a small sable brush.

'Place two of your male mourner-puppets under the gauze. They'll be barely visible,' Caroline directs. 'The monument should be at a slight angle upstage left.'

'I've rented a number of plastic wreaths from College Road Florists. My sister, Philomena, bought a whitethorn bush and a bag of peat moss in the Garden Centre. She gave me this blue dress, which can symbolise Nora O'Kelly's body.' I show Caroline the dress.

'Perfect! Lovely colour!' Caroline replies as Donncha Crowly walks on stage.

'Will this rucksack suit you?' I ask as he helps lift the whitethorn and peat upstage.

'Fine! Thanks. I'll give it a worn-out look later.' He hums *Stabat Mater* and fills the rucksack with nightlights, white napkins and a box of matches.

The Renoir painting, *Les Parapluies*, inspires me to group my mourner-puppets under large black umbrellas suspended upstage right.

'The umbrellas must hang by invisible strings, some high, some low, but the mourner-puppets do not touch the stage floor. We'll need fishing line for them,' I tell Jane, the stage manager.

'I'll buy some in Freeney's of High Street at lunch time,' she replies.

'*Les Parapluies, Les Parapluies*,' I repeat.

'Coca Cola instead of wine in this *Chatauneuf du Pape* bottle' Caroline directs with a smile. 'It's for the picnic on Nora's grave after you've thrown these wreaths into that dustbin, Donncha.' We arrange the plastic wreaths at the foot of the monument.

'Plastic. Plastic! I'll order a bouquet of seven fresh white roses for the foot of the grave,' I say as we cover parts of Nora's blue dress with peat moss.

'Nora O'Kelly, who died of cancer, has been buried in the McAllister grave earlier on Holy Thursday,' I announce. Donncha continues to hum *Stabat Mater.*

Tears fill turloughs in Burren limestone.

'The umbrellas cover sections of the female mourner-puppets' bodies, but will show a number of black skirts with fashionable shoes attached. The end of a mink-like coat will peep from under a smaller umbrella and a fashionable handbag under another.

'*Les Parapluies. Les Parapluies,*' I tell Jane when she returns. She nods in agreement.

'And put the whitethorn downstage left at a lower level. It should be in bloom,' I continue.

Under the whitethorn and parallel to the McAllister grave, we decorate a grave-shaped peat moss rectangle with primroses and bluebells.

'Where will I put this dustbin, Caroline?' Donncha asks.

'Downstage right,' she replies.

'I've got the *Úna Bhán* tape from Grand Airs of Conamara here, Caroline!' I say.

'Give it to Michael at the light-and-sound desk. He'll look after the other effects in your script, the tolling bell, the sound of a car passing and dawn chorus. But the *Stabat Mater, Salve Regina* and *An Droighneán Donn* will be sung by Donncha,' Caroline replies.

Requiem of Love is premiered at the Town Hall Theatre, Galway on 22nd November 2005. On Saturday morning Caroline rings me to say that the production gets a very good review from Patrick Lonergan in *The Irish Times.* In tears I tell her that my sister Philomena has telephoned from hospital saying that she has been diagnosed with breast cancer.

'I'm sure they've got it in time,' Caroline replies. 'We'll keep up the prayers.'

'Thank you very much. I appreciate your concern.'

'Here is the *Irish Times* review. It might help,' Caroline reads aloud.

> *Patricia Burke Brogan's plays have always seemed a little*
> *ahead of their time ... But although Burke Brogan is*
> *exploring new territory here, the moral generosity and*
> *painterly sensibility of her earlier plays remain evident,*
>
> *Burke Brogan presents to us a man whose life has been*
> *ruined because of his own weaknesses – but, by using tightly*
> *constructed images of forgiveness and transformation, she also*
> *leaves open the possibility of redemption for her character.*
>
> *Requiem of Love therefore manages to be rich without being*
> *dense.*
>
> *It draws on a range of allusions to song, visual art, the*
> *natural world, and other cultures' funeral rituals, but never*
> *loses narrative impetus ... the script's haunting tone ... creates*
> *a strong, lingering contrast between O'Kelly's hopeless situation*
> *and the beauty of the language used to describe it.*
>
> *Dr Patrick Lonergan*

Requiem of Love tours to the Pavilion Theatre, Dun Laoghaire in December 2005.

The script of *Requiem of Love*, published by *Wordsonthestreet*, is launched during Cúirt International Festival of Literature on 27 April, 2006 in the Town Hall Theatre.

Requiem of Love is presented during Project 06 Arts Festival Galway July 2006 and in Bewley's Café Theatre, Grafton Street, Dublin from 5 February to 3 March 2007.

Theatre Critic Emer O'Kelly in her review writes: 'She weaves a lyrical web of disappointed hopes, fierce love, and the roaring express train that has been Irish life in the past 20 years ... It's a hell of a panorama and Burke Brogan manages it with skill, accuracy ... without soft-pedalling the crudities of modern vulgarity and self-forgiving mawkishness. It's a well-balanced piece of theatre.'

Theatre Critic Therese McKenna writes: 'The story is both old-fashioned and modern: on the one hand focusing on the undying Irish concern for land, respectability, class and religion and on the other hand highlighting the fascination with mobile phones, environmental destruction and rampant crass consumerism. But mostly this is a love story. ..... The words Burke Brogan uses to paint the scene are heavy with symbolism and magic and each prop almost seems to have religious import.'

Musical

The shrillness of the telephone rips through the night. Holding my breath, I reach out and lift the blackness of the receiver.

'Hello. Yes,' I gasp in fear of bad news.

'Hello, Patricia. It's Martin Murphy. I'm ringing from our restaurant in New York City. A group of us are discussing our dream of producing a musical. From your powerful play, *Eclipsed*, of course! What do you think?'

'Oh, *Eclipsed*. I relax a little as I hear the rattle of cutlery in the background and the hum of merrymakers.

'An *Eclipsed* musical! My friend Rosa here beside me is from New Mexico. She's a composer and she loves your play, Patricia. We attended the off-Broadway production together last night.'

'Thanks very much.' I push another pillow under my head.

'Who's ringing at such an hour?' Eamon grumbles.

'Just New York City. It's OK, Eamon.'

'Have you still got the film rights, Patricia?' Martin's voice is anxious.

'No. The film rights of the play are gone!'

'I told you they'd rob you. What about our musical?'

'It's the middle of the night here in Galway! I'll think about it.'

'Apologies for disturbing you. But this is a great chance for all of us. I missed investing in Riverdance because I didn't move fast enough! Now John Blake, an attorney, here beside me too, is very interested in this musical. John and myself with you, Patricia, will form a production company. He'll draw up a two-year contract and send it on to you.'

'I'm not sure, but I'll read the contract when it arrives.'

'I'm going down for a smoke.' Eamon rolls out of bed.

'Take it easy on the stairs, Eamon. Hold the banisters!'

'Rosa, my lady-composer, says that Maria, her librettist friend in

New Mexico, and herself will start work on what they call the book immediately, Martin continues.

'The book?' I ask, but with an ear for Eamon's footsteps.

'Yes. Maria says that term will be new to us Irish.'

'Huhh! One of those, is she?'

'She's an OK lady, Patricia! She and Rosa will have lots of questions for you.'

'More questions! Send on that contract and I'll read it, Martin. Enjoy yourselves. Goodnight.' I replace the receiver and snuggle into the duvet, but I'm still worrying about Eamon's balance on the stairs.

Later that summer, Martin and Rosa visit Galway City. She presents me with recordings of two of her compositions, *Brigit's Song* and *Mother Victoria's Song*, saying, 'These compositions are my property and are only to be used for my musical!'

'These are excellent songs, Patricia. For our musical only!' Martin adds.

Truth disappears like water from turloughs in Burren limestone.

Months go by as I email answers to New Mexico. I post copies of the BBC documentary *Washing away the Stain* and the RTÉ radio interviews on *Eclipsed* to New York. Before the two-year contract runs out, Martin telephones saying that he'd like it extended. It seems easier to agree. More phone calls and emails. Maria's emails become more arrogant.

Just as the extended contract runs out, Martin, composer Rosa, attorney John and librettist Maria fail to agree on business matters. The romance between Rosa and Martin ends. Maria telephones me from New Mexico. 'Restaurateur Martin Murphy and attorney John Blake are strutting around Manhattan posing as producers.'

Martin telephones, 'Send on another copy of that BBC documentary asap, Patricia.'

More emails from Rosa and a rant from Maria. Martin telephones again,

'Sting's secretary is dining here in my restaurant. *Fields of Gold* Sting, Patricia! A wonderful contact. Also, I've spoken to another top NY attorney. He's very interested and could invest. He'll send you a new contract, sign it and send it back asap.'

More emails, more telephone calls. When this third contract runs out, I write, 'I'm no longer interested in an *Eclipsed* musical, Martin. I've moved on to a different type of work.'

There are no more middle-of-the-night phone calls. No more emails.

Brigit's Song and *Mother Victoria's Song* rest silently in my studio. On 23 August 2012, Raquel Yossiffon telephones from New Mexico. To celebrate her birthday, she has decided to produce a musical of *Eclipsed* in New Mexico. She plans to tour it to Texas and Los Angeles.

I reply that if she sends me the necessary legal forms, I'll give her permission to go ahead with the production.

There was another call from Raquel at the end of Novemebr 2013 with the same result. On 20 December there is another call from Raquel. She asks for a copy of the Rights Option Agreement etc.

Since then there has been no contact from Raquel.

In my studio.

Décollage

Because of the stress of caring for Eamon, I know that my health is deteriorating. I decide not to wait for a publishing date for *Décollage* from Salmon Poetry, so I'm very pleased when Wordsonthestreet publish my *New and Selected Poems*. I choose one of my own paintings, *Where The River Meets The Sea*, for the cover design.

Award-winning crime writer Ken Bruen writes an introduction to my collection. I quote: 'Her body of work is quite astonishing, from her plays to her poems ... she is consistently startling, surprising and above all a true artist. Few poets can blend the commonplace with sheer bursts of pure spirituality and the language like the best art ... grows on you gradually until you rush back to the pages, see if what you realize is true, that here is a master-class in poetry.'

Sculptor John Behan is guest speaker at the launch in Galway Museum on 18 October 2008. I quote:

In Décollage Patricia Burke Brogan has produced a seminal work of sincerity and artistry which proclaims a unique vision.

Each poem in Décollage is distinct in itself yet related to an ongoing pattern of belief and conviction. The poems reflect the thoughts and feelings, embracing millennia, from the monk of Corcomroe to the young who are dying daily in Afghanistan – who are also related to the Gallagh Bog Body in Dublin's Archaeological Museum. There is a sublety of expression and capability, which seems to me to be an indication of a spirit which is all-embracing and beyond the accepted range of the usual literary norm.

Patricia Burke Brogan is an accomplished painter and graphic artist – her love of colour is expressed directly in many poems – as Patrick Kavanagh said, To name the names is enough. The poet mentions for instance – blood colours, crimsons and magenta – terracotta tiles – blasts of dirt-white – shredded crimsons – siennas, burnt umbers, ultramarines, ochres – golden tabernacles, lacquered ceilings – bone-dust of Normans whitens the air – he fell amongst cobalts and ultramarines.

Pilgrims-splodged furze, cadmium and saffron.

Tomb – I've lost him, I've lost my lover – my last painting – we offer chrome yellow, burnt sienna, vermilion – warm umber. Haiku – Camille Souter paints herring flames on a white plate. Picasso eats lobster.

She weaves words and images in her own magical poetic way. She looks into the past to see the present and the future and at times the picture is bleak. It is the combination of sound, colour and landscape, image and meaning which is the strength of her poetry – her gentle yet profound understanding of all the elements that go to make up a poem.

It can be truly said of Patricia Burke Brogan that she is a renaissance person, multi-talented, aware of nature and the frailty of human desires and wishes.

Her work is founded on an understanding of the pagan past, the beauty of Irish Christian art and the spirituality that underpins it.

She is an outstanding playwright whose work has travelled over many continents. Her etchings have been recognised by major awards, yet she remains a modest working artist, a sure indication of a powerful inner belief. In a quotation from Samuel Beckett, To be an artist is to fail, as no other dare fail, at the beginning of her magnificent poem Etched Torso, she outlines a credo that should be constantly in the forefront of all artists – yet one must go on. Again to quote Patrick Kavanagh, To be a poet and not to know the trade, To be a lover yet to repel all women, Twin ironies by great saints are made, The agonising pincer jaws of heaven; is at the core of all poetic expression and I feel that Patricia Burke Brogan in her own way expresses this constant dilemma between the human and the profane with great conviction.

We have here amongst us an artistic talent touched by genius who has not been at all recognised, a multifaceted creator, who deserves our heartfelt thanks.

Dunmore

Mom and Dad buy me a bicycle with shiny wheels and red handlebars. After many wobbles and a few falls, I gain courage to cycle along by the river as far as Currabell.

Later, I push up over Cuckoo Hill to visit a nesting coot.

'You mustn't disturb those birds,' Dad says. 'They might desert their eggs.' I visit the nest again, but keep my distance.

In an old garage near Howley's Bar, my brother and I put on our own story-plays. An older boy directs a film show with the help of a carriage lamp.

'A dangerous game, a fire hazard,' one of the Gardaí reports to Dad.

'Thank you very much. I'll look after that.'

Dad and Mom make plans.

'We're getting a real piano from Piggotts' Music Shop in Dublin!' I boast to my pals, the Fahys and Mooneys. I then jump into the river and show off my swimming skills.

My excitement grows when the piano arrives, is unpacked and placed in our sitting room. I touch the ivory keys gently and listen, eyes closed, to the overtones.

'You and Brendan will take piano lessons from Sister Florence in the Convent,' Mom says.

'One theory lesson and one practical lesson every week,' Dad adds.

'And you'll practise every evening after homework!'

'Yes, Mom.' I sit on our red piano stool and pretend I'm a concert pianist. Dissonance crashes through my fingers.

I breathe in the wax and incense smells of the convent parlour as, seated at the rosewood piano, I play the five-finger exercise.

'Look at the sheet music, not at your fingers, Patricia!' Sister Florence instructs.

'Yes, Sister, I'll try.'

I fall in love with piano music. I forfeit my regular time of diving and swimming for practising scales and arpeggios. Month after month new words are added to my vocabulary.

'Bach, Mozart, Chopin, Schubert, Schumann, Brahms, Beethoven, Allegro, Legato, Allegretto,' I chant as I cycle to and from piano lessons in the convent.

Magdalen Memorial

Four Galway women, Bridie Hogan, Margaret Geraghty, Orla Higgins and myself arrange a meeting to discuss a memorial for the Magdalen women. This memorial would be erected within the site of the original Galway Laundry. We choose a motto, *The Concept of Dignity, The Violation of Dignity – The Magdalenes.* We approach councillors in City Hall. There are many meetings. Financial support is given by the City Council, the Amicable Society and the Chamber of Commerce. A branch of Anglo Irish Bank, which now stands on part of the laundry site, also contributes.

Sculptor Mike Wilkins is appointed by City Hall councillors and attends our next meeting. I present him with my poem, *Make Visible the Tree,* which I wrote in 1990, while the Magdalen Laundry was being demolished. After some time, he shows us sketches of the proposed memorial. He then begins work on a large block of limestone.

A site for the sculpture is chosen at the corner of Forster Street and *Bóthar Breandán Ó hEithir.* The sculptor himself supervises the safe erection of the heavy artwork.

On International Women's Day, 8 March, 2009, the memorial is unveiled by the Mayor of Galway City, Councillor Padraic Conneeely. It's a very special ceremony. Mike Wilkins has given the sculpture the title of *Final Journey.* One year later this title proves ironic.

Here is the text of my address at the unveiling of the Magdalen sculpture:

> Dia Dhuit, Mr. Mayor. Dia Dhiobh, a cháirde. Is aoibhinn
> liom bheith anseo ag ceilliúradh an píosa ealain íontach seo.
> Good afternoon, Mr. Mayor, friends, distinguised guests.
> I'm delighted to be here with you at the unveiling of this

extraordinary sculpture. In memory of our Magdalen women, it stands here on this space, where women were hidden away, their lives eclipsed.

In the history of every people there are areas of great wounding, times when human beings inflicted great damage. History often avoids retrieving these areas especially if recalling them threatens to upset the status quo. I have always been fascinated by layers, layers of time, layers in landscape, layers in the artistic imagination. In the story of this limestone sculpture there are many layers.

Three hundred million years ago the island of Ireland was covered by a tropical ocean. As time went on brachiopods and other marine organisms, skeletal remains of past lives, fell to the seabed and formed a layer. This layer was later crushed under the weight of other layers of rock. Crushed being the operative word here. Isn't it extraordinary that this crushed material, now called limestone, has been carved by sculptor Mike Wilkins into this woman shape, which represents our crushed Magdalen women? The women were sentenced without trial. Their crime was that they had given birth. It's a dark judgement on a society when the act in which woman is most like God, the act of creating new life, becomes a crime. That crime was considered to be so horrendous that its punishment could be advanced without due process. And for that crime the baby was snatched from the new mother. She, the mother, was put away, hidden, crushed under layers of our self-righteousness. Her name and the name of her baby were erased from the discourse of society. This happened in recent Irish history. But this limestone was laid down millions of years ago.

I now move away from sculpture to theatre. I've written two plays set in the Magdalen experience. Eclipsed, first produced in 1992, and Stained Glass at Samhain, produced ten years later. Stained Glass at Samhain looks at the

Magdalen experience from a different angle. Sister Luke in Stained Glass at Samhain, when she comes back to her Magdalen Laundry at Killmacha, speaks of 'the pain held in the earth'.

I quote from Peter Brook, the famous theatre director, 'The responsibility of anyone in the arts is to look, which is more difficult, for the other side of the coin. The moment you see a black side, your obligation is to look for the luminous side. ... The role of the arts is to see what is behind the surface'.

Peter Brook sees theatre as a kind of medicine. 'The theatre artist, like the doctor, must be able to look deeply into a wound before producing an act of healing. Theatre in its origin', he says, 'was conceived as a healing instrument for the city'.

I believe that this wonderful luminous limestone sculpture will heal our city, that the pain held in the earth here in this place of betrayal will be appeased.

Go raibh maith agaibh. Thank you.

Removal

'Have you seen *The Connacht Sentinel*, Patricia?' journalist Bernie Ní Fhlatharta asks on my voice-mail. 'It's about the removal of the Magdalen Memorial to make space for a new bus corridor.' I feel that I'm reliving a nightmare. Is the memory of the Magdalen women about to be violated again! This memorial represents the pain of the women and the pain held in the earth on which it was erected. It's a hallowed space. This memorial gives great comfort to visitors, who place flowers and lights there.

When the journalist rings me again, I tell her that I'd do everything in my power to prevent the removal.

'The sculpture of Pádraic Ó Conaire was moved when Eyre Square was restructured. The City Council promised to bring it back, but it now sits in Galway City Museum,' I continue.

The following morning, as arranged with Philomena, my sister, I travel by train to Dublin to visit the National Museum of Ireland in Kildare Street. I take comfort in the beauty of the lunulae, the gold collars, in particular the Gleninsheen Collar, crafted in Ireland during our early Bronze Age. I'm conscious of the Celtic reverence for motherhood and fertility now eclipsed by some Roman Catholic attitudes and by the major Social Theorists, Plato, Aristotle, Augustine, Aquinas and Marx.

As we return through the Curragh, I salute Brigit, pagan Celtic goddess of sun and fertility, whose image evolved into our Celtic St. Brigit. Ordained Bishop of Kildare by St. Mel, she was the first and, so far, the only Irish woman to become a bishop. Her emblem, Brigit's Cross, is a Christian symbol superimposed on the sun-goddess symbol.

My mobile phone rings as we cross the River Shannon in Athlone. It's Jenny Friel, journalist with the *Irish Daily Mail*. She asks for an interview. On reaching home that evening there were over ten protest messages against the removal on my voice-mail.

Headlines in *The Galway City Tribune* announce, "'I'll chain myself to statue,'" vows playwright. *Former Magdalen nun up in arms over plan to move memorial to tragic women.'*

Truth disappears like water from turloughs in Burren limestone.

'I did not say that I'd chain myself to the memorial sculpture! But I said that I'd resist the removal, with all of my strength,' I tell each interviewer. 'I was a novice, never a nun!'

On reflection, I concede that I'm chained to the memorial in a symbolic way by my plays and poems.

The memorial is now known as 'the statue', which adds to its religious symbolism.

James Smith, Associate Professor to the English Department and Irish Studies Programme at Boston College, joins the protest along with members of Justice For Magdalenes. His volume *Ireland's Magdalen Laundries and the Nation's Architecture of Containment* provides a comprehensive history of the Magdalen Laundries.

Mika Funahashi and Dr. Hiroko Mikami, academics at the University of Waseda, Japan, email their support. Dr. Hiroko Mikami plans to visit Galway City on 25 August and hopes to join our group for meetings. Mika Funahashi had admired the sculpture when she visited Galway City earlier in 2010.

Michael Burke, Environment, Recreation, Amenities and Culture Officer at City Hall, telephones. I tell him that I first heard the news of the removal via the media.

'Why not take a slice from the Anglo Irish Bank building to make space for this planned bus corridor? Buses are really tin boxes on wheels!' I protest.

He apologises for not consulting our group, The Concept of Dignity, The Violation of Dignity, the Magdalenes. He arranges a meeting between us and representatives of Galway City Council, James C. Harrold (City Arts Officer), Joe Tansey (Head of

Transportation), Martin McElligott (Senior Executive Engineer) and Keith Mitchell (CSR Consultants). This takes place on 11 August in the Council Room of City Hall.

We explain our annoyance at the removal of the statue. The Council members listen and speak of their plans for the area surrounding the statue. We thank Michael Burke for arranging the meeting and we thank the members for listening to us. We then leave.

I walk along by the convent walls and stand outside the Anglo Irish Bank. I pause and gaze at the limestone statue across the road. Beside it the wondrous bark of a silver birch glows. Leaves shed tearful shadows on this shrouded limestone woman. I walk towards the church entrance, turn around and gaze again at the sculpture, which has now become a crucifixion image.

Moving onto the pavement, I kneel and whisper my poem, Make Visible the Tree

This is the place of Betrayal.
Roll back the stones
behind Madonna blue walls.
Make visible the tree.

Above percussion of engines
from gloom of catacombs,
through a glaze of prayer,
scumble of chanting,
make visible the tree,
its branches ragged
with washed-out linens
of a bleached shroud.

In this shattered landscape,
sharpened tongues
of sulphur-yellow bulldozers

slice through wombs
of blood-soaked generations.

This is the place,
where Veronica
forsaken,
stares and stares
at a blank towel.

At the only pillar left erect from that laundry gateway, I stand and stare at the cropped hair of this limestone mother as she emerges from an empire of shadows.

Here on bruised earth I make this promise: 'You'll never be hidden away again. Head held high, you'll lead out hundreds of women, who were pushed into oblivion through this gateway. Your voice will tell the Magdalen story to men and women of all cultures and will be remembered as part of human history.'

The branches of the silver birch bow in approval.

Four lines from the second stanza of my poem Make Visible the Tree are inscribed on a limestone plaque as part of the memorial. Situated beside the statue, a large limestone plaque is inscribed with the full poem.

On Tuesday 19 February 2013, during a debate in *Dáil Éireann*, *Taoiseach* Enda Kenny apologises, on behalf of the Irish State, to all survivors of the Magdalen laundries.

I sit in the Public Gallery with a group of survivors, who have travelled from different parts of Ireland, and see the *Taoiseach* break down in tears as he finishes the apology.

Later in the debate, Dara Calleary, TD, Minister of State for Labour Affairs and Public Service Transformation, reads my poem Make Visible the Tree aloud.

'Your poem is now on the records of *Dáil Éireann*,' my publisher says.

One week later, a telephone call from Kennys' Bookshops, Liosbán Estate, says that a large letter addressed to me c/o their Bookstores/Art Galleries will be posted to my College Road address. I wonder if another admirer of my paintings wishes to talk about my work.

Next morning, a cardboard box from Kennys is delivered by our postman. I open the box, then the enclosed envelope, which contains over thirty-five handwritten A4 pages and includes name and address of the writer. I read that the writer has attended the Vigil we held at the Magdalen Memorial on the previous Sunday afternoon. Threats to my personal safety follow.

Obscene words describe the mutilation of my body by Operation Syracuse. Too upset to read further, I push the pages back into the envelope and hurry to the bathroom to scrub my arms, hands and fingers with disinfectant soap.

My sister Philomena arrives for her morning visit. With reluctance, I show her the letter. She, too, cannot bring herself to read beyond the second page. We take the letter to the local garda station. The Gárda sitting behind a protective screen reads a few pages, pushes it back towards me and says, 'Burn it.'

'No! No! I do not want this evil script anywhere near me or my house!' I insist.

'I'll shred it so,' he says and throws it into a dustbin.

We leave the garda station and drive to Mass in the Augustinian Church.

When I tell some of my academic friends about this letter, they say that I should keep it as part of my archives. I'm too horrified to quote the pornographic threats, so they cannot judge my terror or the danger to my life.

Grykes now have razor-sharp edges. Turloughs are full of crimson tears.

At a Committee meeting in the Galway Education Centre, I'm

comforted by the support of the director and all of the members.

'Please ring me at any time, day or night,' Máire says, handing me her telephone number.

Liam writes his number and says, 'Day or night, you'll get me at this number.'

The director rings and repeats his offer of support.

All are pleased that I have an Eircom house alarm,

This letter-writer needs help. Each night I include this person in my prayers

A week later, my sister and I drive to the address given in the letter.

We find a derelict house hidden by an overgrown front garden.

Truth disappears like water from turloughs in Burren limestone.

Mariposa

In August my herb garden is a butterfly tapestry.
Small Tortoiseshells glow like stained glass on blossoms of sage and
thyme.
Painted Ladies, Peacocks and Red Admirals float towards my bay
tree.
My thorntree hums with ultramarines, alizarin crimsons, cobalts
and aubergines.
Alleluia, Alleluia I sing to the Creator of such magnificence.

In September, butterflies gone, I sing a *requiem* for their radiant lives.

Medugorje

At Ireland West Airport in Knock, Co. Mayo, my sister Philomena and I join a pilgrimage to Medugorje in Bosnia Herzegovina.

'Jackets, coats, caps, shoes, mobile phones, keys, handbags in these trays, please!' Security announces. But Brigit, a pilgrim from Clifden, has difficulty undoing her shoes. 'All hair ornaments, loose cash in these trays! Only small amounts of liquids, make-up, medication in see-through plastic bags allowed,' Brigit is told as she puts her opened handbag on the nearest tray.

'All this fuss and trouble because of that yellow-faced Binny Layden and his whiskery rascals from beyond in Afganistan,' Brigit declares.

'Strict security makes us feel safer,' Philomena consoles Brigit.

The flight in a Bosnian aircraft is smooth. I fail to see the lights of sleeping European cities because I'm not near a window.

On arrival at Dubrovnic Airport, we board a coach and travel through the indigo night.

The pilgrimage organiser announces, 'Have your passports ready.'

Our passports are checked and rechecked as our coach weaves its way across borders of Croatia, Bosnia Herzegovina, Croatia and back to Bosnia Herzegovina.

At midnight a petite border guard enters our coach. Her olive-skinned face is stern as she checks each passport against a passenger list.

'The machine-gun she carries is almost as big as herself,' I whisper.

A pilgrim nudges me and, finger on lips, warns me to be silent.

Eventually the border guard leaves the coach. The Adriatic glimmers on our left as our coach climbs cliff-edged roads. After midnight we arrive in Medugorje.

Though sceptical about reported visions, I find an extraordinary spiritual peace in this war-scarred valley. Drenched in prayer, we walk through vineyards to the foot of Cross Mountain, the Mountain of Visions.

On our return to the town of Medugorje, we dine on omelettes and delicious tomato salads in a café near our hotel.

'Evening Mass is at seven o'clock,' Yezelke, our guide, announces.

'There must be a hundred priests concelebrating Mass on the high altar outside the church,' Brigit whispers to Philomena.

Sacred hymns echo across the town and up towards Cross Mountain.

Beneath the peace of this prayer-filled valley, I'm conscious of that blood-stained under-layer of war, when neighbour killed neighbour. The skies here are ominous. Could a fleet of enemy planes suddenly darken the sun?

Amazed at the fervour of thousands of pilgrims, I kneel with them on ochre earth and pray. Beside me a pilgrim falls to the ground, writhes and groans in pain. An exorcist priest and a number of pilgrims pray over this tortured person. Another casualty of that war, I decide. Eventually the man's body quietens and we continue to recite the rosary.

Suddenly a pilgrim exclaims, 'Look, look, the sun is spinning!'

I don't look directly at the sun for fear of damaging my eyesight.

'I told you that I'm an atheist,' declares a bearded American to his blonde companion as he turns away from the spinning sun.

'Why is there something rather than nothing?' his companion replies.

'Come with me to the resurrection sculpture. You'll see tears form on the bronze limbs of the Christ.' She takes him by the hand. They walk away together through crowds of Italians, Bosnians, Croations, Germans and Irish.

Because of years of caring, my shoulders are constantly aching. I book a shoulder and back massage in a small beauty parlour outside the town. As I lie face down on the salon table, Maria, the beautician, pummels my stiff muscles.

'During the war, planes, sent from Serbia to bomb us in Medugorje got lost when The Lady sent a thick blanket of clouds to hide our valley,' says Maria.

'How did any of your people survive that war, Maria?'

'We are a very strong people. The hairdresser next door, who shampooed your hair yesterday, is a survivor from the siege of Sarajevo,' says Maria.

'And that's why her face is so sad,' I reply.

The salon door opens. A voice speaks in a foreign language. The door closes as the caller leaves.

'Do you know who that is?' Maria asks.

'No. Who is it?'

'That's Marija, the visionary. She gave up her appointment for you, Patricia.'

'Such generosity. I'd like to speak with her.'

'She has just gone home to her village.'

'Please thank her for me.'

I roll around and look directly at Maria.

'Do you believe that Our Lady appears to the visionaries?' I ask.

'I'm from their village and I grew up beside them. I never saw anything myself. But I believe them.'

'Thank you, Maria. My shoulders are less painful. I'll book another session before we leave for home.'

'Why don't we hire a taxi to Mostar?' I suggest to Philomena later in the week.

'Do not wander in Mostar! Your body could be dumped from the bridge into the Neretva river and you'd never be heard of again!' a much-travelled pilgrim warns.

'Fifty euro for two passengers, please.' The tall, sturdy taxi driver opens the door of his Mercedes. We sit on the black leather seats and enjoy their exotic smell.

'This karst landscape resembles our own Burren in Co. Clare, 'I remark as we travel through the countryside. I stare at rugged mountains and forests some of which I'd seen on TV during the recent war.

'Herzegovnians fought fiercely and declared independence from

Yugoslavia,' I add.

The taxi driver listens, but does not comment.

In the centre of Mostar a huge rock bears the inscription:
IN MEMORY OF THOSE WHO DIED
1992-1995.

Close by I see the remains of a bombarded seminary.

Our taxi driver guides us over Stari Most, the old Mostar Bridge.

'I must protect you while on this side,' he says as we walk quickly along the front line with its shell-pocked buildings.

'These buildings have not been refurbished. Left like this, they remind us of the damage done by war,' he says.

I look up. Armed Serbian sentries, guns at the ready, watch from rooftops.

We quickly cross the bridge to the less dangerous side.

'Be careful with your wallets,' our taxi driver warns as we purchase gifts from craft shops huddled around the old bridge.

Back in the sacred valley of Medugorje, we again eat omelettes and tomato salads with crusty bread at our usual café.

On our last day in Medugorje, Brigit from Clifden approaches. 'Tonight The Lady will appear to Ivan on Cross Mountain. Won't you climb to the top, Patricia?'

'No, Brigit. I'll climb just as far as the Blue Cross.'

Thousands of chanting pilgrims pass as I wait under the shadow of that Blue Cross.

Mosquito bites swell crimson on my legs because I had forgotten to use an insect spray.

'It must have been like this in the Holy Land, when Christ walked on earth,' says Áine from Galway as she climbs over jagged rocks with the help of a stout stick.

'Will there be an exorcism tonight?' another Irish voice asks.

Elizabeth's ancient prayer of salutation, *Hail Mary, full of grace the Lord is with thee. Blessed art thou amongst women and blessed is the fruit of thy womb* resonates over Bosnia Herzegovina's battle-scarred valley.

From darkness I look towards the mountain-top, where lights are now flashing. Suddenly a great silence descends. Pilgrims kneel. A soft breeze brushes past us towards the summit.

'Gospa!' I say to myself (Mirjana, Ivan, Vicka, Marija, Jakov).

Returning through Dubrovnic airport, Philomena, who has had radiation treatment for cancer, is delayed and searched again. Brigit from Clifden places a large bottle of water beside her shoes, handbag and keys on the security tray.

The security guard takes the bottle and dumps it into a box.

'Liquids not allowed, Madam!'

'But that's not liquid! That's holy water from Medugorje!' Brigit tries to retrieve the bottle, but fails. Áine next in the queue declares, 'Sure, he's a pagan! You can see it in his eyes, Brigit.'

'Last summer didn't I give a naggin of Knock holy water and seven lovely duck eggs to Roy Keane, that grand soccer player from Cork! He was delighted. If he comes this summer, what'll I do?' Brigit sobs and wipes tears from her eyes.

'I've Medugorje holy water in my checked luggage. I'll be delighted to share it with you, Brigit! Philomena consoles her.

At home in Galway I write this poem entitled 'Gospa'.

Eyes on summit,
boots against bloodied karst,
stick grappling support,
I scrunch my way
up through pilgrim prayer
up through war clouds,
up through mountain black
up through body pain,
up through soul darkness,
up through spinning suns,
up beyond world time,
up beyond scientific formulae,
up beyond rational thought.

Rosary rhythms
thousands of thousands
stop.
Throbbing footsteps
thousands of thousands
stop.
Crying babies
stop.
Barking dogs stop.
Breathing bodies thousands of thousands stop, transfigured in silence.

Memorare

On a Sunday afternoon, accompanied by a professed Sister, I visit houses in the nearby terraces. In one cosy kitchen, I take from my big serge sleeves the usual voucher for a loaf of bread and pot of jam.

A young man rises from a window seat. He snatches the voucher and says, 'Where's Sister Pius?' He tears the voucher into pieces and throws it back towards us.

It floats like confetti in the smoke-filled air.

'Sister Pius is visiting another Sister in the hospital,' I reply, trying to keep custody of the eyes.

'She'll be needing hospital treatment herself when I get a hold of her!'

He picks up and puts on his boxing gloves, stands in the middle of the floor and gestures.

'Sister Pius flung a book at my sister Brigit and barely missed her eyes,' he squares himself.

'Thank Goodness she missed,' I whisper as I step backwards towards the door.

'Now she's made up a new Memorare! Puts herself into it!'

'A new Memorare?'

'She orders our kids to say, Remember, Most Pious Virgin Mary instead of

Most Gracious Virgin Mary! Pius, Pius! I'll write and report her to the Pope himself!'

'But there are two different spellings, or she could even mean our saintly Pope Pius,' I protest.

My companion pulls me backwards by one of my big sleeves. We move outside.

'Don't ever come back to this house again, ya crowd of magpies!' he shouts and boxes the door shut with his gloves.

Aoife Kate McGarry

On 2nd December 2009 telephones ring in every home of our extended family.

'It's a baby girl! Congratulations to Eleanor and Pádraig.'

We celebrate the birth of our first grandniece. Baby photographs arrive by post.

'She's the image of Pádraig. Dark eyes just like his. Dark hair.'

'But Eleanor's hair is dark too!'

'Lovely long fingers! She'll be a pianist like Claire, her Granny!'

From Bruges an embroidered christening robe with matching shawl and bonnet arrive for baby Aoife Kate McGarry.

'Why the name Aoife? Must be on your side of the family, Eleanor!'

'It's an ancient Gaelic name!'

'Kate after John McGahern's aunt, Pádraig's Granny McGarry,' she adds.

I go to Dublin for Aoife Kate's christening ceremony.

'I baptise thee in the name of the Father, the Son and the Holy Spirit.' The priest pours holy water on her head. She objects, but Pádraig dries her hair and she smiles as he replaces her bonnet.

Wrapped in her white robe, oils of chrism and catechumens on her forehead, fingers and feet, a lighted candle held high by Pádraig, Aoife Kate is now cleansed of original sin. When the ceremony has ended, I ask the celebrant, 'How could this beautiful baby ever have had a sin on her soul?'

'In the Early Church adults were baptised on Holy Saturday night and were then accepted into the Christian community. The doctrine of Original Sin was dreamt up by Saint Augustine,' the learned theologian replies.

'And what about Limbo?' I ask. There's no reply.

'A perfect baby brother for Aoife,' Claire telephones on 13th

September 2011.

'His name will be Oisin Brendan McGarry.'

'*Deo Gratias* again and again,' I reply.

Oisín Brendan is baptised on 5th February 2012 and is now a member of our Christian community. Saoirse, another sister for Aoife Kate and Oisín Brendan, is born on Holy Thursday … hence her name, which means Freedom.

Saoirse is baptised on 2nd March, 2014.

My sister Claire in the operetta *The Belles of Corneville.*

Irish Human Rights Commission Meeting

Professor Jim Smith phones to say that a meeting in Dublin of the Irish Human Rights Commission on the Magdalen Laundries will take place on 9th November.

'Please attend, if at all possible, Patricia,' he says.

I set my alarm for 5.30 am, take the train from Galway and arrive in Heuston Station at 9.35 am. A taxi brings me to Jervis Street. I'm delighted to arrive in time for this 10 am meeting on the Fourth Floor of Jervis House. I meet a number of young women lawyers. Some of their names are familiar from emails sent by JFM, Justice for Magdalenes.

In June 2009 JFM had asked the Commission to inquire into the treatment of women and girls in the Magdalen Laundries.

Olive Braiden, Commissioner of Irish Human Rights, Dr. Maurice Manning, President, Eamon Mac Aodha, Chief Executive and Sinéad Lucey, Senior Inquiry Legal Officer address the meeting.

During the questions and answers session, Professor Jim Smith of JFM says that the Government must move beyond its 'deny till they die' policy.

A survivor of the Limerick Magdalen Laundry sits silently in the second row.

'An inquiry by this Commission cannot deliver the apology and redress sought from the State for the women,' declares Chief Executive Eamon Mac Aodha.

'The Commission calls on the Government to set up a statutory inquiry into the treatment of women and girls in Magdalen Laundries. It also says that financial redress should be available to the survivors,' he continues.

Commissioner Olive Braiden reminds us, 'We are dealing with a small and vulnerable group.'

Present at the meeting are four TDs from Fianna Fáil, Tom Kitt and Michael Kennedy, Kathleen Lynch from Labour and Maureen O'Sullivan, Independent.

The survivor from the Magdalen Laundry in Limerick still sits quietly in the second row.

'The State cannot abdicate from its responsibilities in regard to these women,' insists Dr. Manning.

'The Government says it has asked the Attorney General to set up a statutory inquiry into the treatment of women and girls in Magdalen laundries. The State must take responsibility. The survivors should get a sincere apology and should be compensated,' says Sinéad Lucey.

'The State must convince the church to acknowledge its part in the scandal and open up its records,' says Maeve O'Rourke, co-author of the group's submission to the Commission.

'I worked in the Magdalen laundry in Galway. I worked there, as a novice, for one week. One week was enough,' I announce during the questions and answers session.

When the meeting is over, Olive Braiden and Maurice Manning tell me that they have not seen my play, *Eclipsed.* I decide to post them copies of *Eclipsed* and *Stained Glass at Samhain.* Both plays are set in a fictional Magdalen laundry.

I'm introduced to Joe Little of RTÉ During a recorded interview, he questions me about my time in the laundry.

This excerpt from the interview is broadcast on RTÉ News At One and introduced by Seán O'Rourke:

'I was a novice with the Sisters of Mercy Order in Galway. I was told to see that the women worked, not to talk to them except on business. I felt I was in Dante's *Inferno.* This huge dark room was full of women. The women seemed to merge with the large washing machines, the greyness, the sweating walls. I was their jailer. As I've said today, I was there for one week. That was more than enough.'

During the adjournment debate in the Dáil that evening, in the absence of Dermot Ahern. Minister for Justice, Tom Kitt, TD proclaims, 'Survivors should receive an apology from the State and a distinct redress scheme should be established for them.'

The following Government Press Statement is issued from the Department of the Taoiseach, *Roinn an Taoisigh* (Minister for Justice, Dermot Ahern was absent):

The Government today was made aware of the assessment report issued this morning by the Irish Human Rights Commission (IHRC) in relation to its enquiry into the treatment of women and girls who resided in Magdalen Laundries. The Commission carried out this work following an approach made to it by the Justice For Magdalens (JFM) in June 2010.

The Government notes that the IHRC has decided not to conduct an enquiry itself in relation to the matters raised by JFM as it is entitled to do under the legislation which established it. It also notes the Commission's recommendation that a statutory mechanism be established to investigate the matters advanced by JFM and in appropriate cases to grant redress where warranted.

The Government regrets that relevant Departments were not offered an opportunity by the IHRC to contribute to the Commission's considerations of this matter to facilitate a fully balanced evaluation of the facts.

The Government is also conscious that the Magdalen Laundries were run by a number of religious congregations.

The Government has asked the Attorney General in consultation with relevant Departments to consider the IHRC's report.

9 November 2010.

We remember the survivor from the Limerick Magdalen Laundry, who sat silently in the second row.

Tears fill grykes and turloughs in Burren limestone.

Sold Out
20 November 2010

I stand at my father's grave.

Above me our skies are bruised and bloodied.

Eyes on his name, Joseph Phelim Burke, engraved on this headstone, I say, 'Dear Dad, I'm sorry for what has happened to your beloved Ireland. You and your fellow idealists have been betrayed. Your country now belongs to strangers.

When I grumbled about tax deducted from my first salary by the Department of Education, you said, 'It's the least you might do for your country.'

Millions of tax-free euros are now stacked abroad by sun-soaked 'friendly bankers.'

In 1921, released after that year on death row in Mountjoy Jail, you returned to your local Sinn Féin meeting. When you saw there people who had spied on your Old IRA Brigade and now had jumped on the new political bandwagon, disgusted, you walked out.

You never returned.

Descendants of those 'new patriots' have sold you out.

Today they stand beside our tricolour and lie to us.

Every year they march to the grave of Wolfe Tone and lay wreaths in his memory.

Truth disappears like water from turloughs in Burren limestone.

I now lay a wreath of Easter lilies on this tricolour, which I place beneath your name.

During my lifetime I have never joined a political party. No 'ism' attaches itself to my beliefs. Human Rights are my priority.

Galway City

The real founders of Galway City, the De Burgos, have been eclipsed by the much publicised Tribes of Galway.

Richard de Burgo, the Red Earl, a descendant of William the Conqueror, erected the first walled castle, which was the origin of our city of Galway.

The Red Earl
(Founder of Galway City)

From my heart pulses the blue blood
of William the Conqueror.
From folded blues of Burren limestone,
pleated blue of Atlantic ocean,
lace-edged blue of river Corrib,
a multitude of blues,
I raise and fortify my castle.

From Dúnebun-na-Gaillive,
my domain stretches
north to Carrickfergus,
south to Waterford,
east to Luchuid,
back to Furbagh of flaming furze.
I inscribe my name,
Richard de Burgh, Lord of Connaught,
on fractured blue of history.

Etching/Aquatint, Richard de Burgo

Maynooth College

During the 1970s a series of workshops for the New Curriculum in Music, Drama and Art are arranged in Maynooth College by the Department of Education. As I've been asked to give one of the workshops, I set off in my off-white Renault 4. I drive from Galway through Craughwell, Ballinasloe, Athlone, Moate and other small towns. Summer skies of cobalts and ceruleans with splodges of near-white clouds overlook my journey.

Barely escaping a collision with an oil lorry as I approach Maynooth, I turn in through the grand gates of the college.

I think of my mother's great-uncle, Eugene Francis O'Beirne, who had come through these gates, but after some time in the seminary, disagreed with the authorities. He didn't leave without a struggle and later went on to write his volume, *An Impartial View of the Internal Economy and Discipline of Maynooth College.* For years afterwards his portrait had hung face to the wall in his home by the River Shannon. However, having read Jeremiah Newman's strange explanation of the case in his *Maynooth and Georgian Ireland,* I can understand Eugene Francis's situation.

The *Árd Cigire* welcomes us and tells us that most of the Professors are away on holiday and that the lay students have gone home. I know that Monsignor Olden, the President, who is a relative of my father, had gone to visit cousins in the USA.

About fifty teachers and a number of *Cigirí* now invade this stone seminary.

Dinner in the once-silent refectory resounds with teachers' voices. I'm hungry after my journey from Galway City and, to the amazement of some, I express disappointment at the food served.

I walk past portraits of bishops and archbishops hanging on the walls of a long corridor. Ruby rings on manicured fingers show under crimson and magenta robes edged with Carrickmacross lace.

Michael, a teacher from Galway, points and says, 'Dr. Crotty, Dr. Montague, Dr. Callan and Dr. Renehan. Sure those guys are all dead and gone! We're walking through history.'

'This too will pass. I quote from ancient Greek wisdom,' John, the poet, says, his arms spread wide. Michael nods in agreement.

'That's the haunted room,' Cáit tells me as we make our way to our cell-like sleeping accommodation.

'Haunted? I don't believe that story, Cáit.'

'The dark hair of a young priest, who stayed overnight in that room turned snow-white,' she confides. 'Come over and we'll peep in.' We turn the door handle.

'Why is it locked?' we say together, then make the Sign of the Cross and quickly move away.

Truth disappears like water from turloughs in Burren limestone.

In a huge lecture hall I stand on the podium and try to inspire my audience of teachers.

I ask them to close both eyes, to close their left hand and hold it out towards me. I demonstrate and check my audience. Then I ask them to open their eyes and left hand and to concentrate on the lines of the left hand.

'Line, shape, volume and light are the basic elements of art,' I say.

I ask them to close their eyes, close their left hand, to open eyes, open hand and to concentrate on the shape of the left hand. Next close your eyes and left hand, open eyes and concentrate on the volume of your fist. Then I ask them to close eyes and hand, open eyes and hand and concentrate on light as it falls on your hand.

'Line, shape, volume, light,' I repeat. 'Now we'll try making lines with a variety of tools. Afterwards we'll experiment with the other elements of shape, volume and light. Choose from those sticks, nails, scissors' points etc. on your desks. Using black ink, make scratches on your paper, then incise your paper with nails, slit with scissors. Next crush a small piece of paper, and again using ink, dab your paper with wrinkles and clusters. Now with coils of inked twine, print on to your paper to get tangles, lattices, silhouettes.'

We take a day trip to Newgrange prehistoric monument above *Brú na Bóinne*.

'Built around 3,200 BC, it's 600 years older than the pyramids of Giza,' the *Árd Cigire* says as he stands beside the milky-quartz outer wall.

I examine the triple spirals on the entrance stone, the twin spirals on the kerbstones.

I look up at the roofbox through which the winter-solstice sunlight enters and penetrates the passage-tomb by shining on to the floor of the inner chamber.

'Here are examples of linear megalithic art,' I say to John the poet.

I walk along the passage and bow in thanksgiving to the *Tuatha Dé Danann*, who built this extraordinary monument.

At the last session in the college, I present my Puppet Show, which is based on Yeats' poem 'Easter 1916'. This combines drama and history with music and painting. I make a series of puppets from papier-maché and knitting-wool. I use pipe-cleaners for Yeats' spectacles. For the backdrop I paint a scene of Dublin's 18ᵗʰ century houses.

'Will you take charge of sound, Cáit, please? The background music is from Seán Ó Riada's *Mise Éire*.' She checks the tape and nods in agreement.

I recite Yeats' poem as I move the Yeats puppet in front of the backdrop.

I have met them at close of day
Coming with vivid faces
From counter or desk among grey
Eighteenth century houses –

and I finish the show with
All changed, changed utterly. A terrible beauty is born.

I pack puppets, backdrop and luggage into my Renault 4, wave *Slán* to the ghostly institution. I salute Eugene Francis O'Beirne and swing out through the great gates.

Under apricot skies dappled with mackerel clouds, catching glimpses of the *Esker Riada*, I drive westwards to a changing life in Galway City.

During the following semesters, I give a series of lectures and workshops on Art in Education to groups of teachers. Arranged by Bernard Kirk, the director, they take place in Galway Education Centre.

I prove that art, though a subject in its own right, can assist and make other subjects more valuable, vibrant and more interesting for teachers and pupils. During these sessions I combine music, drama, painting, puppetry with language skills, mathematics, history and geography.

I speak of the complexity of our Tara Brooch and its golden geometric ratio.

I show the different types of symmetry including mirror images and rotation used repeatedly through the differing aspects of the brooch.

'According to an Irish scholar,' I say with pride, 'the artisans who created pieces like the Tara Brooch could be considered the mathematicians of their time.'

The teachers who attend the courses are very enthusiastic. They adapt their work to suit their pupils' stages of development.

Sardinia

From Dublin we fly southwards over a turquoise Mediterranean to Alghero in Sardinia. This island, populated since Neolithic times, has a history resembling that of our own. Here too, traces of invaders scar the landscape.

In a roofless monastery, shadowed by ancient Nuraghe, we listen as stars echo the rhythms of Paco Pena's flamenco music.

Cloisters of Alghero
From dark caves above Granada,
where entranced Moors sleep,
Paco Pena calls gipsy voices
to the cloisters of Alghero.

Beneath the Tower of Maddalena
oleanders open crimson ears.
Sand-lilies lift silver trumpets.
In the ancient city of Alghero
bougainvilla stains ochre walls.

Chevrons, circles, embossed triangles,
terracotta calligraphy of strings,
olive, jasmine, lemon elipses,
blood-dried earth of Andalucia
in the cloisters of San Francisco.

Ice and flame, laments and love songs,
dark magic on curving strings,
glow of pink on gold Alhambra
under snows of Sierra Nevada.
Along Via Roma and Via Columbano

from Torre Saint Joan,
above the crickets' soft percussion,
under slanting ilex trees,
through the island of Sardegne
flows a red-gold river of flamenco.

They come from that scarred Mountain,
Mountain of Pain, Mountain of Fear.
Ancient people quicken from
shadowed doorways of Nuraghe.

The sleeping youth of Aesculapius wakes
to hear scalloped music.

Phoenicians and Genoese to the Piazza Civica,
zig-zag Romans on white horses,
after them Catalans and Aragonese,
under the Bell-Tower thousands gather,
the Bell-Tower of Sancta Maria.

Chevrons, circles, embossed triangles,
terracotta calligraphy of strings,
olive, jasmine, lemon elipses,
blood-dried earth of Andalucia
in the cloisters of Alghero.

Could this island be the lost Hy Brazil?

That Story

'I'm going to a meeting in the Warwick Hotel, Patricia. Put on your new coat and beret and we'll face the music together,' my sister Philomena says.

'What kind of meeting? Will it be interesting?' I ask.

'Literary, more or less,' she replies. 'Hurry up and we'll catch the Salthill bus!'

I pull the beret down over my ears. My hair has been sprouting since I cast off coif and veil and left the Galway Novitiate.

The meeting has started when we reach the Warwick.

'Please do not sit too near the front,' I say and I glide into a back seat.

Four men sit at a top table facing the audience. We bow excuses for our late arrival.

The snores of a white-haired man on our right punctuates the sound of the central heating.

Suddenly, a man dressed in a tweed coat stands and holds up a book with a bright cover.

'This is a disgrace! In County Clare we burned this book!' he shouts.

'If any of you get a copy of this so-called *Country Girls*, bring it along and we'll burn it in Eyre Square!' another middle-aged man roars.

'Edna O'Brien herself should be burned with it,' a bespectacled woman exclaims.

'Burn! Burn!' three hoarse voices chant. The snoring man gives one last high-pitched snore and wakes up.

'Have any of you read that book?' I say, but nobody hears me in the uproar.

'I must buy a copy tomorrow,' I add.

About a week later, Philomena says, 'We'll go for coffee to the Great Southern Hotel in Eyre Square. You must get used to life on the outside.'

Free now from the custody of the eyes rule, I turn to look at *Loch an tSáile* as the bus brings us through Moneenageisha. I look to the right as we pass the Grammar School and that high wall around the Magdalen laundry on the slope down to Forster Street and Eyre Square.

We enter the elegant foyer of the Great Southern Hotel and go to the bar.

Tom, the gracious barman, serves us as we sit at the wall facing the long counter. Two glamourous women accompanied by two children walk in and greet Tom, who has been dusting bottles of liqueur on the teak shelves.

One woman sits on a bar stool, the other, dressed in green velvet, stands against the bar and speaks in a County Clare accent with British overtones.

'Now, my darlings, your Auntie Edna will treat you to your favourite drink of red lemonade!'

I put down my coffee cup and pay attention to this tall auburn-haired woman.

'It couldn't be!' I say to my sister.

'That woman is used to an audience!' she comments.

Tom pours lemonade into four tall glasses. He adds ice cubes, then pours another liquid into two of the glasses. He stirs the drinks and places them on cork mats.

'Your Auntie Edna and your mother have special drinks, my darlings. Tom knows what we like,' Edna says as she smiles at Tom and turns to survey the room. I nudge my sister and whisper, 'Yes. Yes! It *is* Edna O'Brien! I've a story for her, Philomena! She must hear about the happenings in that laundry up the road in Forster Street.'

'The Magdalen Laundry, Patricia! You said it was the richest branch-house of the order, but that the enclosed women didn't get paid for working there.'

'Yes! That story must be told,' I say. 'I'm sure Edna would be glad to use it.'

I stand up and begin to move towards the bar counter.

'Why don't you write it yourself?' My sister jumps up and takes me by the arm. 'You were always scribbling stories before you entered that Novitiate!'

'Will they burn me if I write it myself? Will those people we heard in the Warwick Hotel sacrifice me out there in Eyre Square?'

'Write it yourself, Patricia. You were the witness.'

I sit down.

I keep my story.

Crossing the bridge beside the novitiate.

Holidays in London

An email from Mika Funahashi says, 'This is the last day of my short stay here in London. I'm writing this message from a carrel at the British Library. ... I'm preparing a proposal for this year's IASIL Conference, which will he held from the end of July through the beginning of August in Montreal, Canada. I would like to consider your work, *Eclipsed*, again from another point of view, so now I'm listening to something from the PC of the library.

I tried many times, but failed, to get tickets for *The Recruiting Officer* by Farquhar, an Irish dramatist.'

I reply to Mika:

'Eamon and I always visited London during our summer holidays. We stayed at the Irish Club in Eaton Square. My days were spent in The Tate Gallery, The Hayward Gallery, The British Museum and The Victoria and Albert Museum. On one visit to the V & A I was amazed by an exhibition of ancient Japanese woodblocks and their prints.

In the British Museum, I studied the handwritten scripts of the great English poets. When, in my excitement, I leant too closely over the glass cases which protected the documents, I was ordered to move away.

After pre-theatre dinners, we attended shows in the West End. We feasted on great productions during our two weeks in London. In the Aldwich, we saw Henrik Ibsen's *Ghosts*. We crossed the city to The Donmar Warehouse Theatre, where Pat Layde and Galway actor Siobhan McKenna were playing in O'Casey's *The Plough and the Stars*.

That 1706 restoration comedy, *The Recruiting Officer* by George Farquhar at The Royal Court was booked out even then. We sat on the stairs of the theatre and waited for cancellations. Eventually, we were delighted to get two tickets, though they were on separate sides of the auditorium. Happy days.'

Next day I send another email to Mika:

'I remember one sunlit morning as I stood in Drury Lane and bowed my head in honour of my ancestor, Bishop Thomas Lewis O'Beirne. His play, *The Generous Impostor*, ran for six nights in 1781 at The Theatre Royal, here in Old Drury Lane. He was born on our family farm in Co. Longford and went on to become an associate of Richard Brinsley Sheridan in London.

His long poem, *Crucifixion*, is preserved in our National Library in Dublin.

According to our O'Beirne family tradition, Thoms Lewis and his brother Denis studied in a Catholic seminary at St. Omer. Thomas Lewis was raised to the diaconate there. He changed allegiance from Catholicism and was ordained a Protestant clergyman in England. In London he was friendly with Charles James Fox and his associates, who were important politicians called Whigs.

Because of his former diaconate, he was chosen to perform the marriage ceremony between the Catholic Mrs. FitzHerbert and the young George, Prince of Wales.

George, on the death of his father, became George the Fourth, King of England.

Thomas Lewis was installed as Church of Ireland rector in Longford town. At the same time, his brother Denis who had remained a Catholic, was appointed parish priest in Longford town.

Thomas Lewis was ordained Church of Ireland Bishop of Meath in 1789.

Goodbye for now, Mika.'

Mika's next email says:

'Thank you, Patricia, for family background information.

Now I quote for you from Adrian Byrne, editor of the *Irish Arts Review*, 1998 and 2010:

"*Eclipsed* is a play which demands to be seen, not just from the Irish perspective, but as a universal exploration of suffering and insidious cruelty within society."

Addendum

In Spring 2013, Prof. Charlotte Headrick, University of Colorado, visits Galway to research the history of productions of *Eclipsed*. She writes an essay on my work with the title of. 'Giving her the respect she deserves.'

I'm delighted when I receive a call from Caroline Lynch and Emma O'Grady of Mephisto, a Galway theatre company, asking permission to produce my stage play, *Eclipsed*. A meeting is arranged. It's decided that the production will run from the 21st to 31st of August, 2013 on the main stage of the Town Hall Theatre, Galway City. I answer questions and give advice. I'm impressed with the professionalism of those involved and I realise how lucky I am that Mephisto has decided to produce *Eclipsed*.

Auditions follow. A very strong cast, directed by Niall Cleary, and an excellent stage-set draw audiences back to Killmacha Magdalen Laundry. They respond with laughter and tears.

In the green room, a four star review from the *Irish Times* and a blog from Patrick Lonergan are greeted with shouts of joy

Reviews in the *Irish Independent*, the *Irish Theatre Magazine*, the *Connacht Tribune and The Advertiser* are also superb and the celebrations continue.

Jane Talbot, stage manager, visits my home and selects a number of my framed monoprints and etchings for an exhibition on the first floor of the Town Hall Theatre.

The exhibition, with the title of *Enclosed*, takes place from 23rd August to the end of September 2013. Guest speaker is James Harrold, Arts Officer.

An email from Manuel Trujillo Lopez Haya in Lima, Peru says he has read the reviews and requests a copy of the script. He plans to produce *Eclipsed* in Lima during April and May 2014.

Eileen Kearney emails to say that she and her husband Dan

Koetting will produce the USA premiere of my stage play *Stained Glass at Samhain* during *Samhain* 2013 in Denver, Colorado.

Dan holds the Chair of the Department of Theatre and Film at the University of Denver.

Because of my cardiac ailment, I cannot accept their invitation to attend, but I nominate Judy Murphy, journalist, to take my place. She had represented me in Urbino a few years earlier when, because of Eamon's illness, I couldn't leave Galway.

However, I'll speak to the audience by Skype after one of the performances in Denver.

Scene from the Denver CO. production of *Stained Glass at Samhain*, Nov 2013.
Photo: courtesy Dan Koetting.

Rustington

At Gatwick Airport I follow signs to the train station. As I struggle down stone steps with my luggage, the Victoria Express flashes past.

'Take the train to Littlehampton and get off at Angmering,' my brother, Fr. Brendan, had instructed.

'Make sure you sit in one of the middle carriages, because the last four divide off at Worthing.'

The Littlehampton train comes in with a chug, chug. I pull on my luggage and find a seat beyond the bicycle carriage. We stop at Haywards Heath, then travel along the coast to Hove, Portslade, Southwick, Shoreham by Sea, Lancing, Worthing, West Worthing, Durrington-on-Sea and Goring-by-Sea.

'Next stop Angmering!'

I stand near the exit. The train groans to a stop and I step out into West Sussex air.

My brother hugs me, then packs my luggage into the boot of his dark blue Ford Mondeo. We drive to his presbytery in Rustington.

'You must be hungry after your long journey, Patricia,' he says when we arrive.

'I'm starving!'

'I'll cook your favourites.' He takes saucepans from a cupboard. 'Fillet steak with Stilton,' he smiles and switches on the grill.

'Mmm. Mmm! Purple-sprouting broccoli and new potatoes,' I say.

'Jersey potatoes with that delicious taste.' He pours boiling water into a steamer.

We chat about our home in Galway City as he moves around the kitchen.

'You've changed your spectacles, Patricia. Nice frames.'

'Yes. I got them in Colette Kelly's shop at the top of Buttermilk Walk.'

'Buttermilk Walk?'

'Yes. The shop is on the corner beside the Augustinian Church. I can change the clip-on sides to suit whatever colours I'm wearing!'

'You like earth colours.'

'Maybe I'll order frames for you on your next visit home.'

'I'm satisfied with my own at the moment. Since my cataracts were removed, I can see colours properly again. Blues in particular.'

'That's wonderful news. I brought my brushes and acrylic paints with me to restore your statue of St. Thèrese.'

'Did I tell you that Céline, St. Thèrese's sister, presented that statue to our church? She said it had the closest resemblance to the Little Flower. She also presented a first-class relic of the Saint, which is now enshrined in our main altar.'

'Why were the statue's original colours covered in white paint?'

'I don't know the true story except that some type of iconoclast here decided that all the statues in our church should be white. Maybe this was a new outbreak of Iconoclasm like those during the 8th and 9th centuries or maybe it was a follow-on from the 2nd Vatican Council. However, you must relax for at least two days before you bring St. Thèrese back to her life-colours.'

After Mass on the first few mornings of my visit, I stroll through the town of Rustington. Its houses are built with local flint-stone, which gives their walls a wonderful texture.

'It's Thursday already. I'd like to have the statue ready for the weekend, so I'll start this morning,' I say when he has finished reading his Breviary.

The phone rings.

'Hello. It's Father Burke here. – The Last Rites – John Patrick Flatt, our Gold Medal Tramp – In Darlington Nursing Home? I'll go there immediately. Thank you.'

'John Patrick Flatt, our Gold Medal Tramp, was born deaf,' Fr. Brendan tells me as we leave the presbytery. 'He was rejected by his parents shortly after he was born and was taught to speak, read and write by an order of religious sisters. During his life he wandered along the south coast, from Eastbourne to Portsmouth. He read *The*

Telegraph and *The Times* from cover to cover every day.'

'Why Gold Medal Tramp?'

'He wore a gold miraculous medal on a rosary around his neck.'

We open the side door of the church, kneel before the tabernacle for a few minutes and then enter the sacristy.

'We've placed her statue on this low table, so you won't need those steps. Here's an apron to protect your clothes. I must hurry to Darlington Nursing Home!'

With a purple stole around his neck, he unlocks the tabernacle, takes hosts from the ciborium and encloses them in a pyx. From the sacristy he takes blessed oils for the Rite of Anointing and leaves.

I put on the apron and look at St. Thérèse's face. Her smile, even though it's covered in white paint, is angelic.

I mix a little yellow ochre, burnt sienna and raw sienna with titanium white until I get a basic skin-colour. Cheekbones, forehead, nose and chin highlighted, I define lips and eyebrows. I stand back, half-close my own eyes, then correct middle tones and shadows. I work on details, eyelids, irises, pupils and eyelashes. I mix ultramarine with burnt umber for the rich dark of pupils. A first coat on veil, coif and habit dries quickly. I rework, stand back again, correct and finish with a matt varnish. When completely dry, John the sacristan lifts the Little Flower back on to her own dais in the alcove near the church door.

'I got there just in time, *Deo Gratias*. Next Thursday we'll have a Requiem Mass for John Patrick, our Gold Medal Tramp. Generous parishioners have offered him a space in their family burial plot. We'll give him a great send-off,' Fr. Brendan says on his return.

'Her statue is now back in the church. In time for his Requiem,' I say.

'Wonderful! John Patrick will be happy.'

'You look very happy too.'

'Yes, Patricia. If I had a thousand lives, I'd live each of them as a priest.'

'A thousand lives as a priest. *Deo Gratias*.' I bow my head.

'The Little Flower is smiling more than ever,' John the sacristan tells me before Requiem Mass begins.

'I'll light a rosary of candles in celebration of all of those extraordinary lives,' I reply.

Parishioners admire St. Thèrèse's statue before they follow John Patrick's coffin from the church and on to the cemetery in Littlehampton.

The following week, I walk past the ancient Norman church, which is surrounded by leaning gravestones, and along Sea Lane towards the sea. I stop to read from a plaque on one of the houses:

THIS WAS THE HOME OF SIR JOHN PERRY, WHO
COMPOSED THE MUSIC FOR BLAKE'S JERUSALEM

I give you the end of a golden string
Only bind it into a ball,
It will lead you in at heaven's gate
Built in Jerusalem's wall.

Inspired by this inscription and by the layered history of West Sussex, on my return to the presbytery, I write:

On Sea Lane
I hold a flint-stone in my hand,
chalk crushed under ancient oceans
stained with crimson of iron.
Bird-shape carved by waves,
ejected as the ice-cap melted,
it resonates with cries
of oyster-catchers and sandpipers
as they skim the tide
and cormorants, wings spread wide,
turning sunwards
to heat their swallowed food.

I place the flint-stone to my ear
and hear Blake's angels sing.

The ghosts of Normans,
who landed on this beach
and built their church of flint-stone,
kneel in prayer.

Canute, attended by his royal court,
returns from shore-line
to join Blake's chorus.
Nelson's warships dip their sails.
Spitfires and Messerschmitts
spiral skywards in salute.

My flint-stone becomes a cello,
a violin, a double bass, a harp
as Parry's opus echoes
and earth revolves on its way to Jerusalem.

I now move into a time-space of great loss.

On Friday 4th March 2011, I follow Eamon's coffin from St. Augustine's Church in Galway City to rest beside his parents and baby sister in the New Cemetery above *Loch an tSáile*.

The Passing

Fr. Brendan

At 10 am on 11th April, 2011, my brother, Fr. Brendan, celebrates Mass for his parishioners in St. Joseph's Church. At 10.45 am his great heart fails.

On 19th April, we follow Fr. Brendan's coffin from St. Joseph's Church in Rustington through woods wreathed in bluebells to Worthing Crematorium. His words come to mind.

In the woods of Worthing,
bluebell clusters
echo Spring gentians
on Burren limestone.
Whitethorn blossoms mirror
my alb's brightness,
lapis-lazuli cruciform
of my All Hallows stole.

If I had a thousand lives,
I'd live each of them as a priest.

Invisible,
I read my Breviary

beside my parents' grave
above Loch a' tSáile.

Every morning,
in Rustington,
I celebrate Mass
for my parishioners,
while swallows bow
their wings
and chant Benedictus
around St. Joseph's Church.

On 6th June, 2012, Claire's husband, Patrick McGarry, dies of cancer.

On 8th June, with Claire and their son Pádraig, we follow his coffin to Oughteragh graveyard in Co. Leitrim.

Are the spirits of Eamon, Fr. Brendan and Patrick among us, or have they returned to that place I remember? That place of happiness, which I mourned, as I came through a tunnel of light to be given my earth-body.

High above our winter-dead hedge,
a rosebud opens its heart,
glows with new hope,
banishes my night-dark.

Meshed in our winter-dead hedge,
a nest of starlings
hums young with music.
burnishes my life.

Some references to my work in books and journals

1. **A Tribute to Patricia Burke Brogan,** Cork Literary Review 2003, Volume Ten. ed. Sheila O'Hagan.
2. **Reaching from the Past into the Future: Patricia Burke Brogan's** *Eclipsed,* IASIL, 2004. National University of Ireland, Galway. Charlotte J. Headrick, Oregon State University.
3. **Crossing Over: Patricia Burke Brogan's** *Stained Glass at Samhain,* IASIL 2004. National University of Ireland, Galway. Eileen Kearney, University of Texas.
4. **Il Concetto Di Dignita Cultura Occidentale (Urbino) The Concept of Dignity in Western Culture, The Magdalen Laundries.**
5. **I Magdalene Laundries Nelle Opere Di Patricia Burke Brogan** (Verona), Sonia Maffina – Prof. Carla De Petris.
6. **Ireland's Magdalen Laundries and the Nation's Architecture of Containment,** James M. Smith.
7. **The Field Day Anthology of Irish Writing, Volumes 4 and 5.**
8. **Irish Women Playwrights of the Twentieth Century.**
9. **Ireland's Women, Writings Past and Present.**
10. **Motherhood in Ireland.**
11. **Unmarried Mothers in 20th Century Ireland.**
12. **A Century of Irish Drama. The Sins of the Mothers.**
13. **Soul Journeys in Contemporary Irish Theatre, Dudes and Beauty Queens.**
14. **The Changing Face of Irish Theatre, Laundry Basket Hearts.**
15. **Visions and Revisions of the Magdalene Laundries in the Drama of Patricia Burke Brogan,** Theatre Journal 1999.
16. **The Power of Visual Elements in Patricia Burke Brogan's Work** (University of Delaware).
17. **Amnesty International Magazine 2002.**

18. **Giving Her the Respect She Deserves**, Prof. Charlotte Headrick, 2013.

19. *Eclipsed (1988/1992)*: **A Theatrical Challenge of the Magdalen Laundries,** *Theatre and Film Studies 2009,* Mika Funahashi, International Institute for Education and Research in Theatre and Film Arts Global, CEO Programme, Theatre Museum, Waseda University.

20. **Interview with Patricia Burke Brogan by Mika Funahashi,** International Institute for Education aand Research in Theatre and Film Arts Global, CEO Programme, Theatre Museum, Waseda University. IASIL 2011.

21. *'Un-Eclipsed'*, an Interview by Jenny Farley and Virginia Garrett, *Irish Studies Review,* August 2010.

22. *The Irish Arts Review* **1998,** Adrian Byrne. See page 284.

23. **IASIL Conference, Leuven 18-22 July, 2011** Theme: Conflict and Resolution in Irish Theatre, Women's Identities.

24. **The Madwomen in the Laundry: Conflicting Femininities & Struggles for Narrative Authorities in Patricia Burke Brogan's Eclipsed,.** Yuri Yoshino Hitotsubashi University, Tokyo.

25. **Memory & Violence in Ireland. The Representation of the Magdalen Laundries in the work of Patricia Burke Brogan,** Victoria Connor, University of Aberdeen.

26. **Anthology of Irish Women Dramatists:** Syracuse Press USA, 2013, Ed. Prof. Charlotte Headrick and Dr. Eileen Kearney.

Glossary

Grykes	Sharp-edged recesses cut into limestone by receding glaciers.
Turloughs	Small lakes which appear and disappear in Burren limestone.
Burren	Karstlike landscape in north Co. Clare.
Corcomroe	Preserved remains of a Cistercian monastery in the Burren.
Gentians	Small ultramarine flowers of Alpine origin found in the Burren.
Annaghmakerrig	Residence of the late Tyrone Guthrie, now an artists' retreat.
Samhain	All Souls' Night. *Oiche Shamhna*, Halloween, when the boundaries between the living and the dead dissolve.
Cigire	Inspector of schools.
St. Brigit's Holy Well	St. Brigit, Abbess of Kildare and Patroness of Poets, had the gift of healing. Holy Wells are named in her honour. St. Brigit was the first and only female bishop in Ireland. She was accidentally ordained by St. Mel, when he visited her Kildare monastery.
Killmacha	St. Paul's Laundry, Killmacha is a fictional place. A combination of pagan and Christian words – kill (cill) is the anglicisation of Gaelic for church or cell/oratory of the early church; Macha, a sun goddess, a life-giving image, a fertility goddess, one of the most important goddesses in ancient Ireland.
IASIL	International Association of the Study of Irish Literature.

CPSIA information can be obtained at www.ICGtesting.com
Printed in the USA
LVOW02s1515280714

396381LV00013B/61/P